Reading the Renaissance

Medieval & Renaissance Literary Studies

reading the renaissance

ideas and idioms from shakespeare to milton

edited by marc berley

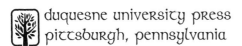 duquesne university press
pittsburgh, pennsylvania

Published in the United States of America by:

DUQUESNE UNIVERSITY PRESS
600 Forbes Avenue
Pittsburgh, Pennsylvania 15282

Library of Congress Cataloging-in-Publication Data

Reading the Renaissance : ideas and idioms from Shakespeare to Milton /
edited by Marc Berley.
        p. cm. — (Medieval & Renaissance literary studies)
Includes bibliographical references and index.
   ISBN 0-8207-0336-2 (alk. paper)
1. English literature — Early modern, 1500–1700 — History and
criticism — Theory, etc. 2. Renaissance — England. I. Berley, Marc. II.
Series.
   PR413 .R38 2002
   820.9′003—dc21

                                    2002009295

∞ Printed on acid-free paper.

for *Edward W. Tayler*

Contents

Acknowledgments

I am grateful to Susan Wadsworth-Booth of Duquesne University Press for her support and guidance. Two anonymous readers for the press helped all of us make this a better book; we remain thankful. Allen Gimbel helped with proofreading. Andrew Armstrong read portions of the manuscript and made valuable suggestions. Vered Sussman, my wife, proffered wise editorial judgments and acts of kindness for which I cannot adequately thank her. For clandestine missions that helped this book to be, I am grateful to Christina Moustakis. Most of all, I thank my fellow contributors, exemplary scholars who made this collection all that it is. Ted Tayler has enriched our lives; this book is but one form of utterable thanks.

Introduction

Marc Berley

"In every work of genius," observed Ralph Waldo Emerson, "we recognize our own rejected thoughts; they come back to us with a certain alienated majesty."[1] A good deal of psychic turmoil is certain to take place when such recognition occurs. Readers may alienate the genius of the writer, transforming the work into something more manageable, attempting to protect against a vulnerability caused by encountering majesty that is not in every respect our own. The forced assertion of prior rejection can seem the only saving course. But it is best to accept that the genius is not our own even if it seems — the true mark of genius — somehow to have come from us. Somehow we must enjoy, not retaliate against, the experience of theft; not to be able to argues no real genius of our own.

Reading is a dangerous act, for how we confront another's genius reveals much about ourselves. Meticulous writers have long understood the likelihood that readers will misread them. Martial, in one of his epigrams, boldly distinguishes the work of the writer from the misprision of the reader: "Quem recitas meus est, o Fidentine, libellus; / Sed male cum recitas, incipit esse tuus!"[2] [The little book you are reading is mine,

Fidentinus; but when you read it badly, it begins to be yours.]
Martial didn't mince his words because he feared his reader
would. If his little book were going to be misread, Martial
knew not only to disown it but also to transfer to his bad reader
ownership of a different, still smaller book. Ben Jonson, who
understood Martial, begins his *Epigrams* with a similar plea:
"Pray thee, take care, that tak'st my book in hand, / To read it
well: that is to understand."[3] The relationship between a reader
and writer, in Jonson's world of seventeenth century lyric, is a
serious one. If the reader slips, the poet and his work are ruined.
It is as much a moral feat to "understand" as it is an intellectual pleasure.

It has long been the task of literary scholars to transmit the
genius of the past to the present — not to steal it back by force
or guile, but to map out the process by which what belonged
to the genius of bygone authors came to be not our own, but
also ours. The goal of such scholarship is to make the writer's
meaning available to readers who, lacking broad and specific
contexts, would not otherwise be able to "understand."

Scholars, though, are readers too, and they work in a tradition that rewards original readings; thus they are capable of
the error discouraged by Martial. Goethe, unlike Emerson,
thought that one of the worst, if inevitable, intellectual errors
is assuming that originality requires the forced rejection of
old truths. Even the best of readers will have trouble keeping
from such error, for human nature has its sway: basic, primordial needs must always be somewhat fulfilled. Consider, for
instance, what scholars used to do with the writer who has
done more than any other to alienate our majesty, Shakespeare.
"What we do is to make him in our own image and then call
him unique," observed Frank Kermode in a 1964 talk at Columbia University.[4] And as with Shakespeare, so with other
great poets. Thus in 1967 the preface to a collection of essays
on Milton by prominent scholars could celebrate "a readiness
to accept that 'our idiom' is spoken by Milton as much as it is
by Donne."[5]

When Kermode delivered his talk on Shakespeare at Columbia University in 1964, Edward W. Tayler was a young assistant professor of English there. It doubtless interested him, since that year he published his soon-to-be-seminal first book, *Nature and Art in Renaissance Literature*, in which he set forth his chief concern as a Renaissance scholar: how a student of literature "may re-create within himself the experience of great and vanishing art."[6] Fifteen years later, in *Milton's Poetry*, Tayler would again show that the best way to mine one's own genius is not to deny the genius that is not one's own: "The grand temptation, as nearly everyone knows, invites us to come upon ourselves in a work of art, finding there our own lineaments of satisfied or unsatisfied desire mirrored beguilingly." Tayler saw no grounds on which to assert that Milton's idiom is our own. Indeed, "one of our stronger reasons for returning to Milton is that he seems, as the writings of Leavis, Pound, Eliot, and others proclaim, so intransigently *other*."[7]

We may, Tayler suggests, discover our own ideas, idioms, and intentions precisely to the extent we engage others on their terms, rather than our own. Under such conditions, our terms may begin to flourish, taking on slowly their own majesty, not an alienated one: "Since books . . . 'preserve as in a vial' the extract of a 'living intellect,' the pleasure of reading first involves understanding another 'self' in its singularities, which incidentally though not unimportantly affords us new perspectives on ourselves as selves."[8] Shakespeare, Donne, and Milton, like Jonson, knew that only a strong self would struggle to "understand" strong lines. These writers challenge readers to understand themselves by first understanding others in their most idiosyncratic terms, whether through characters in a drama, monologues in an epic, or personae in lyric poems. This challenge links the dramatic psychological probing of Shakespeare and the lyric conceits of Donne, and both of these to the epic distillations of grand ideas so common in Milton. In the mind of a literary genius, ideas and idioms — old and new, common and peculiar — shape and reshape each other, crystallizing, as Tayler has shown, in Shakespeare's "glassy essence" in *Measure for Measure* and Donne's "Idea of a Woman" in *The Anniversaries*. Only the process of "understanding" intransigent others can recreate in us the most remarkable intellectual and artistic achievements of seventeenth century English poetry.

When Heminge and Condell collected and published Shakespeare's plays in the 1623 Folio, they, like Martial and Jonson before them, addressed readers with urgency in "To the Great Variety of Readers": "Read him, therefore; and again, and again: And if you do not like him, surely you are in some manifest danger, not to understand him." Reading is a dangerous act because not to understand a great author argues oneself not understood.

A reader might best come to understand what the great Renaissance authors mean, Tayler has shown us, by attending, again and again, to their ideas, idioms, and intentions. "Ideas are heady items," and dealing with them requires "literary tact." It is "part of literary tact to allow a poet to own his own ideas," writes Tayler.[9] Unfortunately, as in the case of John Donne, Tayler observes, "ignorance of the poet's vocabulary . . . has led, over the centuries, to increased misunderstanding."[10]

"I have my own vocabulary," Montaigne asserted. And so he does, and so do Shakespeare, Jonson, Donne, and Milton. And so may we, provided we do not obliterate their vocabularies with our need to have our own. If we cannot account for our unacknowledged sources, how might we ever speak for ourselves? Perhaps the twentieth century, which ushered Modernism in and out, did not make it increasingly difficult to be an individual. But a scholar still had to search for something new to say, to say nothing of having one's own idiom. Thus, the method of indirect self-flattery described by Kermode in 1964 did not persist. The preferred processes of distortion have undergone telling permutations over the last

30 years. Rather than inject themselves into the writers they describe with the unconscious purpose of creating a majestic self-reflection, critics from various schools of criticism began consciously to assert themselves by wresting control of ideas, idioms, and intentions away from their dead authors. In the 1970s, reader-response criticism argued for a superficial supremacy of the reader.[11] At the same time, deconstruction argued language incoherent: ideas implode, intentions miscarry — except, of course, when wielded by theorists. In the 1980s emerged a collective will explicitly to hack geniuses such as Shakespeare down to size, to pulverize pedestals into the manageable dust of ascribed ideology. Into such dust blow the spirits of theory, engendering what they will. The inhumane, though human, need to authorize the self by subduing other imposing selves is demystified by a number of imposing selves, Shakespeare chief among them. So it is not wondrous strange that in the 1990s, no longer New Criticism's reflector of unique genius, Shakespeare became, in the wringing hands of postmodern critics, but an early modern cultural sponge.

New Criticism's privileged text gave way to the privileges of the textualizing critic. And (old) historical criticism — which eschewed the errors of New Criticism while attending to the tangled contexts of intransigent others — gave way, as Stanley Stewart observes below, to wild new historicisms in which unsubstantiated claims, variously juicy and theoretical, become substitutes for evidence. The Martial-like warnings about "understanding" sounded by Renaissance writers gave way to postmodern critics who, seeking to empower themselves with more than a reader's response, could fashion themselves as major authors by representing the works of major authors as mere commentaries on the culture that (in theoretical, chiefly Marxist, terms) "produced" them. We have been witnessing merely the latest way to confront the "alienated majesty" produced by great authors: alienate majesty itself, declare that genius does not exist, steal back all intellectual property, endeavor, after Emerson, to begin anew.[12]

Emerson had been determined to alienate the majesty of Europe, to establish a new, more majestic land. "[T]he children of time do take after the nature and malice of the father," who "devoureth his children," observed Francis Bacon long before Emerson. "[A]ntiquity envieth there should be new additions, and novelty cannot be content to add but it must deface." As Emerson later declared with the air of invention, "New arts destroy the old."[13] Harold Bloom dubbed recent institutionalized resistance to majesty the "school of resentment," the great writers being disconcertingly hard to devour. Critics may be doing only what is natural, but we are obliged to consider the consequences. One consequence of losing the ability to recreate the experience of vanishing art is the diminution of our selves as selves.

Squabbles between ages have ever been thus, and they evoke, in the world of literary scholarship, their peculiar symbolic actions. When Milton wrote that a "good book is the precious lifeblood of a master spirit, embalmed and treasured up on purpose to a life beyond life," he meant it.[14] Such belief by a writer in his symbolic action can heighten in others the need for patricide, which has in our time become no more fierce than it has always been (recall the fate of Cronus at the hands of Zeus), though oddly acceptable as a scholarly practice and critical method recently. Whereas in 1967 Miltonists displayed "a readiness to accept that 'our idiom' is spoken by Milton," in 1987 a collection of essays by prominent scholars, *Re-membering Milton*, punned on the dismemberment of Milton as a necessary part of reconstructing an object worthy of contemporary appreciation.[15] Surely the world is always in need of rebuilding, but when phallologocentrism becomes too overdetermined a target, a giant such as Milton will suffer contemporary displacements, just as his Christ, according to one of the essays in *Re-membering Milton*, must suffer a perfunctory Lacanian mirror "stage."

We do well to observe that there are other experts in psychology, some of them especially relevant on these matters. As D. W. Winnicott tells us, when children make the transition from the parent to another object, the relation — not the object — is significant. One can escape from a majestic intellectual parent, but not free oneself from the process of alienated majesty.[16] Other relationships will mirror the primal one, beguilingly. Perhaps few today are in a position to intone with Montaigne: "It is no more a matter of Plato's opinion than of mine, when he and I understand and see things alike."[17] But if we are too far evolved to affect Montaigne's manner of exemption from "alienated majesty," we are not immune to the consequences of such evolution, however much they may appear to be covered today by the self-fashioning of scholars. It is hard to be new, easy to slip into newfangledness. Emerson, as Goethe knew before him, was wrong to assert that "the past is always swallowed and forgotten."[18] It may perhaps be one or the other, but never both. They knew this on Olympus.

For both scholarly and psychological insights, it is "good occasionally to look to the rock whence we were hewn and unto the hole of the pit whence we were digged," writes Tayler in his first book, where he demonstrates that classical backgrounds have more than academic import.[19] From the beginning, Tayler has hinted at the consequences of neglecting this insight, including the loss of perspective on ourselves as selves.

Tayler's scholarship — focusing on the biggest ideas, attending keenly to idioms and intentions — shows us that how we read says much about us that could perhaps help us to see better rather than to hide our shames. As much as we may try not to, we do wear human nature (which will survive even postmodernism much as a cockroach would survive a nuclear holocaust) on our sleeves. The trouble is that people "become attached to certain particular sciences and speculations, either because they fancy themselves the authors and inventors thereof," as Bacon warned, "or because they have bestowed the greatest pains upon them and become most habituated to them."[20] Habituation, moreover, leads to telling slips. Recent critical schools have habitually sanctioned attacks upon the "arbitrary." Yet nothing has become as arbitrary as whether an author is to be grandly associated with or forcibly rewritten. It depends on the theory, or the particular application of it.[21] Shakespeare becomes at once a giant to be slain (royal apologist, victimizing ideologue), a giant to be cheered (clever subversive), or no giant at all (mere anxious compiler reacting fitfully to every political pressure and social microupheaval). Contemporary critical and theoretical intentions are often naked.

Tayler has always commented insightfully on the progress of scholarly methods. Paying excessive attention to their own idiom, and indulging a need to apply it, critics, he has warned us, can become all too happy to possess a diminutive version of Martial's *libellus*. When one examines the lineaments of desire in the manner of Tayler, it is more than an academic problem that today 'they're not teaching Shakespeare and Milton as much as they used to' or that when they do teach them a germane question is 'Yes, but how?' Many scholars shrink from Tayler's engagement in palpable polemics. Milton, for one, would find such shrinkage "intransigently *other*." In *Lycidas*, yet another poem Tayler has done much to help us understand, Milton foretold the ruin of the corrupted clergy then at their height. With so much archival research and so many ways of reading available, scholars have never been in a better position to read the Renaissance. And it appears bold to announce one's intention to correct scholars at their height: "I aim to set the record straight: about what John Donne meant when he said that 'he described the Idea of a Woman and not as she was,' and about the structure, and therefore the meaning, of The Anniversaries," writes Tayler at the beginning of *Donne's Idea of a Woman*. "Nothing in the various 'new historicisms' can help us define 'Idea,' and nothing in structuralism or poststructuralism can help us understand the 'mimetic' and 'ecstatic' structure of The Anniversaries. Disappointing but true, and not only for these poems." Tayler then expresses "the usual hopes that my mild-mannered polemic may have some effect on the way we read Donne's other poems and other works of the period" (ix). Mild or not, the manner matters less than the punctual nature of the analysis.

Perhaps the act of reading the Renaissance has itself become too strong a reminder of the consequences of living in a world where the center surely does not hold and might not even matter. Readers today have been robbed not merely of faith but of the radical power of doubt. Who can truly say, with Donne, that the new philosophy calls all in doubt? The current mode of academic skepticism is to assent to rather suspect first principles. One of the most notable contemporary habits is the repression of eros (Plato to Freud). Thus we find young scholars becoming, as Anne Lake Prescott has wittily observed, "overstimulated by the now fashionable theory that Renaissance love is not love but politics."[22] This glaring symptom of postmodern criticism — the flight from eros — is one its practitioners dare not probe.

However adept one may be at manipulating lattices of eyes, one cannot, in the end, outbeguile the mirror. For four decades at Columbia, Ted Tayler shook his students into new understandings of themselves as selves. He did this by getting them to pay attention to what authors meant by what they wrote. In his always overflowing undergraduate Shakespeare class, he asked his students to consider why the playwright has Bernardo accost the audience in the first line of *Hamlet*: "Who's there?" Strangely, critical practices appear to have progressed to the point where Shakespeare no longer accosts scholars but scholars unflinchingly accost him. A recent "subscribe now" letter from *Shakespeare Quarterly* offers gratis "the special winter 2001 issue, *Dislocating Shakespeare*" — as if we were truly beyond the labor of locating him, and ourselves. In

fifteen years, the academy progressed from "re-membering"
Milton to "dislocating" Shakespeare, sanctioning the general abandonment of Montaigne's principle of attacking authors "only . . . at their strongest points."[23] Tayler, in contrast,
has remained dedicated to understanding authors where
they are "strongest." And if his dedication has become ever
more against the grain, it has also rendered readings of Renaissance literature that get it, to borrow a word from the
Renaissance, "right."

Reading the Renaissance offers provocative new essays
on seventeenth century literature by Renaissance scholars
dedicated to the principles of literary tact formulated and demonstrated so scrupulously by Tayler. The scholars who have
contributed essays to this collection demonstrate the belief
that the author, not the critic, is supreme — that the aim of a
scholar should be to "understand." These scholars belong to
the authors they consider, not to theories or schools. They are
committed to reading the Renaissance — as opposed to, say,
rewriting it. This commitment, not coincidentally, has led
them to authoritative new readings.

The essays in this book not only reflect Tayler's principles
as they relate to the literary possibilities seized by Renaissance writers such as Shakespeare, Jonson, Donne and Milton;
they also confirm Tayler's influence on some of the field's
major conversations. "We must ascertain as far as possible
what the words meant, and what they now mean," writes
Frank Kermode in "On Certain Verses of Shakespeare." To
understand Shakespeare "readers and auditors must be aware
of the presence in the plays of certain effects that are powerful though hard to describe; the difficulty perhaps being that
they are the consequence not merely of words or even sets of
words but of distinctive rhythms that attend their use." For
the rhythms of use Kermode has an astounding ear, especially
for Shakespeare, who demanded that we hear his patterns of

association with what Wallace Stevens calls "the delicatest ear of the mind."[24]

Marc Berley, in "The 'Idea' of *King Lear*," locates the source of the "Idea" of *King Lear* in Sir Philip Sidney's *Apology for Poetry*. In addition to identifying a new source for the play, Berley examines the anti-Aristotelian poetic Shakespeare used to shape it. What was the purpose of writing such a brutal play? Shakespeare imagined with genius the painfully joyous process of having one's majesty alienated by no less an artist than God.

Michael Mack, in "The Consolation of Art in the *Aeneid* and the *Tempest*," offers a valuable new reading of Prospero's "Art" and Shakespeare's. The power of art owes much to its ability to explore loss. For such exploration Shakespeare borrows themes from Virgil's epic that have not yet been noted by critics. While Virgil and Shakespeare "present art as" a "kind of a refuge against personal loss," they also show art's ultimate inability to console. Only by highlighting that inability, Shakespeare shows us in *The Tempest*, can one achieve consolation "not wholly 'insubstantial.'"

Tayler's significant influence on the way scholars read Donne is also manifest here. In his essay on Donne's *Anniversaries*, Louis L. Martz writes that Tayler's focus on Donne's use of Memory, Understanding, and Will caused him to re-evaluate his own distinguished efforts — as well as those of Hardison, Lewalski, and Manley — to chart the structure and meaning of these complex poems. The result is a momentous essay in which Martz, extolling Tayler's corrective reading, argues for a new, and perhaps even final, account of the structure and meaning of Donne's *Anniversaries*.

Anne Lake Prescott, in "Male Lesbian Voices: Ronsard, Tyard, and Donne Play Sappho," examines a poem that has raised a number of good questions, "Sappho to Philaenis." Whereas some might argue, for reasons having to do with idiom, that John Donne could not have written it, Prescott devotes precise attention to French sources for the poem's ideas and deftly pursues the possibility of related intentions we might trace back to Donne. She provides a valuable framework for examining not only this poem but also large questions concerning the confluence of Renaissance idioms.

Few seventeenth century lyrics have caused as much of a conundrum concerning Renaissance ideas and idioms as John Donne's "Aire and Angels." Albert C. Labriola, in "The *Donna Angelicata* of Donne's 'Aire and Angels,'" demonstrates what happens when a scholar who knows a great deal about both Donne and Thomism visits a twenty-first century cosmetics counter in search of a fragrance for a woman. We are still connected to important parts of Donne's world (a cosmetic is our compacted cosmology, a little part of the little world remade cunningly with dust and essence). In such a world, a woman with a sample atomizer can quickly deliver to a learned scholar the essence of a difficult poem.

Whereas Martz focuses on Tayler's critical acumen in respect to Donne's *Anniversaries*, Stanley Stewart, in "Reading Donne: Old and New His- and Her-storicisms," focuses more broadly on the value of Tayler's historical criticism, offering a provocative, though judicious, evaluation of recent trends in Donne studies as they relate to the effect Tayler has had on our reading of Donne and Renaissance literature more generally. As one of the critics quoted by Stewart observes, a "great deal seems to be at stake in Tayler's book." Stewart's essay shows us what and why. It takes up a central question on which the future of Renaissance (and other literary) study depends: What exactly constitutes "evidence" of a writer's meaning?

Ernest B. Gilman, in "Plague Writing, 1603: Jonson's 'On My First Sonne,'" demonstrates how much we can still learn about long-considered poems when we pursue the kind of historical criticism recommended by Stewart. Gilman provides an important new understanding of Jonson's moving epigram, one that considers the various effects the 1603 plague had on Jonson as father and poet. In the epigram, "emotion is recollected, but not in tranquility," as has long been argued; rather it is a "Roman reframing of the father's very English, peculiarly tangled feelings of grief, anger, and guilt as a plague survivor." Linking the poem to Jonson's "To William Camden," Gilman draws an insightful "living line" connecting "Camden, Jonson, and the young Ben" that would have run "back to Anchises, Aeneas, and young Ascanius," if not for the plague.

Martin Elsky's "Erich Auerbach's *Seltsamkeit*: The Seventeenth Century and the History of Feelings" explores the relationship between ideas and feelings in the Renaissance, including the idea of "feeling" itself. Building on Erich Auerbach's insight into seventeenth century France as "the crucible of emotions . . . where one began to feel like a European feels," Elsky offers a brief history of the idea of early modern emotions — those clouds where idioms chase after intentions.

Anthony Low, in "The Fall into Subjectivity: Milton's 'Paradise Within' and 'Abyss of Fears and Horrors,'" considers with nuance the related consequences of the self's resistance to moving outward toward intransigent others. "Although the inward self can become a paradise, it can also become a hell," writes Low. Indeed, "the autonomous mind cannot, of its own power, even retreat safely within the fortress of its thoughts when fate is outwardly adverse." Once fallen, Adam "cannot escape the two-sided trap and gift of self-consciousness." We may, observes Low, "think of 'alienation' as a modern concept," but Milton "anticipates its modern sense of internal exile and estrangement from community" and our appreciation of "the typically modern condition of man": to find oneself amid "the lonely crowd" with only the refuge of "anguished soliloquizing."

The refuge of "anguished soliloquizing" is the focus of "Bugswords," Edward W. Tayler's epilogue to this volume.

What Tayler meant by "other" in *Milton's Poetry* in 1979 was very different from what so many others meant by the same word in the 1980s and 1990s. The concept of "otherness" became part of a new "discipline"; as literary study gave way to critical "discourse" suffused by political interests, "other" came to be overdetermined, usually in the terms of race, class, and gender. Out of fashion went tailor-made efforts to know other selves; into fashion came a well of jargon serving as oxygenated fuel to every late-model theoretical engine. "Bugswords" is a deeply learned, far-ranging essay that, after considering the condition of literary scholarship in recent years, makes a striking pitch for a new form of attention to authors' ideas, idioms, and intentions. Authorial intention was long ago called into doubt, but as Tayler observes, there is no more rewarding a way to read Renaissance literature and thereby gain new perspectives on ourselves as postmodern selves.

These new essays speak to the enduring value of Renaissance literature and literary study. They encourage new and vigorous engagement with the period and its major authors. If we grapple with Renaissance authors on their turf, struggle to meet them on their terms, perhaps we may come to understand them, and ourselves; perhaps we may alienate neither their majesty nor our own.

1 • On Certain Verses of Shakespeare

for Edward Tayler

Frank Kermode

As Edward Tayler is so well aware, critical comment, however capacious and ambitious, often leaves unexplained bits of language that it might well be thought important to understand. Or they might be glossed, but, as he chillingly expresses it, "glossed impertinently," as in the case of Milton's "ev'ning Dragon" in *Samson Agonistes*.[1] This expression, occurring in the midst of the celebrated closing chorus, was for ages impertinently glossed until Tayler's note gave it a definitive explanation.[2] In much the same way repeated attempts to explain Isabella's "glassy essence" in *Measure for Measure* (2.2.121) were superseded by Tayler's article.[3]

We shall have to wait and see if the world takes serious notice of these corrections. In the present state of the game there can be no assurance that anybody will.[4] I regard this kind of work as primary, though as Tayler complains, that cannot be the view of those who abominate the notion of such limiting glosses and who would either prefer Milton not to be alluding to a precisely definable meteorological phenomenon, or prefer not to know that he was. Tayler, in a moment of almost unforgiveable simplicity, confessed in his fine (and neglected) book *Milton's Poetry* that he had "tried to allow Milton to mean what he said and not 'something else.'"[5] This is an unpopular concession. Similarly inspired and unreasonably hopeful, I myself, almost 50 years ago — to be exact, in 1954 — gave a quite precise explanation of Prospero's term "weak masters," (*The Tempest*, 5.1.41). My Arden edition was superseded in 1999 and the new editors took no notice whatever of my gloss.[6] The assiduous Stephen Orgel, in his Oxford edition did take note of it though stating firmly (and curiously) that my evidence was "not relevant."[7] I could go on, but we old warriors have a Coriolanus-like reluctance to display our wounds.

When the first task is done and we know, in the simplest sense, what the words mean, we may want or need to move to a level above the lexical and ask how, on occasion, words or groups of words interact in ways about which we think we can find something constructive to say. Since the patriarch of such investigations is Walter Whiter, I will here pay him a measured tribute.

Whiter's conclusions may not always appeal to the modern critic, but all the same it must be admitted that the *Specimen of a Commentary on Shakespeare* contains some good suggestions.[8] Whiter, now famous largely for having been resurrected in the twentieth century after suffering well over 100 years of neglect, was a learned classic. He probably needed to be to sustain a close friendship with the great scholar Richard Porson, who also on occasion interested himself in the language of the drama of Shakespeare's period. Whiter was at Cambridge, as student and teacher, at a time when Locke was the philosopher king, and his thoughts ran obediently along associationist lines. He compiled a three-volume *Etymologicon Universale*, a book of great linguistic learning, now forgotten.[9] All languages, he maintained, contain the same fundamental ideas which "derive from the earth." Tracing associations with a view to offering a "universal etymological dictionary," the *Etymologicon* won more admirers than the *Specimen*, which, as its modern editor notes, was thought too eccentric. The associations of ideas he claimed to have discovered existed, it was felt, only in Whiter's head, not in Shakespeare's, and the fact that according to Whiter they might involve reference to such humble matters as kitchen implements, the vocabulary of cookery and the like, was regarded as imputing to Shakespeare a stylistic abasement of which he could not have been guilty, even unconsciously.

Unhampered by any such considerations of decorum, we can now show impartial interest in Whiter's idea that the principle of association can be studied "as it operates on the *writer in the ardour of invention*, by imposing on his mind some remote and peculiar vein of language and imagery" (*Specimen*, 59). The process was not represented as conscious; Whiter agreed that it was he, not Shakespeare, who was aware of the remote connections formed in the ardor of invention; Shakespeare made the connections, Whiter understood them. And the reader may come to understand, as the writer presumably did not, that there is scarcely a play "where we do not find some favorite vein of metaphor or allusion by which it is distinguished" (*Specimen*, lix.n1). Lockean examination of the poet's language will detect ideas that are fortuitously but strongly associated, keeping company, in Locke's own phrase, "as if they were but one idea" (*Specimen*, lxi).

Whiter did not pursue this notion as far as he might have done, for his own associations caused him often to digress and show off his learning in other areas. But there is something in it — not, probably, what Whiter thought, but something. Some of the possibilities he suggested were exploited, at first in ignorance of his work, by such twentieth century scholars as Caroline Spurgeon, Wolfgang Clemen and E. A. Armstrong, all of whom enjoyed considerable esteem in the postwar years. But time and fashion have diminished their celebrity: time allowed their faults to become easier to specify; fashion moved on from "imagery," "clusters" and the like to new territories. The revival of interest in Whiter that accompanied their vogue has also faded — yet there remains something worth thinking about, if not worth imitating. We needn't resume the quest for "clusters" and widely ramified associations, but rather renew the habit of philological devotion to the study of particular words and groups of words in the texts of the plays with no necessary commitment to a philosophical (or indeed to a psychoanalytical) line.

Let me refer to one passage in the *Specimen*. Whiter, as I remarked already, is a garrulous and erratic commentator, turning aside when he feels like it to explicate at great length a verse in Aristophanes or to adduce references in Greek literature to the link between the notion of feasting and the notion of dogs; just the kind of "insertion of foreign topics" he claims to hold in "utter abhorrence" but cannot resist.

This particular excursus arises from a series of remarks on Shakespeare's habit of using figures deriving "from the meanest subjects and the lowest occupations." Whiter notes the distasteful imagery of stale or broken food in *Troilus and Cressida* (for example, "orts of her love, / The fragments, scraps, the bits and greasy relics / Of her o'er-eaten faith" [5.2.158–60]) and turns next to *Antony and Cleopatra* ("I found you as a morsel, cold upon / Dead Caesar's trencher: nay, you were a fragment / Of Cneius Pompey's" [3.13.116–18]).

Noting by the way a similar association in *Two Noble Kinsmen* of broken food with such kitchen expressions as "*lards it*" and "*forces* [farces] ev'ry business" (4.3.7–8), he returns to two particular passages in *Antony and Cleopatra*. In act 3, scene 13 Cleopatra is rejecting Antony's violent attack on her unfaithful conduct and vivid past — "a morsel cold upon /

Dead Caesar's trencher" (116–17). He accuses her of being "cold-hearted" toward him (158), and she replies:

> Ah, dear, if I be so,
> From my cold heart let heaven engender hail,
> And poison it in the source, and the first stone
> Drop in my neck; as it determines, so
> Dissolve my life! The next Caesarion smite,
> Tilt by degrees the memory of my womb,
> Together with my brave Egyptians all,
> By the discandying of this pelleted storm,
> Lie graveless. . . .
>
> (158–66)

Much might be said of this speech, which homes in on the play's insistent leitmotiv of melting or dissolving, as Antony's speech did on that other theme of rejected food. But what first captured the imagination of Whiter was the word "pelleted." It had previously been noted that this word occurs also in *A Lover's Complaint* ("the brine / That season'd woe had pelleted in tears" [17–18]) and what interested Whiter was the fact that since a pellet was, as Steevens had explained, "the ancient culinary term for a *force meat ball*" Shakespeare's imagination is again descending to the kitchen and the banausic business of cooking. Presumably because the word is no longer used in that sense (unless by schoolboys or subalterns throwing bread pellets) the modern editor of the poem does not comment on the word as it occurs in *A Lover's Complaint*, and editors of the play note the parallel with the poem, but again without comment. The *OED* gives the sense of "small globe," certainly including little balls of food, but also the sense, still familiar, of "bullets or small shot," surely more likely here; it doesn't seem likely that Cleopatra's imagined storm contained hailstones resembling forced meat balls (or sweetmeats, as the Arden editor seems to suggest), and the best that can be said about Whiter's conjecture is that it was a little better worth making than modern editors have supposed.

It seems clear enough that when Cleopatra speaks of the pellets "discandying," she was thinking of melting hailstones ("discandying," by the way, is Theobald's emendation of "discandering" — the compositor evidently could not read the unusual word). Whiter, though misled by his passion for tracing Shakespeare to the kitchen, does rather better with "discandying," a nonce-word meaning, as he rightly says, "the dissolving of what is candied." But he still takes "candy" to have the familiar sense of sweetmeat. The *OED* derives it from a Persian word meaning "sugar" and mentions its association with ice only in defining "candied," *trans.* and *fig.* "covered with anything crystalline or glistening, as hoar-frost." It could be and was applied to thin ice on brooks. Cleopatra is not thinking about a bombardment of sweets; the pellets are of ice and will melt in her bosom.

Whiter then draws attention to Antony's speech in act 4, scene 12:

> The hearts
> That spaniel'd me at heels, to whom I gave
> Their wishes, do discandy, melt their sweets
> On blossoming Caesar.
>
> (20–23)

Reading this extraordinary speech, Whiter silently accepts Hanmer's "spaniel'd" for the "pannelled" of the Folio, an emendation still accepted with one or two variations by most editors, though with reluctance by some. It is necessary to Whiter's most famous claim, that in thinking of Antony's deserted condition Shakespeare fell into a pattern of ideas repeated elsewhere in his work: dogs mean "fawning obsequiousness" and they accept sweets that make them slaver, in this case over Caesar. The passage has a metaphorical violence of the sort also to be found in *Macbeth*, as in the metaphorical tumult of "Was the hope drunk / Wherein you dress'd yourself? Hath it slept since, / And wakes it now to look so green and pale?" (1.7.35–37). In this passage from *Antony and Cleopatra* "hearts" is an ironical synecdoche for the courtiers, formerly like dogs at his heels; it makes their past obsequiousness grotesque and unnatural. When they discandy they are not melting like ice but like sweetmeats, and disgustingly offering what is still in their mouths to Caesar. Then the affinity of dogs with trees suddenly supervenes: Caesar is a tree and he is blossoming while Antony, a tall pine, is barked. Unless "barked" is a pun, as one rather hopes it isn't, we have had to abandon the sweets and the dogs and compare trees.

So the word "discandying" in both cases means "melt," though with a different kind of melting: sugar dissolving in the mouth, hailstones bearing poison to the heart as their ice melts. But in either case the figure of melting is involved in a complex of other metaphors, and this in a manner we can take as exemplary of the scope and range of the later style.

For Whiter these examples, especially the spaniel figure, establish his principle of unconscious association, and he lists other passages "deeply impregnated with the same vein of diction and ideas" (*Specimen*, 123). We may share his interest in the word "discandy," for these two uses of it are the total of uses that have been recorded in Shakespeare or indeed anywhere. The two occurrences of the word come within minutes of each other in a play concerned from its first lines with melting, dissolution; the prospect of Rome melting into the Tiber is held up as a figure of impossibility, and the annual swamping and fertilization of Egypt by the Nile is presented as its contrary. After Antony has contemplated the moving, dissolving clouds — "the rack dislimns" (4.14.10), another wonderful nonce-word, another of the play's rich synonyms for "melt" or "melt away" — and when he has reflected on the dissolution of his own "visible shape" (4.14.14), we are moved on toward the impassioned moment when "the crown o' th' earth doth melt" (4.15.63).

When Antonio uses the word "candied" in *The Tempest*

(2.1.279) — "Twenty consciences, / That stand 'twixt me and Milan', candied be they, / And melt ere they molest!" — he is declaring that forces that ought to resist melting, that might be thought to oppose his intention, can melt away, as far as he is concerned, without affecting his choice; presumably he is thinking of blocks of ice, not candy. Here there is no trace of a fawning dog. In *Timon of Athens* "the cold brook" is "candied with ice" (4.3.226) and shows no sign of melting; and again there is no dog in the immediate vicinity, though dogs do occur in the scene and in the play at large, and there is the ghost of one in Apemantus's figure of the trees that will not page Timon's heels and skip at his bidding. It seems that the sweetmeat, sugar-candy sense is there only when there is a dog close by. Whiter is so keen to preserve the association of dog and candy that he professes at great length to find something similar in a passage from the *Odyssey* where dogs fawn on a chieftain as he returns to the banquet from cleaning his hands, which, it is claimed, was done with soft bread, later thrown to the dogs.

I have been discoursing on Whiter a little in his own manner, because although his perceptions are usually beyond belief, his random method maddening and his philosophy unacceptable, he teaches one lesson we should not ignore. We must ascertain as far as possible what the words meant, and what they now mean; and we need also to see with what words they may somehow be associated. And we can say that Whiter, who had not the benefit of a concordance, didn't do too badly, though his purposes were awry (as were Spurgeon's similar studies much later). He was misled, like some of his contemporaries, by Locke, and his adherence to an ideology of higher and lower, and might have agreed with Johnson's strictures on knives and blankets. But he did notice things.

In fact it seems to me that the critics who found unconscious lexical associations, or image clusters, and so on, were sensing something more obscure, more important, that it has proved very difficult to describe. Spurgeon was, so to speak, Whiter without Locke: Shakespeare's imagery is a "revelation, largely unconscious, given at a moment of heightened feeling, of the furniture of his mind."[10] Arthur M. Eastman jokes that since Miss Spurgeon prefers to ignore matters of sex she would probably have catalogued Iago's "beast with two backs" under "Animals, fabulous," and Leontes's Sir Smile fishing in his neighbour's pond under "Daily Life, Sport."[11] Here again we see that these demoded critics, like us, are necessarily constrained by conventions they may not have been fully aware of. But they are still noticing something that needs investigation.

Eastman agrees that although Spurgeon may be smiled at her arguments must not be ignored. But they are ignored. Attempts along the lines of Whiter or Spurgeon are now no longer made, and in general critics have lost interest in them, which is not surprising at a time when so few attend to the actual language of the plays. Other more sophisticated (and less vulnerable) books like R. B. Heilman's studies of *Othello* and *King Lear* are rarely if ever cited nowadays, perhaps because of the obloquy that attends all suspected adherents of the old New Criticism.[12]

All these critics, though they may deserve criticism, may be thought to have been at least trying to talk about something real. And all half-decent readers and auditors must be aware of the presence in the plays of certain effects that are powerful though hard to describe; the difficulty perhaps being that they are the consequence not merely of words or even sets of words but of distinctive rhythms that attend their use. As they inhere in the text of each play where they occur, it is certainly misleading to use them naively for purposes of biography: Shakespeare can't have liked dogs, loved nature, and so on. The motives I have in mind arose after the early period; they may have their origins in the cultivated rhetorical repetitions of the early plays, but they are not themselves susceptible to formal rhetorical description. Often there is a discernible deliberation involved, but usually, I think, this lexical-rhythmical subplotting occurred in the process of composition, or, as Whiter put it, *"in the ardour of invention,"* at a time when dramatic verse had been liberated from the verse of the page, and metaphors might be more like meteor showers than constellations.

The passages including "discandy," adduced by Whiter for his own purposes, provide one instance of what I mean. We can't know, and do not need to know, whether Shakespeare started the play with an intention to use many images of melting, and as he went on saw, on the basis of this prior decision, the potential of a link between the indignant disavowals of Cleopatra in the earlier scene and the despair of Antony a few minutes later. With more certainty we can say he did have in mind the Herculean ancestry of Antony, and put him in the position of that god reduced to femininity by Omphale; we do know that in the source of the beautiful scene where the guards hear music that suggests that "the god Hercules, whom Antony lov'd, / Now leaves him" (4.3.15–16), Plutarch speaks of the god Bacchus, not Hercules; a clear case of deliberate planning. Shakespeare had in mind the topos of the choice of Hercules, a choice between virtue and pleasure, and Octavia is emblematic of the first as Cleopatra is of the second — though not with the emphasis proper to straight allegory. But it is not easy to proceed from such clear cases of a prior scheme to less definite instances that depend on a repeated lexical or rhythmical patterning.

Watching *Macbeth* in a fairly good recent television production, I was struck by what seemed obvious, even redundant, rhythmical emphases, as when Duncan, conferring the title of Thane of Cawdor on Macbeth, says "What he has lost, noble Macbeth hath won" (1.2.67), which when you think of it seems to be forced into the dialogue as an echo of the witch's "When the battle's lost and won" in the fourth line of the play, spoken a few minutes earlier. The point is not simply the obvious one that Macbeth could only be given that title of Cawdor when its holder had been eliminated, but that what L. C. Knights, in a celebrated phrase, described as the "sickening seesaw rhythm" of certain passages is established at a point where the terminal emphases on "lost" and "won" are the more prominent because a little odd, intrusive.[13] And we come to see the whole design of the play as concerned with the equivocating opposites — of present and future, losing and winning, flower and serpent, the plot balanced on the fulcrum of Duncan's murder.

It seems clear enough that such devices, probably more concentrated in *King Lear* and *Macbeth* than anywhere else, could not be used until the mature style, so exultantly free and inventive, had established itself. In my *Shakespeare's Language* I touched, but did not dwell, upon the existence of a semantic "ground bass" in *Love's Labour's Lost*: a set of interactions between the words "wit," "will," and "grace"; scattered about, these come to resemble Rabelais's frozen words, which thaw and can be heard again, speaking in consort with one another and giving new tones to the entire play.[14] These feats of language are most deliberate as well as most apparent in the great tragedies, and may be part of the reason why those plays are valued above the others. But there are other words and ideas that thaw quietly without attracting immediate attention: "becomes" and its derivatives in *Antony and Cleopatra*, "think, thinkings, thought" in *Othello*, where they operate more subtly than the heavily advertised iterations of "honest."

All I have attempted in this sketch is to make a plea for a return to the data of the language of the plays. There was a time when editors sought parallels throughout all Elizabethan and Jacobean literature for Shakespearean usage. Some of the first series of Arden editions were crammed with such parallels; in subsequent replacement editions these linguistic data have progressively diminished, and in many of the latest they have disappeared altogether. The lexicographer and BBC Radio commentator David Crystal reports that he and his colleagues are continually searching through secondhand bookshops for those old editions, for they can provide invaluable guidance to what words actually meant. And as I said at the outset, to do that ought to be regarded as the primary task of literary scholarship. When that is neglected, one can hardly expect the secondary duties concerning the interactions of words to be sedulously performed. "Back to the language!" should be the slogan of a new Shakespearean criticism.

2 • The "Idea" of *King Lear*

Marc Berley

1

For his *King Lear*, Shakespeare would have none of the earthly redemption celebrated by his sources.[1] In *The True Chronicle History of King Leir*, the king bemoans his loss of the "title" of "father" — rather than the power of a king — and rejoins joyously with Cordelia.[2] Cordelia forgives her father, and her husband, the King of France, arms against the other sisters and their husbands "to redress this wrong" (184). And as we read in Raphael Holinshed's account, "then was Leir restored to his kingdom" (5). Where his sources are sanguine, as when Gloucester's wicked son achieves pardon, Shakespeare generally goes the other way. And Shakespeare is singular in murdering Cordelia. Shakespeare chose to make *Lear* not only tragic but brutal, so much so that even audiences unaware of the play's more sanguine sources have chided the great playwright for failing to supply a happier ending. But Shakespeare's reason for refusing the happy ending of his sources has a source of its own,

27

one not known for its specific relationship to *Lear*, as is one of its author's other works, but famous for its general influence on Renaissance poetics. In Sidney's *Apology for Poetry*, and specifically its discussion of "fore-conceit," Shakespeare found a reigning principle of Renaissance poetics, and by ingenious inversion he turned it into the chief dramatic principle of *King Lear*.[3]

Sidney's *Apology* makes a number of grand claims for poetry, not least among them the boast that the art of poetry can surpass nature by bringing forth a conceit — a conception or plan — that with "artificial rules" perfects nature. "Nature never set forth the earth in so rich tapestry," writes Sidney, "as divers poets have done, neither with pleasant rivers, fruitful trees, sweet smelling flowers, nor whatsoever else may make the too much loved earth more lovely." Nature's "world is brazen, the poets only deliver a golden."[4] The skill of the poet consists for Sidney, as for Aristotle, in perfecting nature by the effect of a "fore-conceit," a basic plan, a brilliant conception that weaves out of the chaos of daily life the perfection of a probable plot. The poet, as a maker (from the Greek *poiein*) of fiction (from the Latin *fictio*) and rhetorically gifted distiller of plots, is a supreme artificer precisely because probable fictions surpass nature in narrative design. What is most interesting about Sidney's claim is that he attributes this highest distinction to fiction, and to the poet who creates it, not on the basis of the finished product or the fiction itself, but rather the plan or concept on which it is based. As Sidney explains, "any understanding knoweth the skill of the artificer standeth in that *Idea* or fore-conceit of the work, and not in the work itself. And that the poet hath that *Idea* is manifest by delivering them forth in such excellency as he had imagined them" (16). The delivering forth is doubtless crucial, but the "*Idea* or fore-conceit," the plan, or initial conception, not the execution, distinguishes the poet.

In defining the "fore-conceit," Sidney identifies a skill that is possessed by every great maker of fiction, perhaps none as much as Shakespeare. In *Lear*, after years of using his fore-conceits to reshape his sources into drama, Shakespeare made the idea of fore-conceit the very *idea*, or fore-conceit, of his play. With his characteristic inversion, Shakespeare re-conceived Sidney's conception of fore-conceit, focusing on the relationship between fore-conceit and the "work itself." Inherent in his reworking of Sidney's fore-conceit is one of Shakespeare's grandest, and most brutal, lessons about the relationship between the harshness of life and the sweetness of art.

The idea of *Lear* derives from Sidney's claim that the poet, above "all sciences," is "the monarch" because "he doth not only show the way" from wickedness to virtue "but giveth so sweet a prospect into the way, as will entice any man to enter into it" (38). Like Horace in his *Ars Poetica*, Sidney describes the poet's ability not only to teach but also to delight, thereby to move.[5] Teachers give their students *crustula blandi*, cookies that make the lesson sweeter, writes Horace in his first satire.[6] Similarly, as Sidney explains, poets bring sweet recognition that sugarcoats the unpleasantness of the "most wholesome things by hiding them in such other as have a pleasant taste: which, if one should begin to tell them the nature of *aloes* or *rhubarb* they should receive, would sooner take their physic at their ears than at their mouth." Why? That brings us to the stuff of *Lear*:

> So is it in men (most of which are childish in the best things, till they be cradled in their graves), glad will they be to hear the tales of Hercules, Achilles, Cyrus, Aeneas; and hearing them, must needs hear the right description of wisdom, valour, and justice; which, if they had been barely, that is to say, philosophically set out, they would swear they be brought to school again. (38)

We all know this as the main plot of *Lear*: an old king, hoping against hope "unburdened" to "crawl toward death," childishly demands flattering tales from his daughters, commands his only truthful daughter to sugarcoat her bare, philosophical description of filial duty, and refuses to be schooled by his wise, valorous and just counselor. The old king childishly speeds and burdens his way to the grave. His cradling is painful; he is too old to be brought to school again. There turns out to be no hope for the old king, nor for his youngest daughter. She'll have none of sugarcoating life's most brutal lessons, which somehow she already knows philosophically. She abjures the human need for sugary tales, abjures even more the sugarcoating that people use to take advantage of those who fall prey to the natural need for cradling. She is herself ready for death betimes. Those around her — whom she knows for what they are — attempt vainly to reconceive the nature of the world, to live as if fore-conceits are forecasts of what will be, imaginative presumptions of the eventual reality of works themselves. Says Cordelia, in contrast, "what I well intend / I'll do't before I speak" (1.1.225–26).

It is with their fore-conceits that poets surpass nature. But the power of poets, according to Sidney, is only a distinguished concentration of the power possessed by humankind. "Her world is brazen, the poets only deliver a golden. But let those things alone," Sidney continues, "and go to man, for whom as the other things are, so it seemeth in him her uttermost cunning is employed" (15). Nature's "cunning" is in humankind, and humankind, employing that cunning in turn, can surpass nature. It is part of God's plan for humankind to perfect nature by acting in its likeness to God:

> Neither let it be deemed too saucy a comparison to balance the highest point of man's wit with the efficacy of nature; but rather give right honor to the heavenly Maker of that maker, who, having made man to His own likeness, set him beyond and over all the works of that second nature, which in nothing he showeth so much as in poetry, when with the force of a divine breath he bringeth things forth far surpassing her doings, with no small argument to the incredulous of that first accursed fall of Adam: sith our erected wit maketh us know what perfection is, and yet our infected will keepeth us from reaching unto it.

But these arguments will by few be understood, and by fewer
granted. (17)

Shakespeare understood and granted this. The passage applies
to him as much as, if not more than, any other poet of the
Renaissance. But in *Lear*, as nowhere else, Shakespeare turns
Sidney's celebration of the poet's divine power instructively on
its head, especially his notion of fore-conceit. *Lear* shows us
the danger brought about by infected wills that too quickly grant
the vaunted powers of the poet to themselves. In *Lear*, nature
undoes a man, humbling his art, disabusing him of his most
vain conceit: that he may surpass nature with his fore-conceit.

2

Shakespeare's *Lear* does not merely commence its tragedy with
unprecedented speed; it begins with Lear's attempt to deliver
forth a doomed fore-conceit: the division of his kingdom. Lear
enters and initiates a contest in flattery that, unlike the contest in *Leir*, would benefit only him; he expects his daughters
to surpass nature and deliver to him a golden world. Cordelia
gives her father rhubarb. Goneril and Regan acquiesce to Lear's
demand, but the saccharine quality of their flattery suggests
they are little makers already in the process of delivering forth
fore-conceits of their own. As Kent knows, "good effects" will
not "spring from" their "words of love" (1.1.185).

Lear is a brutally didactic play, dramatic rhubarb perfectly
conceived. Its chief lesson is that fore-conceits work for poets
but not for people shaping lives, even kings. During the English
Renaissance, the relationship between the poet's art and God's
art, as Sidney observes, justifies the comparison of the poet
and "that heavenly Maker of that maker." But attribute that
power to men whose chief conceptions derive more from an
infected will than an erected wit and the comparison becomes
"too saucy." As Gloucester's jocular prelude to Lear's tragic en-
trance in the first scene subtly foretells, saucy conceptions are

proof of humankind's destiny to succumb to nature, not to surpass her with fore-conceits. And they are therefore shameful to acknowledge.

Despite the play's pagan setting, Lear intends to be what Sidney describes as a "maker" made in the image of "the heavenly Maker." Lear, however, is not a poet, but a man; and limitations that poets may surpass with their fictions men must confront in their lives, where even wit, however erected, often cannot contravene. As a man badgered by the brutalizing conditions of human life and their attack upon his crawling psyche, Lear has reason to be ashamed of such brazenness.

The fore-conceit of *Lear* is to demonstrate this unpleasant lesson again and again. We had come to the theater to hear Shakespeare's sweet tongue. But Shakespeare, like Cordelia, purposely fails to speak sweetly. By the end we get only the rhubarb of plain diction setting things out "barely": "Let me wipe it first; it smells of mortality" (4.6.132). And we get renunciation of the human ability to surpass nature rather than succumb to its manner of rubbing us out: "O ruined piece of nature; this great world / Shall so wear out to naught" (4.6.133–34).

Shakespeare's poetic power suffers no such natural enervation; he gets stronger, and more brutal, as the play moves toward its gruesome end. Shakespeare not only grants Sidney's argument but lives it: "Only the poet, disdaining to be tied to any such subjection, lifted up with the vigor of his own invention, doth grow in effect another nature, in making things either better than nature bringeth forth, or quite anew, forms such as never were in nature." Only the poet "goeth hand in hand with nature, not enclosed within the narrow warrant of her gifts, but freely ranging within the zodiac of his own wit" (14). Shakespeare surpasses nature in ways people, even kings, ought never to attempt.

Vaunting the power of the poet described by Sidney, Shakespeare surpasses nature by obeying and perfecting it, making the improbable probable by "inventing the inevitable,"

to borrow Alfred Harbage's apt phrase.[7] Shakespeare forces us
to watch the unmaking of Lear, the brutalizing of Gloucester.
As if this were not more than enough, the needless murder of
Cordelia, original to Shakespeare, comes despite Edmund's late
attempt to remand it. Edmund's penultimate plan is delivered
forth exactly as its villainous author had conceived it. It triumphs over his ultimate — and first good — *idea*, with which
he hopes to surpass his nature: "I pant for life. Some good I
mean to do / Despite of mine own nature" (5.3.244). Just when
Edmund sees his first fore-conceit for the bad idea it was,
Shakespeare delivers it forth with cruel excellency: "Run, run,
O run!" (5.3.248), says Albany. "The gods defend her!" (257).
The moment we most desire it, the idea of justice is not delivered forth. We are merely set up to have some final hope.
Cornwall's death by his servant is enough to make Albany say:
"This shows you are above, / You justicers, that these our nether
crimes / So speedily can vent" (4.2.78–80). It had shown noth-
ing: "Enter Lear, with Cordelia in his arms."

King Lear is no *crustula blandi* for schoolchildren. It is
a bitter pill for adults shaped by the idea that they need to
be brought to school again. The play is conceived to humble
humankind — nay, to humiliate, shame and deride us. The
unmatchable power of the poet to fore-conceive is used repeatedly to belittle the fore-conceits of its characters — and its
audience. *Lear* seeks to brutalize rather than erect our wit,
which, too cunning already, has reason to facilitate the infection of our will.

Samuel Johnson was not one to sit and take this. He com-
plained that "Shakespeare has suffered the virtue of Cordelia to
perish in a just cause, contrary to the natural ideas of justice, to
the hope of the reader, and, what is yet more strange, to the
faith of the chronicles."[8] Frank Kermode observes that Johnson
is "expressing dismay at a cruelty inflicted on him personally,"
pointing out that he "is not alone in feeling like that." The
cruelty is inflicted on all of us, not only intentionally, but with

a brutality available only to a supreme artist. "Cruelty is always a matter of a poet's calculation," writes Kermode, and *Lear* delivers "a cruelty in the writing that echoes the cruelty of the story, a terrible calculatedness that puts one in the mind of Cornwall's and Regan's. Suffering has to be protracted and intensified, as it were, without end."[9] There is glaring calculation in Shakespeare's manipulation of his more sanguine sources. Eventually, we are hoping against hope that the calculations of this calculated play will miscarry. But some larger power than the fallen Edmund sees to it that Cordelia dies. That larger power is Shakespeare, master of fore-conceit, whose *idea* in this play is to turn all fore-conceits against their conceivers, including our ideational demand for justice.

Lear brutalizes us as Shakespeare sets out his lesson barely: fore-conceit is the height of poetic power, and also the seed of human destruction. With the idea of *Lear* in place, perhaps Shakespeare brought forth the work in the easy manner described by Sidney. Shakespeare achieves some of his brutality simply by tweaking his sources in the direction of rhubarb. Near its end, *Leir* has Leir composed enough to say about his suffering: "'Twould make a heart of adamant to weep" (177). Shakespeare, invoking the greater power of showing over telling, simply made his Lear a crumbling soul of weepy adamant. It is hard to witness because the idea of *Lear* is to make its audience withstand the very condition we, in our early judgment of the play's early actions, think Lear should have been able to withstand himself: hearing no sweetness in the ear precisely when one has shown up for the purpose of drinking sweetness in.

Those who, finding *Lear* too brutal, wish Shakespeare had the good sense to write the play more to their liking have long had distinguished company, such as Dr. Johnson: "I was many years ago so shocked by Cordelia's death, that I know not whether I ever endured to read again the last scenes of the play till I undertook to revise them as editor" (240). It took about 75

years for someone to defy Shakespeare's conception and reconceive a play about Lear that people could endure. Nahum Tate's
version of *King Lear*, which ran from 1681 to 1838, deletes the
purportedly indecorous Fool and marries Cordelia and Edgar,
among other things. Deleting the Fool and saving Cordelia does
not merely free the play of its brutality; it obliterates what
Sidney would call its *"Idea* or fore-conceit." The Fool is the
only character who can merge "bare" teaching and decorous
sweetness, which is, as we will see, a distinguishing aim of
Shakespeare's play. Tate was eventually rejected, and audiences
have for almost two centuries preferred a version of *Lear* far
closer to what Shakespeare's company performed, but we all
experience Johnsonian disgust accompanied by a will to reconceive the play.[10]

There is a relationship between the play's focus on fore-
conceit and the will to reconceive the plot that the play
arouses. As Lear stands to nature in the play, so Shakespeare
makes us stand to the play itself: as recalcitrant naysayers who
wish to reconceive things in a way that will resolve our burden. We are to the play as Lear is to the storm, and we have,
like Lear, trouble doing what we are supposed to do: renounce
our will to reconceive the inevitable and suffer patiently. This
can make the play seem "sadistic," a matter, observes Kermode,
of "authorial savagery," *irony* being "too civilised a word for
it" (195). Nature is not ironic precisely because it is not civilized; and Shakepeare's art, in the manner described by Sidney,
surpasses nature's storm.

Lear doubtless requires of us Joblike patience. But why is it
we seem to leave the playhouse with none of our goods restored?
Perhaps, like Johnson, we cannot forgive Shakespeare. But we
might, I think, understand him better if we focus on the *idea*
that not only makes *Lear* brutal but also heightens our reaction to its calculated brutality. Shakespeare's brutality here
serves a purpose that he would attempt in no other play. *Lear*
explores the pedagogical value of setting things out barely, its

chief lesson being that the deepest, most basic psychological truths must be fiercely sought out, however brutal. No one who seeks them, as Freud would eventually remark, can come out unscathed. Shakespeare does not scathe us, I would argue, out of any sadistic motive, but rather a therapeutic one, fierce and proto-Freudian in its focus on the consequences of repression, especially the denial of the powers of nature that human ingenuity inevitably invites.

It takes Lear only 50 lines to express his wish to crawl unburdened toward death. Seventy lines later, he recognizes it will not be fulfilled: "I loved her most, and thought to set my rest / On her kind nursery. . . . So be my grave my peace" (1.1.123–24). For a man so trooped with majesty, the crawl toward death, even on Cordelia's nursery, could never be "peaceful." But Lear ensures that it will be the least peaceful possible. Lear appears to have been staring into the abyss. Wishing to shrink from it, but gleaning the cowardice of such a wish, he jumps into it as a man so eager to master the loss of mastery that his bravery makes him foolish.

Lear is a play about repression, conceived in Shakespeare's brilliant terms. Repression in *Lear* is archetypal: the refusal to relinquish an idea that can never be delivered forth, and the consequent impulse toward self-deception to hide one's shame. The bare philosophy of *Lear* digs humankind into the places we would not willingly go, even though we are already there. Hamlet, unlike Lear, is himself too brutal to resort to repression. But he is also too clever to cure himself, and the play is not concerned with curing him. *Hamlet* is concerned with the difficulties of diagnosis, intent to pose, in a perplexing new style, some of life's most perplexing questions. *Lear*, in contrast, is a play of brutal answers that explores the difficulty of accepting a cure. Kent quickly diagnoses Lear's error, then barks at him the cure: "What wouldst thou do, old man?" "See better, Lear, and let me still remain / The true blank of thine eye" (1.146, 158–59). If you don't see well, says Kent, see well enough to let me see for you; master your loss of mastery; being weak, don't seem so, lest the world find superfluous opportunities to beat up on your shadow. The play then makes us suffer Lear's resistance to cure. And with far more brutal treatment than Kent proffers Lear, it engages its audience in its own resistance, which is rooted in a need to see better, and conceive better, than the play. As a result of the excessive mixture of fear and pity we experience, we may sit and blame the character of Lear for failing to come to grips more quickly with things as they are, even while we suppress our inability to accept the manipulations of a playwright in his theater for what they are, "inventions of the inevitable." My aim here is not only to appreciate the *idea* of *King Lear* but also to justify the brutal ways of Shakespeare in unfolding it.

3

Becoming childish, needing cradling, wishing to hear sweet tales rather than bare truths — this describes Lear. Bringing people to school again and setting things out barely — this describes *Lear*. Tensions between sweet and bare teaching fill the play; they are deepened by a focus on conceptions — doomed fore-conceits, misconceptions and general faults — and the shames they engender. "Great persons," writes Francis Bacon, are "the first that find their own griefs, though they be the last that find their own faults."[11] Lear sees his children, his natural conceptions, as causes of his grief. His children, he thinks, prevent him from accomplishing his "fast intent":

> Give me the map there. Know that we have divided
> In three our kingdom; and 'tis our fast intent
> To shake all cares and business from our age,
> Conferring them on younger strengths while we
> Unburdened crawl toward death.
>
> (1.1.37–41)

It is noble to know when to relinquish one's power and "crawl toward death," and hardly unnatural to want to keep one's power too. But the crawl is certain to be heavy, and the "fast intent" to conceive it as "unburdened" is repressive and destructive. Shakespeare's mixture of the voice of the man with the voice of the king early reveals one cause of the latter's repression; the crutch of royal trappings makes it hard for him to go from three legs to four. ("They told me I was everything" [4.6.103–04].) In the deep recesses of his soul, Lear wants to be ready for the transformation from king to man, from man to child, and — as Edward Tayler has shown us — from everything to nothing.[12] But he is not ready.

"The art of our necessities is strange," beyond our conception, as Lear comes to learn. It is one of the cruelties of the play to transform Lear's fear of his burden into a greater one, just as it transforms his healthy willingness to relinquish power into an irrational need for a puissance that is gone. Such cruelty is Shakespeare at the height of his psychological acumen, as is Lear's hamartia, or tragic error. It takes only 100 lines for Lear to mar his favorite daughter's fortunes and thereby his own, thus destroying the grand fore-conceit with which he enters the stage. When, fewer than 150 lines into the play, Lear attacks Kent, we witness the implosion of a man unable to apprehend the error of his fore-conceit and unwilling to acknowledge his impotence to deliver it forth "with such excellency as he had imagined" it. When Kent approaches Lear in a manner that appears to forget his royal power, Lear has in fact just relinquished it; Kent only seeks to tell him that he has done so foolishly. It is Kent's hope that Lear will recant. But Lear is consumed by the majestic power of fore-conceit, and already well into the hopeless phase of delivering it forth. Lear will soon go to war with Nature, but first he disowns or banishes anyone who suggests that his worst plan is powerless to defeat her. "The bow is bent and drawn; make from the shaft" (1.1.143), Lear warns Kent. The threat vividly relates fore-conceit to Lear's inability to bring his forth. Lear tells Kent what he means to do, and Kent dares him to do it: "Let it fall . . ." (144). Lear is angry because in botching the delivery of a bad idea he is stripping himself of his ability to deliver forth any future ideas: "Only we shall retain / The name, and all th' addition to a king," says Lear. "The sway, Revenue, execution of the rest, / Belovèd sons, be yours" (1.1.135–38). Lear's manner is grand, but he relinquishes the "power, / Preeminence, and all the large effects / That troop with majesty" (130–32) precisely because, as he will later come to accept, he no longer truly owns them. Kent seeks too early "to come betwixt our sentence and our power," which, says Lear, "nor our nature nor our place can bear" (170–71).

By giving power to Goneril and Regan, Lear conceives his most painful unmaking. It is a foolish act, as the Fool tells Lear upon his arrival. Lear first literally conceived and now unwittingly conceives two little makers who will first unmake the world he wanted them to preserve and then destroy themselves attempting to create a world shaped to their lust for power, especially the power to conceive. "Conceive, and fare thee well" (4.2.24) Goneril will say to Edmund, wishing to impregnate the play's great conceiving villain with her own machinating seed. Lear early sees Goneril's lust for conception, which she inherits from him.[13] Thus his curse:

> Hear, Nature, hear; dear goddess, hear:
> Suspend thy purpose if thou didst intend
> To make this creature fruitful.
> Into her womb convey sterility,
> Dry up in her the organs of increase.
>
> (1.4.266–70)

Lear apostrophizes Nature, asking her to "suspend" her grand fore-conceit. He at first appears concerned that Goneril will conceive "unnatural" children that will further corrupt the world.[14] But he shifts: "If she must teem, / Create her child of spleen, that it may live / And be a thwart disnatured torment to her" (1.4.272–74). Lear wants Goneril to suffer what he suffers, to feel the "serpent's tooth" of "a thankless child," one's natural conception gone painfully awry. He does not know it yet, but Lear is more at war with Nature, the arch conceiver, than with his daughters.

Regan refuses Lear "addition" that might keep his mind from his stark nature. "I gave you all," says Lear. "And in good time you gave it," replies Regan (2.4.245). On the matter of servants, she reasons him down to "What need one?" No servant means no mastery. And mastery, as Freud would later explain, having learned in this and other matters from Shakespeare, is related to sexual impulse. Regan's cold zero sends Lear's mind not as much to the poor returns of a woman's nothing as to his impoverished ability to conceive a fore-conceit:

> you unnatural hags!
> I will have such revenges on you both
> That all the world shall — I will do such things —
> What they are, yet I know not; but they shall be
> The terrors of the earth.
>
> (2.4.273–77)

Revenge against thankless daughters turns into revenge against the earth, the will to do "such things" Lear cannot even conceive — as his cracking syntax (a shadow of his royal command) indicates — and has no power to do. What he will do is suffer, and Shakespeare will make sure his suffering is among the greatest chronicled suffering of the earth.

The idea of conception is linked to Lear's loss of mastery, the cause of his shame, the source of his repression, themes that merge in the play's opening lines as Gloucester describes his sport begetting Edmund. Like Lear, Goneril, Regan and Edmund have excessive ambition, infected will. According to Freud, as Shakespeare had shown, "the impulses of sexual life are among those which, even normally, are the least controlled by the higher activities of the mind."[15] In *Lear*, the higher activities of the mind are overcome by the sexually inflected will to conceive. Lear desires to check the conceptions of his "unnatural" daughters, but he is not undone by his daughters as much as by his own impulse to conceive, beyond human powers, the natural course of things.[16] After threatening to conceive "such revenges" but perceiving his inability to do so, Lear says he could become womanly. "No, I'll not weep," he says, choosing rather to be broken "into a hundred thousand flaws," choosing first to acknowledge that his plans miscarry, then to go mad instead: "O fool, I shall go mad!" (2.4.274–81). It is not weeping that threatens to make Lear womanly; it is Nature. And refusing to weep won't stop Nature in her course.

For too long, Lear's excessive faith in his power to conceive escalates his war with Nature and exacerbates his suffering. On the heath, reacting to Nature's inconceivable power and fertility, Lear becomes what today one might callously describe as a walking piece of phallologocentrism who unwittingly conceives his own deconstruction:

> And thou, all-shaking thunder,
> Strike flat the thick rotundity o' th' world,
> Crack Nature's moulds, all germains spill at once,
> That makes ingrateful man.
>
> (3.2.6–9)

The ill-conceived command to spill all seeds at once confirms defeat, the child's feeble reaction against the great mother, Nature, whom, unlike the poet, he cannot surpass or impregnate with his intentions. "Fear of the archaic mother," Julia Kristeva observes, "turns out to be essentially fear of her generative power."[17] As we might expect from someone angry at Nature's power to conceive, Lear commands what is already too true. He demands that the power that has already undone him be unleashed. It is a brutal inversion of Sidney's "fore-conceit of the work."

Renaissance notions of embryology generally see the womb as a fallow field ready to accept a man's seed. "He ploughed her, and she cropped," says Agrippa of Caesar and the Egyptian queen in *Antony and Cleopatra* (2.2.229). But it is women who "conceive," as Gloucester puns in the play's first scene, and once they do, whether the father wishes to acknowledge his "breeding" becomes a question. "I cannot conceive you," says Kent in response to Gloucester's cryptic acknowledgment of Edmund. "Sir," replies Gloucester, "this young fellow's mother could; whereupon she grew round-wombed." Gloucester invites Kent to "smell a fault." But Kent says, "I cannot wish the fault undone, the issue of it being so proper." "The whoreson must be acknowledged," says Gloucester just after he has tried, feebly, to obscure him. Gloucester, who early speaks of coming to acknowledge his fault by being "brazed to't" will later have cause to say: "Our flesh and blood, my lord, is grown so vile / That it doth hate what it gets" (3.4.136–37). In *Lear*, the round womb is the mysteriously powerful place of a man's undoing, or ciphering, by Nature. It is where the spiller of seed relinquishes, by the very act of conception, his power to "conceive."

The power of *Lear* derives from the artistic perfection with which Shakespeare upbraids the conceptions of his characters. Lear's aversion to the sexual act derives from his anger at the way its products escape one's control. It is a symptom of his repression of the deeper knowledge that he must suffer nature's conceptions. Lear's disgust with sex is very different from Iago's in *Othello*. Whereas Iago's is an ingrained and perverse attitude toward the act, Lear's is a vengeful reaction to the consequences of sexual union, not to the sexual act itself. When Lear sees a good consequence he praises fornicators: "Let copulation thrive; for Gloucester's bastard son / Was kinder to his father than my daughters / Got 'tween the lawful sheets" (4.6.113–15). Of course, his facts are in error. Where conceptions are concerned, Lear cannot get anything right.

Beaten by the power of nature, Lear begins to understand that it is not nature that corrupts a man, but rather the "addition" he conceives: "unaccommodated man is no more but such a poor, bare, forked animal as thou art" (3.4.101–03). The fact that Edgar is only playing Tom makes this important recognition no less true. But, like others, it is a truth Lear evades. He still clings to the value of "addition." "You, sir, I entertain for one of my hundred," Lear tells Tom, "only I do not like the fashion of your garments. You will say they are Persian; but let them be changed" (3.6.76–79). Lear notes the poor man's need to reconceive the world after his fashion, but he still cannot identify his own pitiful impulse to do so.

As Lear learns on the heath, Nature alone offers protection to her creatures. Where Nature is most brutal, she is, by her inversions, also strangely sweet: "This tempest will not give me leave to ponder / On things would hurt me more" (3.4.24–25). To the pain of experience Nature administers amnesia (senility); to the pains of the mind and the heart she administers anesthetic (bodily pain); and to loss, such as the loss of mastery or competence in general, she administers false autonomy of the last resort (repression). Repression, of course, is eventually helpless against facts. And when anagnorisis becomes too intense for repression, as it does for Lear, Nature doles out, as if it were a self-administered morphine drip, her nearest panacea, the ability to float in and out of madness. Shakespeare's *Lear*, however, offers its audience no such protection.

4

King Lear presents a line of brutal teachers: Cordelia, Kent, Lear's Fool and, finally, Lear himself. Cordelia and Kent set things out barely in their naive belief that what is obvious to them will be obvious to the person they seek to teach. People like Lear seem to require bare teaching, there being no other way to shake them into their proper cares. Sidney observes that bare teaching, like philosophy, teaches only those who already know. Such Aristotelian wisdom, however, does not cover the case of Lear, who knows basic truths but is yet unready to acknowledge them. When it thrusts truth at such people, bare teaching shames. It does not let one come to one's own conclusions; thus, it deprives one of mastery and heightens the repression of that shame.

Cordelia's answer to her father's pressing question is bare and philosophical even to the point of cold pedantry. Lear asks: "[W]hat can you say to draw / A third more opulent than your sisters? Speak." "Nothing, my lord," replies Cordelia, who then goes on to say too much (1.1.85ff.). "But goes thy heart with this?" asks Lear. "Ay, my good lord," answers Cordelia. Lear importunes Cordelia ("our joy, / Although our last and least") to ignore certain aspects of reality. But might she not simply deliver the truth more sweetly, and communicate her disappointment that the truth is so brutal? We are made to wonder how different things would be if she answered "no." Lear could well understand a heart nay-saying the grimmest reality. Conversely, he cannot brook one that does not. "So young, and so untender?" "So young, my lord, and true." Lear's suggestion that Cordelia "mend" her speech "a little" seems to be a wrangle over method. Perhaps Lear would be satisfied with the kind of sugared truth described by Sidney, and would discern it as different from the falsehoods he hears from his two oldest daughters. But when Cordelia gives Lear her purposeful rhubarb, setting out barely her love of her father ("You have begot me, bred me, loved me"), she indulges her need to dispute her sisters' falsehoods, and attack even more fiercely her dear father's acceptance of their lies, his demand that they quantify their love:

> Why have my sisters husbands if they say
> They love you all? Haply, when I shall wed,
> That lord whose hand must take my plight shall carry
> Half my love with him, half my care and duty.
>
> (1.1.99–102)

Cordelia takes from Lear half the filial love he treasures long before Goneril takes half his train. Whereas Goneril and Regan begin by offering all, then half, then nothing, Cordelia begins by offering "Nothing" and ends by offering half.

Cordelia's one "small fault" is a hatred of lies that leads her to set truths out far more barely than a weak heart can endure. She shames her father and makes him hate what is true, shame being, as Freud would later observe, an even nastier problem than guilt. Only a horribly ineffective teacher, contra Sidney, goes after shame with the bluntest edge of truth. Cordelia lacks "that glib and oily art," as well as appreciation of its potential value. Words hurt. As Lear reports to Regan, Goneril "struck me with her tongue / Most serpent-like upon the very heart" (2.4.155). When they engage the heart in the theater of the mind, words are actions. Saying is doing.[18] Thus Cordelia early: "what I well intend / I'll do't before I speak" (1.1.225–26). But Cordelia's words to Lear do what she least intends. She does first with brutal words what her sisters do later with brutal action: wrest from Lear what he clings to, his authority. Inversions make a tragedy all the more tragic, as Aristotle observed. Cordelia's intentions miscarry; she is her father's daughter.

Kent, an even blunter teacher than Cordelia, furthers her lesson. Kent works earnestly to serve Lear, but he is undone by Lear's error; he compounds Lear's shame by urging him to regain something he has already lost, self-mastery.[19] And in refusing to "make from" Lear's "shaft," Kent becomes even more brutal. "Be Kent unmannerly / When Lear is mad. What wouldst thou do, old man?" (1.1.145–46), says Kent, focusing on Lear's declining powers. The severity of Lear's condition, says Kent, justifies his bluntness. Like Cordelia, Kent is not a teacher who could successfully set Lear to school again. Rather than teach Lear the simple lesson that he cannot at once give all away and yet retain it, they induce him to give it away to the wrong people. Rather than teach Lear that his crawl toward death cannot be "unburdened," they induce him to make his crawl all the more burdened. Failed teachers who are banished, Cordelia and Kent both reappear later as pupils; but first they reappear in different roles, as better teachers. With Cordelia gone to France, banished Kent presents himself to Lear, posing as "a very honest-hearted fellow" who would serve the king. Kent tries to give back to Lear precisely what he had bluntly said was lost: "you have that in your countenance which I would fain call master." "What's that?" asks Lear. "Authority," says Kent (1.4.17–29). Having learned that bare teaching humiliates in a way that is counterproductive, Kent quickly hones the art of flattery. He must call himself "honest-hearted" but may not be so honest. Kent lacks, however, the skill to bring an old man back to school. That mastery belongs to the Fool. Cordelia gone, Lear's Fool arrives to replace her, played by Robert Armin, who almost certainly played Cordelia. The Fool is more sweet than Cordelia, but also more brutal. His skill is to deliver brutal truths in a manner that makes painful lessons endurable.

The play's master teacher, the Fool, is an expert in both pedagogy and psychology. His lessons are endurable not because he has arbitrary license but because his riddles offer Lear a new mode of learning. When the Fool is about, Lear is as a child ready for his playful lessons. The routine is to listen to what the Fool says and ask him to explain his foolishness. This has the important effect, among others, of demonstrating to Lear, by his own questions, that he has no way to explain his recent foolishness. The lessons are philosophical, but they are too witty to be bare. "Dost thou call me fool, boy?" asks Lear. "All thy other titles thou hast given away; that thou wast born with" (1.4.141–43), answers the Fool. The Fool's riddles probe Lear's troubles in circuitous ways that give the feel of sugaring. Once Lear recognizes truths he doesn't like, he is too deeply into their mazes to repress them. The Fool helps Lear reach his own conclusions, and thus allows him to accept his shames.

The Fool, though, is dealing with the great repressive hero of Western literature. He must take Lear, again and again, through the anagnorises he delays by repression. Hence, even the Fool cannot slant sufficiently some of the principal lessons: "When thou clovest thy crown i' th' middle and gav'st away both parts, thou bor'st thine ass on thy back o'er the dirt. Thou had little wit in thy bald crown when thou gav'st thy golden one away. If I speak like myself in this, let him be whipped that first finds it so" (1.4.152–57). A bare lesson, the Fool knows, must be followed immediately by a perplexing song about the comparative value of fools and wise men. And when Lear evades even the Fool's calculated evasion — "When were you wont to be so full of songs, sirrah?" (162) — the Fool knows to get bare again: "I have used it, nuncle, e'er since thou mad'st thy daughters thy mothers" (163–64). There is a psychological rhythm to brilliant teaching.

The Fool's duty, to help Lear confront painful truths, is one he has trouble fulfilling: "Prithee, nuncle, keep a schoolmaster that can teach thy fool to lie. I would fain learn to lie" (1.4.170–71). The pain endured by the honest teacher is potentially one of the play's few civilized ironies. Lear's riposte turns it brutal: "An you lie, sirrah, we'll have you whipped" (1.4.172). Lear has what it takes to become what to this point he has most failed to be, the play's best student.

The Fool brings about humility in Lear, not humiliation. Humiliation is the domain of nature, and the villains it engenders. Shakespeare gives not only the Fool but also the play's villains what Cordelia and Kent lack: expertise in pedagogy and psychology. Villains exploit this knowledge. Unlike Cordelia and Kent, the villains know to be sweet before they are brutal. Flattery makes any fool, especially an old one, more susceptible to brutality directed at the wound the flattery is meant to soothe. Thus, eventually, Regan: "I pray you father, being weak, seem so" (2.4.196). Goneril and Regan borrow Satan's method: seducing by lies, conquering with truth. Good characters don't know until after they succumb. Thus the play's deepest pedagogical and psychological wisdom must come from the mouths of villains: "O, sir, to willful men / The injuries that they themselves procure / Must be their schoolmasters" (2.4.297–99).

Determined to make things easier for Lear, Kent must struggle to subdue his plainness. He knows it will shame Lear to find his new servant in the stocks, and Gloucester says twice it will be "ill taken" (2.2.153), but plainness — indeed, "saucy roughness" (2.2.92) — is Kent's nature. "What's he that hath so much thy place mistook / To set thee here?" asks Lear upon seeing Kent in act 4, scene 2. "It is both he and she, / Your son and daughter," says Kent, naming them each twice — and somewhat more if you count the force of "both." Lear's lingering inability to accept disparagement leads Kent to revert to brutal didacticism. "No," says Lear. "Yes," says Kent. Lear: "No, I say." Kent: "I say yea." Kent's chiasmus appears less an artful lesson than a downright cruelty. "No, no, they would not," Lear again counters. "Yes, they have," says Kent. "By Jupiter, I swear no!" "By Juno, I swear ay!" Kent's persistence in negating Lear's negations appears to justify the hyperbole of Lear's final pronouncement: "They durst not do't; / They could not, would not do't. 'Tis worse than murder / To do upon respect such violent outrage" (2.4.11–23). Kent worsens Lear's shame at finding him in the stocks. He cannot distinguish "sweet" and "bare" teaching, and he has the fatal pedagogic flaw: the casual observation that cuts too deep: "How chance the King comes with so small a number?" asks Kent upon Lear's exit to speak with Regan. "An thou hadst been set i' th' stocks for that question, thou'dst well deserved it," scolds the Fool. Kent is shameless: "Why, fool?" The Fool admonishes Kent not to send an old man back to school again: "We'll set thee to school to an ant, to teach thee there's no laboring i' th' winter." Kent comments not on the Fool's wisdom but the manner by which he gained it: "Where learned you this, fool?" It is a foolish question. The Fool, expert in setting old fools to school, must offer Kent one of his trenchant lessons: "Not i' th' stocks, fool" (2.4.61–83). A bare teacher, Kent is also the play's worst pupil. Though younger than Lear, Kent is, as he tells Cornwell, "too old to learn" (2.2.122).

By the end of the play, Lear assumes the role of the play's ultimate teacher. He has learned from the Fool to teach "bare" lessons with riddles.[20] "We'll go to supper i' th' morning," says Lear. "And I'll go to bed at noon" (3.6.82–83), says the Fool. Lear's education is complete. The Fool's role is finished; Cordelia must return and finish the role as Lear's "poor fool." Having internalized the Fool's philosophical wit, Lear becomes the play's new artificial fool. "Thou must be patient. We came crying hither; / thou know'st, the first time that we smell the air / We wawl and cry" (4.6.175–77), Lear tells Gloucester. An inversion of the first scene, it shows us that psychological maturity comes, here tragically, when one is finally brazed to primal shames. Lear comes to understand that he is no different from anyone else in being a "natural fool of fortune" (188). His wisdom starts to hurt us. "Why, this would make a man a man of salt, / to use his eyes for garden waterpots, [Ay, and laying autumn's dust]" (192–94). Lear not only accepts burdens and realities he once evaded; he teaches us that we must accept them. "I will die bravely, / Like a smug bridegroom" (194–95), says Lear, continuing, in a new vein, the fertilizer metaphor. Lear recalls the puissant king of the first scene who, regarding his words as self-actualizing intentions, expected to impregnate the world with his conception. The old man likens, with the wit of "smug bridegroom," the temporary death of a man's inseminating organ and the absolute death he will soon enough die. The little death will become the big one; and the little maker may rejoice in his large limitation, for it will set him free from the burden of conceiving. "What, I will be jovial! / Come, come" (195–96). But acknowledgement is hard; all loss is not all gain. "I am a king; masters, know you that?" (196) asks Lear. His emphasis is on the word *king* and the degree to which it suits him as he fades. A Gentleman loyal to Lear knows to observe that the word doesn't wear out its truth until the king dies: "You are a royal one, and we obey you" (197). Lear then flames the fire of our hopes even more than his own: "Then there's life in't. Come, an you get it, you shall / get it by running. Sa, sa, sa sa!" (198–99). We must chase after him, if we believe in life.

The sweetness of Lear's teaching is uncannily bare. This reversal is a fore-conceit that Shakespeare, inverting Sidney, delivers forth with too much "excellency." Once captured, Lear's greatest attribute is his hope. There is no more fighting villains, who are as the time is. Lear appears both mad and wise. He speaks of the final dissolution that attends him and Cordelia: "He that parts us shall bring a brand from heaven / And fire us hence like foxes." (22–23). He offers no more fore-conceits attempting to surpass nature. Rather, he appreciates the therapeutic value of verbal conceits that resign playfully to things as they are. He could still use kind nursery, but he knows instead to give it: "Wipe thine eyes. / The goodyears shall devour them, flesh and fell, / Ere they shall make us weep! We'll see 'em starved first. / Come." (23–26). This is not evasion. It is manly nursery for a father to give his prisoner-daughter hope. Lear's hope will end only if Cordelia dies. To make an audience cling to Lear's hope even after Lear's "poor fool" is hanged is a crueler part of the fore-conceit of the play.

5

"The finest kind of recognition [anagnorisis]," writes Aristotle, "is accompanied by simultaneous" reversal of fortune (peripeteia), as in Sophocles' *Oedipus*.[21] Recognition of a reversal of fortune, especially the tragic hero's recognition of his tragic error (hamartia), is the center of good tragedy. For the playwright, anagnorisis is the moment of delivering forth with excellency his fore-conceit by thwarting the fore-conceit of his character. For the character, in contrast, anagnorisis is the antithesis of his fore-conceit, and peripeteia is the antithesis of delivering forth one's fore-conceit with excellency. Anagnorisis occurs at the moment a character recognizes that his fore-conceit has been trumped by the fore-conceit of a higher power. A character's devotion to the power of fore-conceit despite recognition of reversal of fortune is repression.

Shakespeare's *Lear* reworks Aristotle. No play since *Oedipus* is more concerned with, or more skilled at, anagnorisis than *Lear*. But *Lear*, unlike *Oedipus*, purposefully separates reversal and recognition in a way that makes the recognition more painful. *Lear* is a play about repression, and Lear's resistance to recognition is the protracted tragic action of the play. *Lear* is, in many respects, an inversion of *Oedipus*. Lear's reversal comes almost immediately, a result of his own foolish action. The recognition also comes early, so early and in so casual a manner we are invited to miss it:

> Fool: Thou canst tell why one's nose stands i' the' middle on's
>   face?
> Lear: No.
> Fool: Why, to keep one's eyes of either side's nose, that what a
>   man cannot smell out he may spy into.
> Lear: I did her wrong.
> Fool: Canst tell how an oyster makes his shell?
> Lear: No.
>
> (1.5.19–23)

Anagnorisis just occurs, without the fanfare of ironic warnings. There follows no immediate action, such as the howling of Oedipus. When Lear does howl, later, on the heath, the recognition has been repressed, the blame displaced. He howls not in the agonizing mastery of self-punishment, but in finger-pointing anger at the requirement to accept his shame. Lear argues that he is more sinned against than sinning. Such baleful disorder he had expected Nature to prevent. Shakespeare conceived a new kind of drama, examining repression with an attention we may call modern.

King Lear, more than any other of Shakespeare's plays, engages its audience's impulse toward repression. "The essence of repression," writes Freud, "lies simply in the function of rejecting and keeping something out of consciousness."[22] It is an

enormous responsibility to be in charge of keeping things out
of the consciousness of others, as Edgar is for Gloucester, or to
be in charge of keeping things in consciousness, as Shakespeare
is for us. Aristotle warned playwrights to keep brutality off the
stage, and to narrate any violent actions required by the plot. In
Lear, Shakespeare would have none of this, just as he would
have none of the optimism of his sources, and none of Sidney's
admonitions against bare teaching. The play is an anti-Aristotelian coup. "The revenges we are bound to take upon your
traitorous father are not fit for your beholding," Cornwall tells
Edmund (3.7.7–9). But somehow they are fit for us. We must
watch the vile blinding of Gloucester, a horridly protracted act.
No simultaneity, just botched premeditation. It takes a while
to accomplish "both, both." Of course, a simultaneous peripeteia and anagnorisis immediately follow: "O my follies! Then
Edgar was abused. / Kind gods, forgive me that, and prosper
him" (3.7.91–92). But Gloucester's last simultaneous peripeteia
and anagnorisis, when he learns the good news that the gods,
who treat men as wanton boys do flies, have prospered Edgar,
we may not see. Edgar must narrate:

> But his flawed heart —
> Alack, too weak the conflict to support —
> 'Twixt two extremes of passion, joy and grief,
> Burst smilingly.
>
> (5.3.197–200)

If done right, Shakespeare shows us, narrative can be more violent than spectacle, words more powerful than deeds. The passage ends "smilingly," but the graphic word order has its
brutality; it suspends us in the extremes. Actions cannot do
that. Words must wield such crucial matters. Else we would not
see them feelingly, and our fear and pity would not be extreme.

   It moves even Edmund. It is remarkable poetry, beautiful.
With *Lear*, Shakespeare, long before Freud, gives us deep pains
that are strangely pleasurable. Maynard Mack describes the

cause of gratification in broad terms: "Lear's 'new acquist' of self-knowledge and devotion to Cordelia, the majesty of his integrity and endurance, the invincibleness of his hope."[23] True enough, but, as Tayler observes, when "proleptic form . . . at long last coincide[s] with plot," Cordelia's lips bring us the play's "promised end," and with it Lear's knowledge — and ours — that nothing can come of nothing. "It is," writes Tayler, "Lear's apocalypse, the theatrical 'image of that horror,' and the un-folding of the deepest and most final of truths."[24] And it is too much for us to bear. Doubtless "there is something appalling about the thought of an author who will submit his characters and his audiences to" the events that are *Lear*, as Kermode writes (194). But in art, if not in life, sweet and brutal may lose distinction. *Lear* makes the pain it produces pleasurable in a deeply uncomfortable way. We can tolerate Shakespeare's art, but not the inevitabilities he invents. We can appreciate the fore-conceit of *Lear*, but not what it brings forth.

In this play about the loss of its protagonist's mastery and his repression of it, there is too much brutal mastery of the audience. Shakespeare's homage to nature in *Lear* anticipates Freud. We cannot enforce our meanings on the world, cannot impregnate reality with meanings we conceive, cannot deliver forth fore-conceits with excellency. We identify with impatient Lear, thwarted in his mastery by Nature. We identify, too, with patient Cordelia.[25] The audience is mastered, rendered passive, or womanly; and neither men nor women like it.

Shakespeare not only considered these matters long before Freud; he analyzed a problem regarding the mastery of art from which Freud himself would suffer: "[W]orks of art do exercise a powerful effect on me. . . . This has occasioned me, when I have been contemplating such things, to spend a long time before them trying to apprehend them in my own way, *i.e.* to explain to myself what their effect is due to. Whenever I cannot do this, as for instance with music, I am almost incapable of obtaining any pleasure," writes Freud. "Some rationalistic, or perhaps analytic, turn of mind in me rebels against being moved by a thing without knowing why I am thus affected and what it is that affects me."[26] Such a need for mastery is related to our adverse reactions to *Lear*.

In "man," writes Sidney, nature's "uttermost cunning is employed" (15). During the Renaissance, people were, as John Donne asserted, "little worlds made cunningly." Cordelia, similarly, obeys God's art, which unfolds human ingenuity and shames those who believe in its ultimate power: "Time shall unfold what plighted cunning hides, / Who covers faults, at last with shame derides, / Well may you prosper" (1.1.280–82). Cordelia might seem early to deliver the fore-conceit of the play and refer to its two contexts, its two conflicting meanings. In the Christian worldview to which the pagan Cordelia seems anachronistically to allude, she adheres to the only fore-conceit in which humankind can trust, God's plan. In the world of the theater, however, where she is only a character on a stage, the Christian playwright gradually derides the fore-conceits of all of the conceited, world-shaping characters out of which he shapes his play. When Cordelia delivers these portentous lines, we are heartened, for we already wish to see Goneril and Regan shown for what they are. Most important, we think the playwright has let us in on his *idea*, the key to understanding the play that will ably guide our expectations. We are happy to trust theological and theatrical time to cohere as co-fathers of truth. But by the play's end, our trust is betrayed. Time unfolds the plighted cunning of villains, but not before they kill Cordelia and mangle our souls. Cordelia's trust in what appears to be the Christian fore-conceit of the play is the one Shakespeare most brutally obstructs. "We are not the first / Who with best meaning have incurred the worst" (5.3.3–4), says Cordelia in prison, when the worst, to paraphrase Edgar, is yet to come. "Is this the promised end?" asks Kent. Then Edgar: "Or image of that horror" (5.3.264–65). The playwright, surely, is too much a master of us all.

The relationship between nature and art in Shakespeare's day has been well described by Kermode and Tayler. "The chain of command, as we say, is perfectly clear. Art imitates nature, and Nature is the Art of God," writes Tayler. Human ingenuity partakes of God's art. But although this relationship is the basis of the power of the poet described by Sidney, it also prescribes limits. Even for powerful Renaissance poets, Kermode observes, acceptance of this "Christian dogma" means "the end of their autonomous art."[27] The art of the poet partakes of God's divine art, but the limitation of the poet's human powers must be understood, and granted. In *Lear*, Shakespeare shows us how brutally nature dominates human ingenuity. Still, as Sidney suggests, a poet may be a better teacher than nature: Shakespeare surpasses nature in teaching us the lesson that humankind cannot surpass nature. The play's setting had to be pagan: the conflict between its pagan realities and the Elizabethan audience's Christian expectations maximizes the crucial rubs.

Cordelia could not let Lear deliver forth his fore-conceit. And we have our difficulties allowing *Lear* to deliver forth Shakespeare's fore-conceit. Shakespeare repeatedly teases us by letting us think we can have our fore-conceit for the play, a happier ending; then he purposefully fails to delight us. In its day, the pagan context engaged — most ironically (and cruelly) — the Christian audience's fruitless hope for redemption. Even today, like Lear in act 2, we are susceptible to baseless conceptions of "good hope" (2.4.183). Finally, the lesson of the play is too bare: we must deliver forth no fore-conceit for an alternative experience to the play. In life, as opposed to art, fore-conceit is "addition," a human attempt to act like Sidney's poet and surpass nature with precisely those powers that nature possesses to the exclusion of humankind. So Lear strives "in his little world of man to outscorn / The to-and-fro-conflicting wind and rain" (3.1.10–11). This describes a man, a microcosm, unable to bring order to the insurrection in his mind, let alone wage successful war against nature. Says Edgar to Gloucester, "Men must endure / Their going hence, even as their coming hither; / Ripeness is all" (5.2.9–11). For the poet, in contrast, as Sidney describes it, fore-conceit is all. Shakespeare possessed, above all poets, the power of fore-conceit. But he knew, as a man, the necessity of conceding to Nature her insuperable power.[28] Human beings cannot create out of nothing; and when they try to recreate or obliterate something — especially Nature, God's art; but also perhaps a poet's art — they court trouble.

The idea of *King Lear* is to render Nature's greatest power: her defeat of human ideas or fore-conceits. Shakespeare surpasses Nature only in the sense that he perfects artistically her manner of wearing us out with what she sets forth, defeating our hopes, brutalizing what is best in us.[29] By making the improbable probable, Shakespeare pays homage to Nature's power to rub us out. And there isn't any one of us, his admirers, who doesn't somewhat hate him for this singly brutal abandonment of the poet's duty to sugarcoat, to create a golden world. Poetry is supposed to teach by delighting. But it may teach even more by refusing to delight. We evade bare truths at our peril. Often we need the villains we empower to tell us: "to willful men / The injuries that they themselves procure / Must be their schoolmasters."

3 • The Consolation of Art in the *Aeneid* and the *Tempest*

Michael Mack

Starting with J. M. Nosworthy's groundbreaking essay on the narrative sources of the *Tempest*, critics have uncovered more than a few parallels between the *Tempest* and the *Aeneid*.[1] Between the opening tempest, which is akin to the storm Juno causes to shipwreck her enemy Aeneas, and the climactic discovery of Ferdinand and Miranda playing chess, the conventional activity for Aeneas and Dido in at least one medieval iconographic tradition, a half dozen or so episodes in the *Tempest* can be seen glancing back at passages in the *Aeneid*.[2] Critics most often have given central importance to the relation the parallels develop between the tragedy of Dido and the happy marriage of Miranda.[3] Indeed, it has frequently been pointed out that the shipwrecked Ferdinand's first words to Miranda, "Most sure the goddess / On whom these airs attend!" echo the shipwrecked Aeneas's first words to a beautiful maiden (who happens to be his mother in disguise), "O dea certe!"[4] With Ferdinand as the new Aeneas, Miranda, it follows, is a new Venus, and a new Dido. The new lovers reenact Virgil's moving episode, but with a difference: whereas the union of Dido and Aeneas is lustful and barren, engendering only lasting enmity between Rome and Carthage, the marriage of Miranda and Ferdinand is chaste and fruitful, promising to unite the two kingdoms of Naples and Milan in peace. Although it is less obvious and has received less attention, the relation between the revenge of Pallas, which occurs at the end of the *Aeneid*, and Prospero's revenge plot is also significant. As Robert Wiltenberg has shown, just as the tragedy of Dido is transformed in the marriage plot of the *Tempest*, the revenge of Pallas is transformed in Prospero's revenge plot, which does not end in vengeance but in mercy. Whereas Aeneas banishes thoughts of mercy and kills the vanquished Turnus in fury, Prospero overcomes his fury and chooses to forgive his enemies when they lie at his mercy.[5] In reworking this Virgilian material, Shakespeare unquestionably succeeds in transforming tragedy into tragicomedy, and in writing a play that not only attains the status of literary "work," but also deservedly takes a place in the lofty epic tradition.

When one views the *Tempest* as (at least in part) a reworking of Virgil's epic, other parallels emerge. One that critics have not yet noted is the similar way each work of art calls attention, within itself, to works of art. The most famous example in the *Aeneid* is the passage on the shield of Aeneas, which is the Roman world in miniature, with the victory of Augustus at Actium in the center. Also important is the description in the opening book of the temple of Juno, where Aeneas finds carved episodes from the Trojan War. In the *Tempest*, Prospero's magic is, of course, his "art," and its most obvious artistic production is the play-within-the-play, the betrothal masque for Ferdinand and Miranda. Although the resemblance between these instances is not immediately apparent, both of these works of art in the *Aeneid* are occasioned by loss: Vulcan produces the shield when Aeneas is downcast about the impending war and his premonition of Pallas's death, and the scenes in the temple of Juno depict the painful loss of Troy, which Aeneas has just suffered. Although the occasion of the masque is a happy event, the betrothal of Miranda is a loss: Prospero's loss of his daughter. Each of these works of art also offers some consolation for the loss that is its occasion. Whereas the shield depicts the great victory of Augustus over Antony and Cleopatra, the tragic scenes in the temple show Aeneas that his fame has preceded him and that in this strange land he will not find barbarians but people capable of sympathy and kindness. And the masque presents Prospero, who is about to give away his daughter in marriage, a vision of a timeless world in which parents do not lose their daughters.

As I will argue, in each of these cases, the consolation of art turns out to be only a seeming consolation. In the *Aeneid*, art may promise kindness, but in the end it much more surely brings about passion. Virgil's epic opens with the temple of Juno, but it closes with Aeneas thrusting his sword into Turnus after seeing a different work of art, the belt of Pallas. In the *Tempest*, Prospero's art was once a consolation to him, a retreat from political life. But by the start of the play, Prospero understands something that was never clear to Aeneas: art offers no real consolation. Prospero's dedication to his secret studies, however seemingly consoling, was in fact the occasion of loss, the loss of his dukedom. By the end of the play, Prospero will not place any false hopes in his art. Whereas Aeneas saw in art an expression of human kindness, Prospero expresses his kindness not in art but in his action, specifically, the act of renouncing his art.

In playing variations on the material it employs, the *Tempest* resembles all secondary epics; but in boldly reversing the outcome of the story it inherits, the *Tempest* is particularly

Virgilian, for Virgil does the same with the story he receives
from Homer. Transforming a Trojan refugee into the founder
of Rome, Virgil turns those defeated at Ilium into those who
would eventually rule not only their Greek conquerors but
the entire known world. Although this transformation of loss
into victory is most certainly propaganda for the empire, it is
also part of an extended and far more subtle — even ambiguous — treatment of the relation of gain and loss. Within the
larger arc of loss turned into victory are many episodes illus-
trating the loss that accompanies victory. On the way to founding Rome, Aeneas suffers lost, time and again. Home, wife
and father are all taken away from him; and then instead
of having Dido taken away as well, he is required — much
worse — to sacrifice her for the sake of a Rome that does not
yet exist and that he would be happy to forget.

In the climactic episode in Virgil's presentation of the ironies of glory, Aeneas descends to the underworld, where
Anchises shows him the future heroes of Rome. They are, of
course, mere shadows of their future selves. Moreover, the
future glory of these shades is brought into relief by the dark
knowledge that, like the Greeks before them, the Roman heroes will experience the painful cost of glory. Indeed, Rome
will suffer its greatest loss precisely in the time of its greatest
glory. Although Augustus "shall bring once again an Age of
Gold / To Latium," he will suffer the loss of his chosen successor, Marcellus (6.792–93). "In shining armor, but with
clouded brow / And downcast eyes" [fulgentibus armis, / sed
frons laeta parum et dejecto lumina voltu], Marcellus, the
destined heir, is fated to die young (6.861–62). His loss would
cast a cloud even over the glory of the deified Augustus. And
it casts a cloud of grief over Anchises as well, who is reminded
that Ascanius will suffer the same fate as Marcellus, failing to
succeed Aeneas. In Virgil's poem, the tears well up in Anchises
as he narrates this history in which political victory flows
into personal loss, and tradition has it that the historical

Augustus wept as Virgil read the passage to him. In the end, the glory of the heroes of Rome, as Virgil reflects it in his poem, will be that people will read their story and weep.

In the *Aeneid* the grand theme of victory-in-loss cannot be separated from the countermotif of loss-in-victory, the nuanced development of which gives the work its darker tones, its pervasive sense of the deep irony of things. To understand the victory of Aeneas is to understand not only his accomplishment but his loss. And to understand the *Tempest* is, in part, to understand Shakespeare's reworking of Virgil's sense of the heavy personal cost of political victory. Prospero's success, like that of Aeneas, has something hollow about it. In his famous epilogue, Prospero argues that one reason the audience should forgive him is that he has recovered his dukedom, which confirms what has been increasingly clear throughout the play: political victory is not his ambition but his penance. Like Aeneas, Prospero is not glory-seeking but duty-bound. And like Virgil's hero, his victory comes at a high price. Although he regains his political power, he forsakes the far more extraordinary power of magic. And although he secures a lineage through his daughter's children, he must release his daughter from his care and let her experience the world of political wrangling, which he knows from bitter experience to be neither brave nor new. Giving up his daughter, whom he calls a "third of [his] own life," Prospero will return, albeit victorious, to a place where every "third thought" will be his "grave" (5.1.312). It is against this backdrop of loss that art offers consolation.

In their respective artistic monuments, Virgil and Shakespeare seem to present art as a kind of a refuge against personal loss. The shield of Aeneas, with its depiction of the future glory of Rome, seems to offer Aeneas some refuge from his personal loss. He loses himself in the marvelous vision just as readers lose themselves in the extended ekphrasis. Just as Homer fit the whole Greek cosmos onto the shield of

Achilles, so too Virgil places the whole Roman empire, with
the sea in the middle of the lands, on the shield of Aeneas. At
the center of the shield of Aeneas is the naval victory at Actium,
and the depiction of the defeated Cleopatra recalls the demise
of Dido. This parallel makes Aeneas's freeing himself from
Dido the type of Augustus conquering Egypt, and thus Aeneas's
more modest and more personal success foreshadows the great
political victory at the foundation of the empire. But in the
analogy, Aeneas is not only Augustus. Having been charmed
by a woman into forgetting his duty, he also is Antony. His
victory over Dido therefore is really a victory over himself,
and on this shield that glorifies Rome, Aeneas is reflected in
both victor and the vanquished.

This aesthetic treatment of loss and glory, though it does
not do away with pain, might nevertheless offer some sense of
consolation. By incorporating pain into a larger pattern, whose
beauty can be contemplated through tear-filled eyes, the shield
could help make sense of suffering. Although pain mixed with
joy would be an appropriate reaction to the scenes depicted,
in the work of divine craftsmanship Aeneas finds unalloyed
joy. His response lacks the appropriate complexity for one
simple reason: he does not understand what he sees. At the
end of the passage, Virgil makes it clear that the wonder Aeneas
experiences is not matched by understanding:

> All these images on Vulcan's shield,
> His mother's gift, were wonders to Aeneas.
> Knowing nothing of the events themselves,
> He felt joy in their pictures, taking up
> Upon his shoulder all the destined acts
> And fame of his descendants.

> [Talia per clipeum Volcani, dona parentis,
> miratur rerumque ignarus imagine gaudet,
> attollens umero famamque et fata nepotum.]

> (8.729–31)

For Aeneas the history of Rome is not yet history. Ignorant of
the significance of Actium, he is also ignorant of its relation

to his own story with Dido. If the work brings him consolation, it is because he does not understand it. It does, however, achieve the end for which it was created, to prevent Aeneas from hesitating to battle Turnus. As will the belt of Pallas, it moves Aeneas to action, though it fails to provide him knowledge of the future or of himself. Finding joy not in things but in pictures — images of things that do not yet exist — Aeneas happily takes the shield, which represents the world, upon his shoulders. Not knowing that he is carrying a burden that Atlas did not wish to bear, pious Aeneas here seems duped by the gods into so lightly taking upon himself the weight of future glory, of an empire and a world he so little understands. As an implement of war, the shield offers a most certain defense in battle; as a work of art, however, it offers no refuge from battle. In scene after scene of future conflict, the shield offers an immortality that is an unending war, and the "fame" and "fortune" of his descendants will be like his, to fight eternally. Not understanding what he sees, he does what the gods have decreed: he goes into battle.

In the opening book of the *Aeneid,* on the other hand, when Aeneas beholds the marvelous works of art in the temple of Juno, he understands their subject matter as few could. Entering the temple after having just survived a tempest which Juno inflicted on him, Aeneas finds the struggles of the Trojan War (already) depicted. These scenes encompass the *Iliad* in the *Aeneid,* and they transform the song of glory into what is for Aeneas a tragic spectacle. Marveling at the "*miranda,*" the "wondrous sights" of his own defeat (1.494), Aeneas finds a strange consolation. With tears in his eyes, he asks, "What region of the earth is not full of the story of our sorrow?" Seeing himself as others have seen him, he wonders that

> Even so far away
> Great valor has due honor; they weep here
> For how the world goes, and our life that passes
> Touches their hearts. Throw off your fear. This fame
> Insures some kind of refuge.

[quae regio in terris nostri non plena laboris?
en Priamus! sunt hic etiam sua praemia laudi,
sunt lacrimae rerum et mentem mortalia tangunt.
solve metus; feret haec aliquam tibi fama salutem.]

(1.460–63)

He is consoled to know that through these works of art others
have identified with his suffering, and that they have been
touched by the "lacrimae rerum," the tears of things, and by
thoughts of mortality.[6] The recognition that the world is passing thus becomes a source not only of pain but also of consolation, insofar as Aeneas realizes that others share the same
recognition. In this shared recognition, tears of sadness are no
longer a subjective response; they are part of the objective
nature of things. Things do not provoke tears, they possess
them. And nothing is more filled with sorrow than the defeat
of the valiant, which is seen in the fall of Troy.

It is truly a great artistic accomplishment to show that the
nature of things is as fluid as it is poignant. But despite the
power of the insight they convey, the images in the temple of
Juno are no more substantial than the sad and evanescent glory
they enshrine. Like the shades Aeneas will see in the underworld and the picture of the naval victory at Actium that will
decorate his shield, the images in the temple are images of
what is not present. Immediately after Aeneas says that their
fame will bring them some refuge, Virgil describes the scenes
not as "wonderful sights" but as an image that is empty,
"pictura . . . inani," and he says that Aeneas is feeding his soul
on this unsubstantial picture: "animum pictura pascit inani"
(1.464). When he marvels at the scenes in the temple or on
the shield crafted by Vulcan, the consolation Aeneas finds
proves as insubstantial as the images he takes in. The fact
that others have been moved by his suffering is something
beautiful, but not something that will save him from suffering.
Dido's compassion will become, thanks to the meddling of
Venus and Cupid, a furious and consuming passion, turning

sympathy into enmity. Indeed, in the temple of Juno, what Aeneas takes to be a recognition of valor and a sign of sympathy looks, to the less sophisticated viewer, like the portrayal of the humiliation of Troy, like propaganda for his spiteful goddess-enemy. So too, on closer inspection, the "fame" that precedes Aeneas and that is figured forth in the temple carries a note of insubstantiality, as that of mere "rumor" or "report." As Mercury makes clear to Aeneas, his mission will allow no refuge except Italy (where, of course, he will go to war). With layered irony, Virgil shows Aeneas finding comfort and refuge in defeat, but comfort and refuge that will prove as hollow as the cave in which he and Dido escape the storm. In an exquisite work of art, a work that becomes one of the core texts of the Latin West, Virgil presents the consolation of art as ultimately insubstantial, and its power as largely the power to deceive.

Like Aeneas, Prospero knows that the consolation of art is not lasting. For Prospero, his magical art once seemed to offer a refuge from the toil of political life. When he was duke of Milan, his library seemed dukedom large enough, and there he retreated into the study of magic. But his books of magic were only a seeming sanctuary from the travails of political life, for it was when he lost himself in his Art that Prospero suffered his greatest political ordeal, usurpation. In the 12 years between his being usurped and the start of the play, Prospero has clearly adopted a different approach to his art. No longer characterized by the *otium* of the liberal arts, it is all business. The opening tempest is a powerful work executed with practical consequences in mind, the most important one being to initiate his plot to regain his lost dukedom. Whereas Aeneas is diverted from his mission by a tempest conjured by his enemy, Prospero conjures a tempest in order to divert his enemies and to reclaim his mission as ruler. Combining the tempest of the *Aeneid* with the tragic art in the temple of Juno, Shakespeare's opening tempest and shipwreck are

emblems of misfortune, a tragedy in epitome, and they evoke
the same response as the *"miranda"* in the temple of Juno.
Herself a wonderful sight in her innocent, woeful admiration,
Miranda responds to the spectacle not only with words of
"amazement" but also with a perfect expression of sympathy: "O! I have suffered / With those I saw suffer" (1.2.5–6). It
is just this kind of sympathy that Aeneas attributes to the
Carthaginians who have heard the story of his suffering and
been moved to immortalize it in art. Although Miranda will
stop her "amazement" when her father assures her that the
shipwreck was only an illusion, her sympathy, unlike that of
Dido, will not fail.

Like the initial tempest, the other spectacles that Prospero
produces with his Art are as insubstantial as they are powerful. The banquet that he presents the hungry courtiers van-
ishes before their eyes; and the sumptuous clothing hanging
on the line with which he lures Stephano and Trinculo is the
embodiment, as it were, of appearance without substance. The
betrothal masque that Prospero presents Miranda and Ferdinand is similarly insubstantial, enacted by "airy spirits." It
stands apart, however, from the previous spectacles in that
it captivates not only the intended audience but also Prospero himself, who loses himself in the wondrous vision —
until he recalls the business at hand, interrupts the masque,
and gives his famous "Our revels now are ended" speech.
Having felt the dangerous charm of this work of his art,
Prospero rejects the escapist consolation of the masque and
instead seeks the consolation of philosophy. Referring to the
aborted masque as a "baseless vision," he shifts from aesthetics to metaphysics and meditates instead on the world as
an "insubstantial pageant." Prospero realizes what Aeneas
did not: the insubstantiality of artistic images. Whereas art
moves Aeneas to passion, Prospero calms himself by contemplating the insubstantiality of art, and he is consoled not by

the poignant consideration of the "tears of things" but by the thought that the world, with all of its passion, suffering, and tears, is passing.

Although Prospero's earlier spectacles, the original tempest and the banquet spoiled by the harpies, are obvious borrowings from Virgil, the betrothal masque has a more subtle and complex relation to the *Aeneid*. Reworking material from Ovid as well as Virgil, Shakespeare transforms the tragic outcomes of his ancient sources into the harmonious vision of a betrothal masque. The production of the masque is not, however, without its obstacles; and these obstacles are not without thematic significance. To produce the masque, Juno, the goddess of marriage, calls on Ceres, the goddess of increase and plenty; but Ceres hesitates for fear that Venus and Cupid may be present. Only after she is assured that Venus and her blind boy will not interfere does Ceres join Juno.[7] The most obvious explanation for this complication can be found in the *Metamorphoses*, specifically in the episode of the rape of Ceres's daughter, Proserpina, by the god of the underworld, Dis. In this story Venus is annoyed that Proserpina insists on following the example of Diana, and she dispatches Cupid to shoot Dis — which clearly explains Ceres's hard feelings toward Venus in the *Tempest*. As well as explaining Ceres' anxiety, Ovid's story accounts for the changing of the seasons, which is the theme of Prospero's masque. After the abduction of Proserpina, Ceres will not allow anything to grow on the earth until a return of her daughter is negotiated. When an arrangement is finally made, Proserpina spends half the year with Ceres and half the year with Dis, during which time Ceres withholds her bounty and we have the barren season of winter. In Shakespeare's reworking of Ovid's story, the masque of Ceres presents a golden world in which spring follows immediately upon the harvest. This world without a winter, a world in which parents never have to give up their daughters, is the dream of both Ceres and Prospero, who in fact says that the spirits "enact" his "present fancies" (4.1.121–22).

This transformation of the Ovidian source provides a timeless vision in which both cupidity and loss are excluded. This ideal world is, of course, mere wishful thinking, something Shakespeare makes abundantly clear when he allows the timeless vision to suffer an untimely interruption. The play within the play is interrupted when Prospero recalls Caliban's "plot" (4.1141). Presumably, the plot is that of Caliban, Stephano and Trinculo to take over the island. This, however, is not the only plot in Prospero's painful memory: Prospero also remembers the earlier plot of Caliban to rape Miranda, a plot Prospero just barely foiled (1.2). Out of the "dark backward and abysm of time" Prospero recalls Caliban's plot, and the recollection interrupts the masque exactly at the point when winter would set in, the point of the year at which Proserpina would descend to the realm of her abductor, Dis. It is, of course, fortunate that reality intrudes upon this idealized vision, for it reminds Prospero that he must set in motion his own plot to foil that of Caliban. Whereas the timeless vision fails, and even places Prospero in jeopardy, his timely action is effective — not in eliminating Caliban, but in controlling him.

Though elegant, Shakespeare's use of the mythological material supplied by Ovid is rather obvious. His handling of Virgil, on the other hand, is more subtle and more sustained. After the myth of Proserpina is used to illuminate the scene, what remains unclear — and something that recourse to Ovid cannot resolve — is the reason Ceres thinks Venus may be attending Juno. Since Juno has no part in the rape of Proserpina, there is no obvious reason for Ceres to think that Venus and Cupid should be with Juno. But in the *Aeneid*, Juno does in fact ally herself with Venus to plot the marriage of Aeneas and Dido.[8] As the enemy of Aeneas, Juno tries to prevent his founding of Rome, first by arranging for the tempest that puts him in Carthage and then by orchestrating his marriage to

Dido. In the *Aeneid* the alliance of Juno and Venus made for a marriage marked by passion and fire. The substitution of Ceres for Venus in Prospero's masque, on the other hand, betokens a chaste and fruitful marriage for Miranda and her brave new Aeneas, Ferdinand.

The masque celebrates qualities notably absent in the marriage of Dido and Aeneas. Enacted by "temperate nymphs," the masque seamlessly unites temperance and timelessness. In overcoming disorder of unrestrained passion and defying the insatiable appetite of time, who eats all things (*tempus edax rerum*), temperance is the key to not only a pure but also a lasting love. Juno's blessing of the lovers calls for temporal happiness to be enjoyed eternally: "Hourly joys be still upon you" (4.1.108). "Still" here means "ever," and the implication is that their chaste love will never fade. This time-conquering temperance is that of *Sonnet* 18, in which the beloved, "more temperate" than "a summer's day," will escape the decay brought by time and will enjoy an "eternal summer." Whereas the love of Aeneas and Dido was a short-lived and self-consuming passion, that of Ferdinand and Miranda will be a temperate love that will not fade. At least that is the dream of Prospero until time, and Caliban's plot, break in. Again, if Miranda is to be saved from the wiles of Venus, Caliban, and their ilk, it will be by Prospero's timely action rather than his timeless art.

When Prospero extends his art to encompass the art of the theater and produces the masque of Ceres, it is by all accounts truly wonderful. Before it is enacted, Prospero memorably calls this betrothal gift "Some vanity of mine Art" (4.1.41). Although a conventional expression of modesty, Prospero's litotes also states the simple truth. The masque, enacted by airy spirits, really is nothing. Though a charming work of artifice, it is one that Prospero "bestow[s]" only "upon the *eyes* of this young couple" (4.1.40, emphasis mine). Once the "timeless" vision is cut short, Prospero describes the "vision" as "baseless" and "insubstantial" in an attempt to comfort Ferdinand. Although his words clearly provide Ferdinand little comfort, Prospero himself does find a strange consolation in the fact that not only the masque, but even

> the great globe itself,
> Yea, all which it inherit, shall dissolve,
> And, like this insubstantial pageant faded,
> Leave not a rack behind. We are such stuff
> As dreams are made on; and our little life
> Is rounded with a sleep.

$$(4.1.156–58)$$

This speech is, on the one hand, metatheatrical, with Prospero acknowledging that he is only a fictional character whose performance will end. But his meditation, Stoic and existential, takes him beyond the limits not only of the theater but of life itself. Prospero finds consolation in the consideration not of the possibility of permanence but in the certainty of impermanence. He understands the real world to be, like the "baseless vision," something "insubstantial" that shall itself "dissolve" (4.1.159–60). Fully accepting what the masque tried to exclude — time, passion, mortality — Prospero now sees clearly the baseless and fugitive nature of life. His meditation on the "nothing" that lies behind the insubstantial world succeeds where the masque fails. It is a *memento mori* that provides, ironically, a truly timeless vision.[9] Prospero recognizes what Lear would not: "thou art an O without a figure," "thou art nothing" (1.4.192, 194). He has attained the same wisdom that Richard II gained through suffering the loss of his kingdom: "Nor I, nor any man that but man is, / With nothing shall be pleased till he be eased / With being nothing" (5.5.39–41). Prospero has what Wallace Stevens much later would call "a mind of winter," the mind of one who, "nothing himself, beholds / Nothing that is not there and the nothing that is."[10] Although Shakespeare is hardly original in asserting the "vanity" of the world or of art — Ecclesiastes had long before given a thorough presentation of the former, Agrippa more recently of the latter — he presents the theme with a sophistication and power that had never been seen before, except, perhaps, in the *Aeneid*.

Although both Virgil and Shakespeare know well that the past and the future are at best shadows of the present moment — no more substantial than artistic images — they are also well aware that the memory of the past bears heavily on present action. In the opening book of Virgil's epic, Aeneas makes a rhetorical argument based on the proposition that in the future the present will be the past, and he tells his companions that in the future they will look back on their present hardships and perhaps (*forsan*) find pleasure in recalling them (1.203). Even if time transforms experience and there is in fact pleasure in the memory of past hardships, Aeneas does not really believe that the pleasure will be worth the pain it costs. He presents the consoling idea when pain is unavoidable, and he suspects that it is little more than a coping mechanism for epic heroes. Like all such devices, it works best for those who think least, and although his men are heartened by his words, Aeneas is not. He is inventive enough to argue that memory will transform the present, but he is realistic enough not to believe his own conceit. Shortly after his speech to his men, Aeneas does in fact have the chance to look back on his suffering, in the temple of Juno. The scenes that recall his past suffering do offer consolation, but a consolation that holds out the false hope of finding a refuge in Carthage. Virgil shows that although memory can transform pain, it provides no shelter from it.

Although he knows that through his pain he is to attain future glory and will live in the memory of all Romans, Aeneas nevertheless has no more taste for his mission as founder than Prospero has for his role as duke. When he is with Dido, he is happy to forget about the future, and Jupiter must send Mercury to remind Aeneas of his mission and of the future glory

that depends on his reaching Italy. Pious Aeneas sets out because it is his duty, and because he is *reminded* of it. Despite
his personal reluctance, when he is reminded of his obligation to the future he acts in the present.

Aeneas receives an even stronger impetus to act from the
memory of the past at the end of the epic. When Aeneas is on
the verge of killing Turnus, he wavers. The words of Turnus,
"If you can feel a father's grief . . . then / Let me bespeak your
mercy for old age," make Aeneas think of his own father, and
how Anchises would have felt if he had seen Aeneas killed.
Out of sympathy for the father of Turnus, Aeneas is on the
verge of sparing the life of his son. But as he wavers, he sees
the belt of Pallas, and is reminded of the pain of the loss of his
friend: "Aeneas raged at the relic of his anguish / Worn by this
man as trophy," and standing over Turnus, "terrible in his
anger," Aeneas shouts,

> You in your plunder, torn from one of mine,
> Shall I be robbed of you? This wound will come
> From Pallas: Pallas makes this offering
> And from your criminal blood exacts his due.
>
> (12.947–49)

The memory of what Turnus had done to Pallas moves Aeneas
not just to action, but to furious action. In the next instant,
Aeneas plunges his sword into the chest of Turnus, and present
vengeance exacts the due for past violence. The personal
memory of his friend moves Aeneas with a passion that the
memory of his vision of the future of Rome cannot match.
More powerfully than the words of Mercury is the desire
to avenge.

In the *Tempest*, as well, memory has the power to convert
past suffering into present action. In the long second scene,
Prospero prepares Miranda and the audience for the "present
business" by exhorting his daughter to look into the "dark
backward and abysm of time." When he supplies the details

of their exile that were lacking in her memory, she exclaims

> Alack, for pity!
> I, not rememb'ring how I cried out then,
> Will cry it o'er again. It is a hint
> That wrings mine eyes to 't.
>
> (1.2.132–35)

Miranda's wonderfully innocent memory responds to the mere "hint" of past tears with new tears. The guilty memory of Alonso is neither as sensitive nor as simple. Alonso's guilt remains buried in his memory, and it takes a prodigy to bring it to the surface:

> O, it is monstrous! Monstrous!
> Methought the billows spoke, and told me of it;
> The winds did sing it to me, and the thunder,
> That deep and dreadful organ-pipe, pronounc'd
> The name of Prosper; it did bass my trespass.
> Therefore my son i' th' ooze is bedded; and
> I'll seek him deeper than e'er plummet sounded,
> And with him there lie mudded.
>
> (3.3.95–102)

When the past deed surfaces in his present circumstances, he suffers a crisis of conscience. Through anamnesis, Alonso recognizes that he deserves — and even is responsible for — the present evils he suffers. Remembering things as they really were, in all their monstrosity, Alonso is changed. He wishes to suffer the evil effects of the evil deeds he has committed, and if only possible, he would take upon himself the suffering of his son, whom he thinks is drowned and buried in the mud of the sea floor. To his newfound misfortune he responds with his newly felt guilt and present penitence. His brokenheartedness and his desire to be buried and befouled is a perfect image of atonement, and in him Prospero has achieved his "purpose." His enemies "being penitent, / The sole drift of [his] purpose doth extend / Not a frown further" (5.1.28–30). Insofar as Alonso's mishap causes him to feel the pain of conscience that he previously failed to experience, it is for him a fortunate misfortune. For in his willingness to suffer for his previous unkindness and for the human cost it has exacted, his heart of stone is replaced by a human heart, one that can suffer with others, one that can give and receive human kindness.

If Alonso suffers as a penitent for his past misdeeds, Prospero suffers as a victim of those same misdeeds. Unlike Alonso, however, he has no need to remember the past events, for he has never forgotten them. But although he remains "strook to th' quick" by the "high wrongs" of his enemies (5.1.25), he overcomes his own "fury" and thirst for vengeance and chooses mercy. In choosing forgiveness, the "rarer action," Prospero shows that his "affections" are in fact made "tender" by the suffering of others (something Ariel doubted). And like Miranda's woeful suffering with those she saw suffer in the opening of the play, Prospero's sympathetic tears at the sight of Gonzalo are an emblem of human sympathy and kindness: "Holy Gonzalo, honorable man, / Mine eyes, ev'n sociable to the show of thine, / Fall fellowly drops" (5.1.62–64). The "holy" and "honorable" Gonzalo is crying at the sight of the just suffering of unjust men; in joining him Prospero shows an even greater sympathy than that of Miranda or of Gonzalo insofar as he suffers with those who, far from being "brave," have injured him. Here Prospero does just the opposite of the victorious Aeneas, who, when moved to sympathy by the words of the defeated Turnus, was reminded of his anger by the sight of the belt of Pallas. Aeneas experiences a moment of kindness but, because of memory, is moved to furious vengeance; Prospero is tempted to fury but, despite his bitter memory, chooses kindness. For Virgil's hero, Roman duty trumps human feeling until the last episode, in which Aeneas's fury coincides with his duty as founder of Rome. For Shakespeare's hero, Machiavellian *virtù* seems to master Christian "virtue" until

the final act, when Prospero's sympathy finally matches his
duty to forgive.

   Closely united to the "rarer action" of forgiveness at the
conclusion of the *Tempest* are the "rare affections" that develop between the young lovers when they are lost to their
parents. Before presenting the pure affection that the young
lovers have for each other, Shakespeare alludes to the unhappy
marriage of Claribel, which was the occasion for Alonso and
his party coming within Prospero's sphere of influence. Designed with an eye for political expedience, and nothing else,
this marriage was not preceded by an exchange of affection.
There is no evidence that any consideration was given to human feeling, and presumably Claribel was at least as unhappy
with the arrangement as her father Alonso clearly was. This
loveless marriage is compared, to the confusion of critics, to
that of Dido and Aeneas. Uniting the marriages is not only
their common location, but their common hollowness.
Whereas the marriage of Claribel and her new husband is without love, that of Aeneas and Dido was void of the due rites
linking the two parties — Aeneas reminds Dido that he "never
held the torches of a bridegroom, / Never entered upon the
pact of marriage" (4.338–39). These marriages, each empty
in its own way, stand in contrast to that of Ferdinand and
Miranda. This happy union duly observes the outward forms,
which Dido's did not, and, unlike the marriage of Claribel, it
is not without love, the proper stuff of marriage. Although
also an arranged marriage, the arrangement was for the two
young people to fall in love and to marry for love, without any
knowledge of the political benefits that their union would
bring. Unlike the empty marriages of Dido and Claribel, that
of Miranda is real, and it has as its substance love.
   Shakespeare uses yet another Virgilian device to highlight

the "rare affections" of Ferdinand and Miranda. The device is the ring composition, which is a symmetrical arrangement, designed to call attention to a significant central scene. In imitation of Homer, Virgil uses this ring composition to frame the story of the Trojan horse. Although it is not possible to say with certainty that Shakespeare was thinking of Virgil when he plotted out the scenes for the *Tempest*, there is no question that the scenes form a ring composition.[11] The characters on stage in the first scene match those of the last scene, the second mirrors the penultimate, and so on; and the matchless middle scene is that in which Ferdinand and Miranda pledge their love to each other. Striking is the contrast between what each author frames. Whereas Virgil calls attention to the paradigmatic act of deception, Shakespeare highlights the simple and sincere pledging of troth. Virgil portrays conquest, Shakespeare mutual submission. Ferdinand and Miranda do have a contest, but one in which each struggles to deprive the other of the menial task of bearing logs. Unlike the Greeks and Trojans, the young lovers compete not to win but to lose. Instead of the hollow gift of the Trojan horse, Shakespeare shows two lovers offering one another nothing less substantial than their very selves.

When the progression of scenes in the *Tempest* is viewed from above, from the perspective of eternity, the lovers are the substantial core. As the central image of the play, their exchange of "rare affections" is the one thing that stands out from the flow of time, the one thing that does not pass away. But just as the lovers have the privileged position in the center of the play, they also have the privilege of appearing at the end of the play. Their discovery playing chess is the final spectacle of the *Tempest*, and the first wonder worked by Prospero after abjuring his wonder-working art. Enacting in different circumstances the same mutual submission found in the central scene, the lovers are once again competing to lose to each other, but this time using deception: each is trying to lose without the other knowing it.[12] When viewed from within, from inside the flow of time, the lovers are no longer the central vision; they are, rather, the ultimate vision. They are a regenerative vision that has the power to "content" Alonso, who had become aware of his own hollowness (5.1.170). Unlike all of Prospero's previous spectacles, this one is not the product of his Art but of human nature. Transforming loss into gain and tragedy into tragicomedy, the vision of the lovers offers just the opposite of what Aeneas found in the temple of Juno and what the Trojans found in the hollow horse: an image that has substance, an image that can bring contentment that will not fade, an image that can convert the "baseless fabric" of human existence into something that, finally, is not wholly "insubstantial."

4 • Donne's *Anniversaries*
The Powers of the Soul

Louis L. Martz

Edward Tayler's book on Donne's *Anniversaries* (1991) is the most important study of Donne's poetry to appear in the past decade. It is unfortunate that it was published just too late to be included in the volume of the *Donne Variorum* devoted to the *Anniversaries*; the editors closed this commentary with the year 1989, although the volume did not appear until 1995. It would, I think, have been wise for the editors to have included at least a brief mention of Tayler's book, since it serves as a firm corrective to Barbara Lewalski's influential book on these poems.[1]

Tayler corrects Lewalski on two major points. First of all, he shows the fallacies in her attempt to alter the five-part and seven-part movement of these poems by coalescing clearly defined sections so as to produce poems in four parts and six parts. As Tayler shows, the division into five and seven parts is clearly marked by Donne's use of refrains and also, one should add, by the marginal notes for the *Second Anniversary* supplied in 1612 by someone (probably Donne himself) who had read the poem closely and understood its structure. Lewalski ignores this evidence of structure, apparently in order to remove indications of Roman Catholic tradition, thus clearing the way for her interpretation of the poem's treatment of Elizabeth Drury as the regenerate image of God according to Calvinist theology.

This larger point is also refuted by Tayler through his analysis of the poems in accord with the Augustinian doctrine that sees the image of God as an interior trinity of powers: Memory, Understanding and Will, powers that for Augustine work through free will restored by the sacrifice of Christ. Lewalski has made an important point when she sees that Donne's "Idea of a Woman" must relate to the theory of the image of God as created in man and woman. But Calvin's view of the role of that image is quite different from Augustine's and from Donne's, as Jeffrey Johnson has shown in his recent study of Donne's theology.[2] Calvin, with his stress on the absolute sovereignty of God, sees only two powers in the soul, Understanding and Will, thus omitting the power of Memory, which for Donne plays an indispensable role in salvation. Donne's theology, as Johnson shows, is trinitarian throughout his career, and thus the tripartite movement in the *Anniversaries* is consistent with the theology demonstrated in his sermons, early and late.

Calvin's omission of the power of Memory is no doubt traceable to his view that the powers of the soul are totally corrupt, and thus cannot work toward a restoration of that image, a restoration that can only be performed by the workings of grace within certain selected individuals. For Augustine, however, the action of grace available to all human beings allows the individual to cooperate to some extent in his own restoration of that image. As Augustine says,

> We must find, in the rational or intellectual soul of man, an image of its Creator planted immortally in its immortal nature . . . we may be sure that from the first beginning to be of

so great and marvellous a creature, that image always remains, whether it be so faded that scarcely anything of it is left, whether it be obscured and defaced, or clear and fair. . . . Human nature is a great thing, but because it is not the highest it was liable to spoiling; and although liable to spoiling because it is not the highest, yet because it has a capacity for the highest and is able to become partaker in it, it remains great.[3]

"We must look then," he adds, "in this image of God, for a trinity of an unique kind — trusting in the help of him who made us in his image." In this view grace will always be available to enable the soul to accomplish, in some measure, its meditative progress toward a restoration of that original purity and harmony imaged in the figure of Donne's transcendent "Shee."

The passages that Tayler cites from Donne's sermons on this interior trinity make it clear that Donne's view of free will is quite in contrast with the Calvinist doctrines of election, regeneration and predestination. He might have added references to the many places in Donne's sermons, early and late, which strongly attack Calvinist doctrine.[4] Now Lewalski is uneasily aware that these differences exist. "For Donne, somewhat untypically," she says, "Christ's incarnation argued for the possibility of salvation to all, not for a Calvinistic predestination of the elect" (132). This view is "untypical" of a Calvinist orientation, but it is quite typical of traditional Christian thinking shared by many Protestants who did not agree with strict Calvinism. Again, she notes that Donne "perhaps envisioned a more complete restoration of the soul's faculties than Calvin would admit" (133). The "perhaps" is not needed: Donne's sermons on the image of God make it clear that the powers of the soul, aided by grace, can to some extent "cooperate" in the process of restoration.[5] Such a view is anathema to strict reformers, since it may sound like a residue of the old religion — but we will never understand Donne if we do not see that certain aspects of his early upbringing never left him, while he, like many other believers in the freedom of the will, remained firmly Protestant.[6] Recent studies of the theological and ecclesiastical conflicts that emerged in England during Donne's maturity make plain the many deviations from strict Calvinism that existed within the Church of England.[7]

Tayler's book presents one major argument that has led me to yet another reconsideration of these great poems, with regard to the tripartite structure into which the *First Anniversary* divides its five main sections, each main section being clearly demarcated by the explicit refrain, while the *Second Anniversary* similarly, though much less obviously, subdivides its seven main sections. Tayler picks up the view first set forth by Frank Manley and later followed by me, that this tripartite movement within each section represents the action of the three powers of the soul, Memory, Understanding and Will, the Augustinian trinity that forms the basis of the Jesuit *Exercises.*[8]

Manley and I took this sequence in the usual order followed in the Jesuit *Exercises* and in methods of meditation adapted from those *Exercises*: first, a Memory of the corruption of this world, then, in the eulogies of "Shee," an Understanding of the nature of the soul's original goodness; and finally, a resolution of the Will, to leave behind this rotten world. But Tayler argues (84–89), following Donne in some of his sermons, that Donne places the Understanding first. This, he points out, is the procedure set forth by Donne's colleague Joseph Hall in his *Arte of Divine Meditation* (1606), where he declares: "Our Meditation must *proceed* in due order. . . . It begins in the understanding, endeth in the affection; It begins in the braine, descends to the heart; Begins on earth, ascends to Heaven; Not suddenly, but by certaine staires and degrees, till we come to the highest."[9]

Now Joseph Hall, according to Ben Jonson, was the author of the introductory poems to the *Anniversaries*, where, as Leonard Tourney has argued, Hall shows that he "recognized that the *Anniversaries* were meditations, didactic and affective in purpose."[10] Donne's knowledge of Hall's interest in the Art of meditation may well be a major reason why he chose Hall to introduce his poems, realizing that Hall was well equipped to understand the poems' structure by "certaine staires and degrees" — that is, by deliberate steps. Donne may also have recognized in Hall's *Arte of Divine Meditation*, published five years before the *First Anniversary*, a certain kinship with the *Exercises* that Donne presumably learned in his boyhood, under the influence of his Jesuit uncles. For Hall's treatise, as Hall acknowledges, is deeply influenced by the "Scala Meditatoria" published in the *Rosetum* of Joannes Mauburnus (1494), a method of meditation that exerted a formative influence on the Jesuit *Exercises*.[11]

Hall does not entirely omit the action of the Memory. Following the preparatory steps in the "Scala" of Mauburnus, Hall advises an opening "wherein the minde, recollecting it selfe, maketh choice of that Theme or matter whereupon it will bestow it selfe for the present; settling it selfe on that which it hath chosen: which is done by an inward inquisition made into our heart, of what we both doe, and should thinke upon: rejecting what is unexpedient and unprofitable" (chap. 15). This is what Mauburnus advises in Hall's marginal translation from the "Scala" (chap. 16), explaining the "modus recolligendi" and "Gradus Praeparatorii": "1. *Question*. What I thinke. should thinke. 2. *Excussion*. A repelling of what I should not thinke. 3. *Choice or Election*. Of what most necessarie. expedient. comely." This is essentially an action of the Memory, as Mauburnus indicates by describing the first step in the "Degrees of proceeding in the understanding" as "*Commemoration*. An actuall thinking upon the matter elected." This is followed by "A redoubled Commemoration of the same, till it be fully knowne." This is the full action of the verb *commemoro*: "to recall an object to memory in all its particulars."[12] So the three powers of the soul are all invoked by Hall, but not explicitly: to do so would invite comparison with the Jesuit *Exercises*.[13]

Still, Hall's strong emphasis upon the Understanding and Donne's practice of giving priority to that power clearly represented a Protestant variation upon the Jesuit method, where the dramatic "composition of place" provides an imaginative setting for a meditation upon an event in the life of Christ, or upon the Four Last Things. To begin with the Understanding bypasses all this sensory detail. Yet the method is still essentially Augustinian, for Augustine in his *De trinitate* does not recommend any particular order in the action of the three powers: he tends to see them acting together in a mysterious unity comparable to the higher Trinity. "This triad of memory, understanding, and will," he explains, "are not three lives, but one; nor three minds, but one." Then, in a witty rhetorical flourish, he adds: "But they are three inasmuch as they are related to one another. . . . I remember that I possess memory and understanding and will: I understand that I understand and will and remember: I will my own willing and remembering and understanding. And I remember at the same time the whole of my memory and understanding and will" (88). Memory must provide the material upon which the Understanding works, and the Will may be said to be both first and last in the sequence, as Augustine explains:

> When we come to deal with the temporal we can suppose will first to proceed from the human mind, making a search for what may be called an offspring when it is found: with the "getting" or "begetting" of this, the act of will is completed, coming to rest in its object, so that the pursuit of the will that sought becomes the love of the will that enjoys; and this love now proceeds from both, from the begetting mind and the begotten idea, as from parent and offspring. (175)

Thus all three powers are present in what we see as the working of any one power, since the temporal dominance of that power involves the presence of the other two.

This principle may help to explain why Donne, in passages from his sermons cited by Tayler, speaks in some places of the sequence "Reason, Memory, and Will" and in other places of "Understanding, Will, and Memory."[14] The latter sequence is explored at great length and with great eloquence in his second sermon on the Image of God, where he sees the Understanding as representing God, the source of power, the Will as representing the Son, Wisdom, the power to choose and assent, and Memory as the Holy Ghost, representing Goodness. The three powers interact to form a culminating unity:

> So then in this first natural faculty of the soule, the Understanding, stands the Image of the first Person, the Father, Power: and in the second faculty which is the Will, is the Image, the Attribute of the second Person, the Sonne, which is Wisdome: for Wisdome is not so much in knowing, in understanding, as in electing, in choosing, in assenting. . . . And then, in the third faculty of the soule, the Memory, is the Image of the third Person, the Holy Ghost, that is, Goodnesse. For to remember, to recollect our former understanding, and our former assenting, so far as to doe them, to Crowne them with action, that's true goodnesse. (9.84)

This flowing together of the three powers will explain why, in the last two sections of the *Second Anniversary*, the tripartite movement is barely discernible, though it is there. Tayler argues that after the fifth section the poem "leaves behind its three-part meditations" as "the poet identifies one faculty with another, substitutes one faculty for another, and makes them, in effect, into interchangeable parts" (111, 104). But this subtle intermingling, as previous citations from Augustine have shown, is essential to the workings of the three powers. The barely discernible distinction between the three powers in the last two sections of the poem shows that the process of meditation has reached its goal of unity.

Tayler appears to see the sequence Understanding, Memory and Will as operating throughout the *First Anniversary* and the first five sections of the sequel. And I would agree that this movement is working throughout the *Anatomy* and the first two sections of the *Progress*, where Donne is taking great care to link his second poem with the structure of the first, enforcing the poem's function as a sequel. As Tayler shrewdly points out, Donne at the outset of his second poem gives us several clues to his procedure by using the words "memory" and "remember." Thus in the first section of the *Second Anniversary* Donne concludes the action of the Understanding by saying "Men thus lethargique have best Memory." Then at once he begins the next movement, the Eulogy, by urging: "Looke upward; that's toward her, whose happy state / We now lament not, but congratulate" (64–66). The word "Memory" thus leads into the Eulogy of the "Idea of a Woman" — representation of what a soul, fully restored, might be.

Now in the poem's second section we hear the insistent repetition of the word "Thinke," resounding at least 30 times throughout the next two sections:

> Thinke thy selfe laboring now with broken breath,
> And thinke those broken and soft Notes to bee
> Division, and thy happiest Harmonee.
> Thinke thee laid on thy death bed, loose and slacke;
> And thinke that but unbinding of a packe,
> To take one precious thing, thy soule, from thence.
>
> (90–95)

This insistent repetition should have long ago suggested that Donne was beginning each section with the Understanding. But, preoccupied with the sequence beginning with Memory, I did not recognize what now seems obvious.

After this deathbed meditation (the first movement of the second section), Donne again hints at his procedure: "Thinke these things cheerefully: and if thou bee / Drowsie or slacke, remember then that shee" (121–22). And so Memory moves into its representation of the ideal soul.

Now in the third section a subtle shift occurs, marked by a special marginal note: "Her liberty by death," as Donne imagines the soul's voyage through the spheres, concluding, "This must, my soule, thy long-short Progresse bee," and moving at once to the Memory of the perfect "Shee:" "To' advance these thoughts, remember then, that shee" (219–20). Here we have indeed a threefold sequence, but the order of the three powers of the soul has changed: now the Understanding leads into the desire of the Will to dispatch "in a minute all the way / Twixt Heaven, and Earth" (188–89), until at the close of this voyage, the soul arrives at the Memory of a perfect being of whom we might say

>   we understood
> Her by her sight, her pure and eloquent blood
> Spoke in her cheekes, and so distinctly wrought,
> That one might almost say, her bodie thought . . .
>   (243–46)

This movement of Understanding, Will and Memory occurs in all the following sections, but is most obvious in sections 5 and 6, where the meditation of the Understanding upon the ills of earthly life is followed by an exhortation of the Will: "Up, up, my drowsie soule, where thy new eare / Shall in the Angels songs no discord heare" (339–40). From here we move to a view of "the blessed Mother-maid," the patriarchs, the prophets, the apostles, the martyrs, with the exhortation "Up" repeated five times, reaching a climax with the lines that bind together the Will and the Memory:

> Up to those Virgins, who thought that almost
> They made joyntenants with the Holy Ghost,
> If they to any should his Temple give.
> Up, up, for in that squadron there doth live
> Shee, who hath carried thether, new degrees
> (As to their number) to their dignitees.
>   (353–58)

Then, the goal of this whole meditative sequence is reached as the Eulogy of section 6 reveals the process of repairing the

image of God in man and woman, as far as this can be done in
earthly life, for now the "Shee" is one

> Who kept, by diligent devotion,
> Gods Image, in such reparation,
> Within her heart, that what decay was grown,
> Was her first Parents fault, and not her owne . . .
>
> (455–58)

It is clear from this climactic passage that the human "Shee"
has powers that "by diligent devotion" enable her to repair in
some measure the decay that the triune Image of God has suffered from original sin. For Donne, regeneration begins with
Baptism, a rite available to all, while subsequent grace, accom-
panying human action, leads to a process by which, as Johnson
says, "justification comes through faith and works operating
in concert" (126–27).

Finally, I should note that reading Tayler's book has made
me aware of a major weakness in my earlier efforts to chart
the structure of the *Anniversaries*: I labeled the divisions of
each section of the *Anatomy* as "Meditation," "Eulogy" and
"Refrain and Moral," and the later sections of the *Second
Anniversary* as simply "Meditation" and "Eulogy." But one
should not limit the term "Meditation" only to the first part
of the section. The whole threefold sequence of every section
is a meditation by the three powers of the soul, while the whole
five-part or seven-part sequence constitutes a complete meditation, with the *First Anniversary* clearing the ground for the
"Progress" envisaged in the sequel.

Remembering all this, I should like to make one last attempt
to chart the progress of the *Second Anniversary*:

Introduction, 1–44
Meditation 1, 45–84
   1. Analysis by the Understanding, 45–64: "A just disestima-
     tion of this world."
   2. Action of the Memory, 65–80: Eulogy of the image named
     "Shee."

3. Resolution of the Will, 81–84: Refrain and Moral ("Shee, shee is gone").

Meditation 2, 85–156

  1. Analysis by the Understanding, 85–120: "Contemplation of our state in our death-bed."

  2. Action of the Memory, 121–46: Eulogy of the image named "Shee."

  3. Resolution of the Will, 147–56: Vestigial Refrain, with Moral.

Meditation 3, 157–250

  1. Analysis by the Understanding, 157–78: "Incommodities of the Soule in the Body."

  2. Exhortation of the Will, 179–219: The soul's "liberty by death."

  3. Action of the Memory, 220–46: Eulogy of the image named "Shee."

  4. Resolution of the Will, 247–50: Vestigial Refrain, with Moral.

Meditation 4, 251–320

  1. Analysis by the Understanding, 251–89: The soul's "ignorance in this life."

  2. Exhortation of the Will, 290–300: "Up unto the watchtowre get."

  3. Action of the Memory, 301–14: Eulogy of the image named "Shee."

  4. Resolution of the Will, 315–20: Vestigial Refrain, with Moral.

Meditation 5, 321–82

  1. Analysis by the Understanding, 321–38: "Of our company in this life."

  2. Exhortation of the Will, 339–55: Of our company "in the next" life; "Up, up, my drowsie soule."

  3. Action of the Memory, 356–75: Eulogy of the image named "Shee."

  4. Resolution of the Will, 376–82: Vestigial Refrain, with Moral.

Meditation 6, 383–470: "Of essentiall joy in this life and in the next."

  1. Analysis by the Understanding, 383–434: "What essentiall joy canst thou expect / Here upon earth?"

2. Exhortation of the Will, 435–46: "Then, soule, to thy first
pitch worke up againe." (definition of "essentiall joye,"
available only in heaven).

3. Action of the Memory, 447–70: Eulogy of the "Shee" as
one "Who kept, by diligent devotion, / Gods Image, in
such reparation" as is possible in this life.

Meditation 7, 471–510: "Of accidentall joyes in both places."

1. Analysis by the Understanding, 471–86: "All casuall joye
doth loud and plainly say, / Onely by comming, that it
can away."

2. Exhortation of the Will, 487–96: "Onely in Heaven joies
strength is never spent."

3. Action of the Memory, 497–510: Eulogy of the image
named "Shee."

Conclusion, 511–28

The double appearance of "Will" in sections 3, 4 and 5 suggests that this power, as Augustine indicates in a passage cited
earlier, really underlies the whole section, emerging at the
close in a short passage growing out of the Eulogy — a conclusion noted by O. B. Hardison in his excellent chart of this
poem.[15] Thus many of us have worked together in the effort to
describe the action and meaning of these complex and enigmatic poems. As for myself, I would like to conclude with
Donne's own words near the close of the *First Anniversary*:
"Here therefore be the end."

5 • The *Donna Angelicata* of Donne's "Aire and Angels"

Albert C. Labriola

1

Walking through a local department store seeking a gift for a woman, I noticed a store employee pacing along the outside of a glass display case with a countertop. A salesperson, she walked the length of the display case to engage passersby and to promote the sale of products. Her associate on the other side of the same case accessed the items under glass and sold them when the passersby became customers. This twosome functioned like the setter and the robber — the highwaymen of old — the one acquiring information about the prospective victims, the other eventually disburdening them of their money. The only difference is that there was an exchange at the display case, products for cash, though I overheard one customer complain that the markup on the products was "highway robbery."

The two salespersons, officially called fragrance promoters, were armed with atomizers. By squeezing a rubber ball attached to a bottle of perfume, each one of them would force a blast of air into the liquid, some of which emerged from a slender nozzle as tiny droplets and quickly disappeared to become vapor. The transition from the liquid to the gaseous state occurred instantaneously or, one might say, in a puff. Indeed, the word "puff," usually pronounced "poof" in such circumstances, is the very sound of the blast of air expelling the liquid from the bottle after the rubber ball is squeezed. Calling the device an atomizer identifies its use in disintegrating a quantity of liquid into smaller units — that is, droplets. Naming it a vaporizer highlights the rapidity whereby the droplets, separated from the larger quantity of liquid, evaporate into air. Referring to the device as an aerosol indicates that a (liquid) solution has entered the air, only to be assimilated into the gaseous state.

As a passerby who became a customer, I was invited by the sales associate behind the counter to choose "the fragrance that best fits the woman for whom it would be a gift." But as the conversation continued, I learned that I was really being urged to select the fragrance that best fits *my perception* of the woman for whom it would be a gift. More than that, I was being told that a fragrance, in effect, would change the woman into my image of, or for, her. If, in the language of the promotional brochures, I wished her to project "the sensuality and ardor of an impassioned woman," I should present her with Obsession by Calvin Klein. Presumably she would become obsessed with me, the outlet for her "sensuality and ardor." If I wished her to accede to my more subtle overtures, I should present her with Say "Yes" by Lancome. If I preferred a woman both "good" and "bad," "hot" and "cool," "body" and "soul," then Calvin Klein's be (cK be is the trademark) would enable her to project such a persona, one in which seemingly opposite characteristics or moods are not reconciled but manifested alternatingly. The woman, in other words, would be virtuous and mischievous, passionate and aloof, carnal and sublime. She would be sufficiently free to adjust to my changing perceptions of her and to engage opportunely the manifold range of my needs.

Though a woman may wear and exude a fragrance that has been presented to her as a gift, she may have her own ideas about the persona that she strives to manifest. In line with her own preference, she will choose a particular fragrance, one to appeal to, and attract, the kinds of partners whom she wishes. By doing so, a woman exercises some degree of control over her suitors, even to the point of promoting or intensifying in them the response that she seeks. To give a demonstration, the woman behind the display case produced an atomizer and expelled a puff (or "poof") onto herself, thereafter urging me to lean across the countertop and inhale, while she recounted her begotten image and persona and dictated how my senses and imagination perceived her. She did so by reciting from the promotional literature for that particular fragrance. To dramatize the kaleidoscopic potential of various fragrances, she gave me one card after another — to draw down on a tab, scratch on a surface, or to peel away a cellophane cover. In case after case, I inhaled, then turned the card to the opposite side and read silently the impression being induced in me by the fragrance.

The ultimate demonstration, however, dealt with a product by Estee Lauder, the Golden Angel Compact Collection. Twelve circular compacts make up the collection, the cover of each engraved with an image of a golden angel, each compact with a shimmering faux birthstone clasp for that respective month, and "each filled and refillable" with a fragrance. In their external appearance, the compacts resemble oversized golden coins, so that one might liken them to British angels. The promotional literature reports that the fragrance will transform a woman who wears it into the image of the angel visualized on the compact; or to put it differently, the woman who wears the fragrance enlivens the graven image of the angel on the compact; or to render it another way, a man who responds to the fragrant air beholds an angel or angelic woman in its mi(d)st. In this instance, moreover, the effect of the fragrance and the influence of the birthstone are conjoined. Indeed, the promotional literature reports that the effect of the fragrance on a man and the celestial influences captured in, and exercised through, the gemstone collaborate to beget his "very own angel," "an angel in the palm" of his "hand." So I learned firsthand after the woman at the counter dusted herself with the scented powder from a golden angel compact and exuded thereafter a fragrance in the air, which, as it reached me, induced the impression that I was being touched by an angel.[1]

In a curious way, fragrances in the air, whether as vapor or as scented powder, and one's resulting perception of the woman who emits them recapitulate the encounter of the speaker and his beloved in John Donne's "Aire and Angels." While such an outlook at first may seem outlandish, it actually emerges from, and remains consonant with, the most traditional commentary on the poem. That traditional commentary invariably includes Thomas Aquinas's explanation of how and why angels appear to humankind. Angels are pure spirits who manifest themselves to human perception, presumably at the behest of the godhead. They assume bodies in order to be movable and viewable, thereby becoming intermediaries between heaven and earth. As subsisting forms and incorporeal or immaterial beings, angels, though they have no need for bodies, assume them primarily to serve as representatives of, and messengers for, the godhead. In assuming sensible bodies, angels fashion them fittingly, in a manner commensurate with their nature and form as spiritual beings. Accordingly, Thomas Aquinas contends that angels assume rarefied bodies of condensed air in order to be visible to humankind; and the condensed air, like that of clouds, may be shaped, colored, and illuminated, whether naturally by the sun or moon or supernaturally by an aureole. In such cases, the appearance of an angel may be flammeous.[2]

Using the foregoing Thomistic commentary, interpreters of "Aire and Angels" focus on one of the central analogies of the poem: the speaker likens his beloved to the rarefied appearance of an angel.[3] While reexamining the central analogy of the woman as an angel, the present essay aims to adjust traditional commentary on "Aire and Angels" by incorporating a frame of reference that complements Thomism. Thomas Aquinas's commentary on angels is a philosophical and theological explanation of recorded appearances of these spiritual beings in Scripture, not the result of the "angelic doctor's" firsthand encounter or actual experience with them. I contend that encountering an angelic woman was a commonplace happening and a firsthand experience for many poets in the seventeenth century, commonplace then and now, as it was for me at the fragrance counter.

In effect, Donne wittily transubstantiates the Thomistic angel, a philosophical and theological creation of the "angelic doctor," into a *"Donna Angelica"* or *"Donna Angelicata,"* a real presence and a firsthand experience.[4] Donne accomplishes this transformation by ascribing to the beloved in the poem the very angelic presence that women manifested in their interactions with him and other men. This angelic presence results, of course, when a woman assumes the "air of an angel." By that assertion, however, I mean that a woman becomes redolent with, and emits, the "air" (the fragrance and aroma) of *"angelica,"* a family of plants whose roots, stalks, leaves, flowers, and fruits were, and are even today, used to add flavor to food and drink, to create herbal and medicinal potions and oils, to make candied victuals, and, of prime importance, to produce perfume. By extracting the "essences" from this family of plants and using them in any one or more of the ways stated above, a woman could and did exercise potent influence over a man at his intake of food and drink, in his reaction to herbal potions and oils, and during his response to a fragrance that she exudes. Whereas the Thomistic angel assumes air, perhaps even ether, and condenses and illuminates it when appearing to humankind, women affect men by (par) and through (per) the fume that they emit. In Donne's poem, in other words, the speaker reacts to the "air" of a woman perfumed with *angelica*. To advance the foregoing thesis, the present essay will unfold in three stages: first, a brief Neoplatonic and Paracelsian overview of herbal and floral essences and fragrances, with emphasis on *angelica* and its properties; second, a survey of herbal fragrances in poems by one of Donne's contemporary lyricists, Robert Herrick; third, an analysis of "Aire and Angels."

2

Neoplatonic and Paracelsian views of the *anima mundi* or *spiritus mundi* provide a context for understanding the effect of herbal and floral essences on humankind. Among others, Marsilio Ficino in his late fifteenth century treatise, *De vita libri tres*, which includes *De vita coelitus comparanda* (originally a separate composition), speaks of "the Power of Attracting Favor from the Heavens." To illustrate his point, Ficino cites "solar things," namely "gems and flowers which are called heliotrope because they turn toward the Sun." Enumerating examples, he concludes: "The above-mentioned things can be adapted partly to foods, partly to ointments and fumigations, partly to usages and habits." Focusing on botanical life, Ficino contends: "by a frequent use of plants and a similar use of living things, [one] can draw the most from the spirit of the world." He continues: "For all herbs, flowers, trees, and fruits have an odor." And because of "this odor, they restore and invigorate [one] on all sides, as if by the breath and spirit of the life of the world." Even the "natural motion of the air, which goes perpetually round and round . . . laps [one] freely and penetrates [one] purely." As a result, one's "spirit is filled by the spirit of the world."[5]

The source of this so-called spirit of the world rests in the stars. Avoiding the extremes of determinism and idolatry, Ficino cautions his readers

> not to think we are speaking here of worshipping the stars, but rather of imitating them and thereby striving to capture them. And do not believe we are dealing with gifts which the stars are going to give by their own election but rather by a natural influence. We strive to adapt ourselves to this multifarious and occult influence by the same studied methods we use every day to make ourselves fit to receive in a healthy manner the perceivable light and heat of the Sun. But it is the wise man alone who adapts himself to the occult and wonderful gifts of this influence. (357)

In the foregoing commentary, Ficino specifically cites the *anima mundi* or *spiritus mundi*, its source in the stars, its transmission to and throughout the earth by the movement of the air, its presence in various forms of botanical life, and its availability to humankind, whether through the odor and fragrance of plants or by other extracts from them.

Consistent with the Neoplatonic views of Ficino, Paracelsus speaks further about the transmission of heavenly influence to humankind. The transaction whereby the potency "is taken from one thing and given to another" is called *influxion* or influence, a natural process important to the practice of medicine. For "nature herself can take the medicine in water, or in the earth, or in the stars and contain them in one *corpus*, in a plant or a stone." And "what nature has taken from every-where, she gives to human beings in a plant or a seed," in which the potent essence of the *influxion* or influence is deposited. The practice of medicine, which Paracelsus perceives as a form of white magic, depends on the exercise of "art [that] can extract both medicine and power from plants and can bestow a person with them." Significantly, Paracelsus denominates as "angelic" the naturally formed things, including plants, stones and gems, that receive and retain potency, then release it to humankind who practice the art of magic. Transporting influence from above and bestowing it on humankind below, such a naturally formed thing was called *"angelicum,* for its effect in nature was regarded as like that of an angel," also a medium between heaven and earth.[6]

Focusing on a prime example of a plant that acquires, stores and dispenses heavenly influence, Paracelsus singles out the "root of angelic thistle," which "extracts power from another" (whether a person or a thing) and "at the same moment" also "confers it upon one who carries" the root. Indeed, "angelic thistle has a power ordained by natural *Influxion.* For that is its *praedestination,* in which it should be. It is *praedestination* when God wishes to effect something special which is above nature," while doing so "by means of nature." "Such is a special *secretum* or other *magnalia.*" Accordingly, "the *praedestination* in angelic thistle is from nature, but it is ordained by God that it should be so." Similarly, Paracelsus contends that persons, notably prophets and apostles, are "conducted by means of *praedestination* toward that which has been determined, and these have also been supernaturally gifted by God to the same end." While persons have the latitude to accept or to resist God's plan for them, "unintelligent plants" are by nature endowed with "powers [that] must manifest themselves in a particular way" (118).

Paracelsus, therefore, identifies *angelicum* and angelic thistle as having magical and miraculous properties ordained by God. Whereas the former is a general term for a medium between heaven and earth, the latter is a specific instance of a family of plants that captures heavenly influence and yields it to knowledgeable users on earth. In calling the family of plants "angelic thistle," Paracelsus refers to the pointed, prickly or serrated leaves, or to the periodic radial frames that grow from the stems, each frame resembling the spokes of an umbrella. Atop the ribs or spokes and usually from May to August, greenish and white flowers grow, whose proximity to one another creates the appearance of the hood of an upraised umbrella. Aptly, these spreading clusters of flowers are termed umbels. Generally, these plants are biennial or perennial, with hollow fluted stems between three to seven feet high. The cultivated variety, commonly named European angelica (or *Angelica archangelica*), belongs to the apiaceous family of plants, including parsley, parsnip, celery and the carrot. *Archangelica* designates the superiority or greater potency of the one plant to the other species in the genus. One of the "most highly praised herbs in old herbal texts," *archangelica* typically "was used in all northern European countries for protection against contagion, for purifying the blood, and for curing every conceivable malady; it was considered a sovereign remedy for poisons, agues, and all infectious maladies."[7]

According to "one legend, *archangelica* was revealed in a dream as a cure for the plague," and the name of the plant derives from the fact that it blooms "near May 8, the feast day of Michael the Archangel."[8] The background to this legend and its relationship to healing derive from several appearances by the archangel. On May 8, 492, Michael "appeared on the summit of Mount Gargano, and the cave where he had appeared became the most frequented place of pilgrimage in southern Italy," a site associated with miracles of healing. Approximately 100 years after the event at Mt. Gargano, while the plague was overwhelming Rome, Michael appeared in a vision to Pope Gregory, who saw the archangel "sheathing his flaming sword to signify that he would put an end to the scourge" (369). And near Constantinople, at a place called the Michaelim, the site of a church built in honor of the archangel, Michael appeared to a man named Aquilinus, near death because of a fever, and imparted to him the ingredients of a balm that cured the affliction.[9]

At first glance, these apparitions and the service of Michael as a healer, together celebrated on his feast day of May 8, seem unrelated to the archangel's militant triumph over Satan, who is visualized as a dragon (Rev. 12.7), the major event celebrated on Michaelmas Day (September 29) and the scene engraved on the Renaissance English coin called the "angel." But Satan and his forces of evil use various means to oppose the godhead — not only direct confrontation but also the affliction of God's creatures, most notably humankind, by painful maladies, poisonous contamination and the plague. Combating these various means of affliction is Michael, the miraculous healer whose very name means "like God."

While the connection of *archangelica* to Michael remains clearcut, its relationship to the other two angels named in Scripture, Raphael and Gabriel, drives home the universal perception of the plant and of its extracts as healing agents and as antidotes of evil, whose potency and efficacy, Paracelsus contends, are granted by God. *Archangelica* "is named after the Archangel Raphael, who, according to a tenth century French legend, revealed [its] secrets to a monk for use during a plague epidemic."[10] To be sure, the Book of Tobias recounts Raphael's ministrations to humankind, which are related to the significance of his very name, "healer of God."

According to other legends *archangelica* "became associated with the Annunciation," not only with Gabriel, whose name means "strength of God," but also with the Holy Spirit in their encounter with the Virgin Mary.[11] As the harbinger of the Holy Spirit at the Annunciation, Gabriel at times carries a bouquet of flowers, including lilies but often *archangelica* and other flowers; or *archangelica* may be seen in the landscape or in a cultivated garden in the background, evident through a partly opened door or window at the back of the interior setting where he visits Mary; or it rests in a vase inside the room, oratory or chapel where he encounters the Virgin Mary. In the same context, *archangelica* (or *herba angelica*) was called "'the root of the Holy Ghost,' so named (when or by whom does not appear — used by Brunfells in 1530) on account of its repute against poison and pestilence, prob. from the fragrant smell and aromatic taste of its root" (OED, "*angelica*"). Thus perceived as "one of the most valuable herbs of Protection, with a long history of use in work against spells, enchantments and all forms of evil," *archangelica* signifies the holiness of the environment in which the Annunciation took place, the purity and modesty of the Virgin Mary, and her imperviousness to the onset of any and all evil.[12] Not to be overlooked in its manifold associations with angels, *archangelica* grows bipinnate leaves. Derived from the Latin word for feather and wing (*pinna*), a bipinnate leaf has lateral parts on either side of a common axis, like vanes of a feather.

Angelica — whether the roots, stalks and stems, leaves, flowers or seeds — has an aroma like that of musk. As such, it joins a long list of plants and herbs with remarkable potency even when their fragrance from a natural landscape is wafted by air in spring and summer. By various means — for instance, piercing the roots or pressing the leaves — one may extract the essence, usually an oil, resin or balm, of a plant like *archangelica*. The concentrated potency of the extract, when used as the prime ingredient of perfume, begets an enhanced reaction in others.[13]

3

To explain this phenomenon of aromatherapy in Donne's "Aire and Angels," one may first examine other seventeenth century lyrics to determine how and why the extract from plants and herbs becomes the essence of a perfume. Most notable are Robert Herrick's lyrics from *Hesperides*, which celebrate perfumes: their aura or the invisible emanation, exhalation or distinctive atmosphere that they generate; the flammeous appearance of this aura when it radiates light; and the resemblance of a perfumed woman to female divinities, who, likewise fragrant, induce awe and wonder in men and wield supernatural power over them. In one of his lyrics, Herrick recounts the impact of masked dancers, women for whom the "oyle" of flowers becomes "sweets" and "sweat," which, when "let . . . fly [,] / . . . so Perfume / E'ne all the standers by" ("A Song to the Maskers," 3–8).[14] Focus on the power of a fragrance also occurs in "On a perfum'd Lady," where Herrick speaks of both *"Powders* and *Perfumes"* as fragrances, the former referring to the ground powder produced from dried parts of a plant, the latter to a recently harvested plant whose fresh parts were fashioned into a bracelet or amulet pierced with holes. Referring to perfumes in "To the most fair and lovely Mistris, Anne Soame, now Lady Abdie," Herrick urges onlookers to "smell those odours that do rise / From out the wealthy spiceries" (1–2) and to "smell those bracelets, and those bands." (15). A similar reference to "a Bracelet richly Redolent" (2) appears in "The Pomander Bracelet," which is "kist" (3) by the male admirer. Pomander was a commonplace admixture of various fragrances, including *archangelica,* the aim being to ward off misfortune and infection. The potency was so great that the influence of the admixture, while issuing from the lady, also accompanied her shadow: "How can I choose but love, and follow her, / Whose shadow smels like milder Pomander!" ("Another on her," 1–2).

In his poem on Lady Abdie, previously cited, Herrick also discusses the interplay of fire and fragrance, whereby scented bracelets and bands, at times gifts from the lady to her suitors, are "enkindled," and "thus . . . they transpire / A noble perfume" (17–18). Issuing from the fire into which her suitors have placed her bracelets and bands is an illuminated cloud of fragrance. This cloud envelops the admirers of the woman, who continues to exercise influence over them despite her absence. But even when she is physically present, a woman may appear to be flammeous, a condition cited in Herrick's "To his Mistresses": "While other Gums their sweets perspire, / By your owne jewels set on fire" (5–6). Here the effulgence from her jewels is so radiant that the mistress basks in the glow of a bright light, an aureole, while she continues to exude her fragrance. In such a situation, she becomes a luminous cloud of fragrance; and if she were to speak, her voice would emanate from a fiery presence, akin to several biblical manifestations of angels speaking on behalf of the godhead.[15] And the beloved, a source of fragrance and light, serves to lead her lover, as in Herrick's "Being once blind, his request to Biancha":

> and I shall well
> Follow thy Perfumes by the smell:
> Or be my guide; and I shall be
> Led by some light that flows from thee.
>
> (5–8)

Finally, Herrick actually elevates the woman from a guide to a goddess, using imagery of fragrance, air and fire to suggest divinization. In "Upon Julia's unlacing her self" (8–10) the woman resembles "Great Juno [who] goes perfum'd. / Whose pure-Immortal body doth transmit / A scent, that fills both Heaven and Earth with it." And in "To Electra" (9–10) the lover wishes that his lady would follow the example of Juno, who collaborated with Jupiter to manifest her likeness in a cloud, which Ixion, who lusted after her, embraced: "Till, like Ixion's cloud you be / White, warme, and soft to lye with me." In "Love perfumes all parts," the beloved, akin to a goddess, becomes the very site at which the lover worships her. At her "brest," he can "smell the Phenix nest" and in "her lip, the most sincere / Altar of Incense" (1–4). In sum, "[h]ands, and thighs, and legs, are all / Richly Aromaticall" (5–6). Etymologically, of course, "incense" means to burn or to inflame; and the legend of the phoenix, associated with the beloved, involves the incendiary brightness of the sun igniting the herbal pyre of the fabulous bird, which sings. Surrounded by flame and sounding forth from the midst of a cloud of herbal fragrance, the phoenix, wings outstretched, furnishes an apt analogue of several angelic appearances in Scripture.

4

In view of my prior discussion, Donne's "Aire and Angels" depicts a lover whose awe and wonder during his encounters with his beloved cause him to perceive her as an angel, a supernal guide, and a quasi divinity. While the Thomistic understanding of angels explains the rarefied appearance of the lady in "Aire and Angels," a supplementary explanation from the Neoplatonic and Paracelsian contexts that I have recounted and from the poetry of Herrick, cited above, enriches understanding. Broadly speaking, a commonplace view of Neoplatonists and Paracelsians alike centers on *influxion*, whereby influence from above (whether from the heavens or from heaven and the godhead) was imprinted on air, then descended below. Because nature in its various forms on earth, including plants, captured this influence, Neoplatonists and Paracelsians focused on botanical means, among others, to release this supernatural power to humankind.

One family of plants, in particular, drew extensive attention, *angelica*, whose very name derives from the miraculous properties that caused it alone to be associated with three of the principal angels in Scripture — Michael, Raphael and Gabriel. Those properties, moreover, and their association with one or more of the angels cited above recur in the literature of the Renaissance and seventeenth century. For instance, du Bartas, as translated by Thomas Winter, asserts that those who clench and "bruse" angelica — "a heauenly simple by an Angell brought" — gain protection against the "Syrens with their subtil-charming rimes" and against "the dankish noysome gales from Southerne climes."[16] In a similar vein, du Bartas, as translated by Joshua Sylvester, contends:

Th'inchanting Charmes of Syrens blandishments,
Contagious Aire ingendring Pestilence,
Infect not those that in their mouthes haue taen
Angelica, that happy Counter-baen,
Sent downe from Heau'n by some Celestiall scout,
As well the name and nature both avow't.[17]

W. Denny asserts that the miraculous properties of various herbs and flowers, including angelica, "live in the fragrance of their perfumes, and are said to be a medicine for all things."[18]

Issuing from the contexts cited above, one discovers that the lady in "Aire and Angels" becomes a *Donna Angelicata* as she perfumes herself with the essence or extract of this family of plants, diffuses it into the *air* around her, and affects her lover as if she were an *angel*. In line with the woman's expectation, the lover collaborates by reacting to the fragrance: he sublimates his perception of the lady and he exaggerates her appearance through hyperbole. To do so, the lover uses language akin to what recurs in Herrick's poems. It follows, therefore, that the speaker in "Aire and Angels" will liken his beloved not only to an angel but also to its legendary analogue, the phoenix: she is "a shapelesse flame," "[s]ome lovely glorious nothing," "[e]xtreme, and scattring bright," all conventional descriptions of the flammeous bird (3, 6, 22).[19]

While she manifests herself only partially to his sensory perception, her rarefied appearance accords with that of several of the women in Herrick's poems cited above: she appears in a bright and fiery cloud from which her voice is heard. All such hyperbole emerges from the lover's idealization of his beloved, whose appearance is akin to that of "*[a]ngells* [that] *affect* us oft, and *worship'd* be" (4, emphasis mine). Presumably, "affect" has at least the following twofold significance: the lady *influences* him after the manner of angels, who, in interacting with humankind, *assume* or *feign* a rarefied human appearance of air and fire. Likewise, "affect" (*OED*, 5.2.4) means "to make a material impression on; to act upon, influence, move, touch or have an effect on." To illustrate such meaning, the *OED* cites examples from seventeenth century texts that refer to olfactory impressions. In such a sublimated state, the lady, like the angels whom she resembles, is "worship'd" because, in part, she affects the lover with the air that she has assumed and that she exudes. Indeed, in its definition (no. 7) of "air" as a noun, the *OED* indicates an "exhalation *affecting* the sense of smell; effluvium, odour, redolence; the 'atmosphere' sensibly diffused by anything" (emphasis mine). In many ways, a counterpart of the lady in "Aire and Angels" is Milton's Raphael, who in *Paradise Lost* descends from heaven to alight in Paradise: "Like Maia's son he stood, / And shook his plumes, that heav'nly fragrance filled / The circuit wide" (5.285–87).[20] Adam engages this "godlike guest" (5.351) "with submiss approach and reverence meek, / As to a superior being, bowing low" (5.359–60). In effect, Raphael's effect on Adam recapitulates the beloved's impact on the speaker in "Aire and Angels."

When in "Aire and Angels" the lover apprehends the lady as angelic, he infers that such a perception issues chiefly from his soul, not from his senses, which have not brought his beloved into full corporeal realization. In other words, he concludes that his soul or spiritual nature must have been, and continues to be, operative to engage her as a spiritual being. He strives, therefore, to bring her within the fuller range of his sensory perception, an objective to be achieved by refashioning her materially, by making her incarnate. What informs his effort is the realization that his own soul or spiritual nature "takes limmes of flesh" (8) and thereby assumes bodily presence. In such circumstances, so that he may be fulfilled, the loving outreach to his beloved will require that she assume a nature akin to that of her lover, one in which her spiritual being must "take a body too" (10).

If the speaker succeeds in this endeavor, he would eliminate the mystery surrounding her presence as an angel, a mystery that prevents him from knowing her "face or name" (2) or, as he tells her, "what thou wert, and who" (11), respectively her physical presence and nominal identity. To procreate her materially will be a function of the love issuing from the speaker's body. In the procreative endeavor that he imagines, he likens his body to the "parent" (9) and her body to the "child" (7). The body that he will impart to her is hypothetically possible so long as the material manifestation harmonizes with her spiritual being.

Imparting materiality to the beloved — whereby she acquires "lip, eye, and brow" (14) — succeeds as procreation, but the materiality does not harmonize with her spiritual being. In effect, the lover's bodily desires for a fuller material presence of his beloved result in "loves pinnace overfraught" (18). Typically, commentators have glossed "loves pinnace" as a light sailing vessel overweighted beyond the burden of ballast, thereby resulting in a sunken ship. Such a gloss of "loves pinnace" communicates the view that the beloved has experienced a disharmony in her dual nature. Because the material nature that the speaker imparts to his beloved would coarsen and degrade her spiritual being, she dissociates from the procreative outcome of his bodily desires; for his representation is antithetical to her sublimity as a *Donna Angelicata* and would vitiate her role as a medium between heaven and earth. In retrospect, the speaker acknowledges that a single strand of hair was too material a representation of his beloved, for it alone, not to mention the speaker's fabrication of other parts of her body, would have disrupted the equilibrium that she had achieved between her angelic nature and its material manifestation only in illuminated or flammeous air.

Because the air that envelops the woman is scented with the perfume of *archangelica*, the aura and influence that issue from the miraculous plant purge the environs of communicable disease, such as the pestilence, and, what is more important, of the power of evil, including sensualism. The plant and its miraculous properties associated with a triad of angels celebrated in Scripture — Michael, Raphael and Gabriel — highlight the woman as a *Donna Angelicata*, who will neither be tainted by nor yield to the bodily impulses of the speaker, who seeks to refashion her more materialistically.

While recognizing that any endeavor to bring his beloved into greater material realization cannot be fulfilled, the speaker relinquishes his plan to do so, thereby accepting the presence of the woman as flammeous air, the only visual representation of her to his senses and the only one compatible with her status as *Donna Angelicata*. Accordingly, the sensualistic love that he sought to arouse in himself, to manifest to his beloved, and perhaps to consummate with her has failed: "For, nor in nothing, nor in things / Extreme, and scattring bright, can love inhere" (21–22). The former — "nothing" — is the purely angelic form of the lady, inaccessible to human perception; the latter — "scattring bright" — is her manifestation as flammeous air, accessible to human perception but not subject to further materialistic embodiment.

Because the lover, presumably by the end of the poem, accepts the beloved as a *Donna Angelicata*, he will sublimate his relationship with her. As such, he requests that her "love" may be his "loves spheare" (25). By such a wish, he identifies her love as the province or domain in which her influence finds scope and exercise ("sphere," *OED*). Since the speaker falls within the aura of his beloved, he has, in effect, been touched by an angel, as the concluding triplet of the poem recounts: "Just such disparitie / As is twixt Aire and Angells puritie, / 'Twixt womens love, and mens will ever bee" (26–28). If the last two lines correlate "Aire" with "womens love," and "Angells puritie" with "mens" love, then those correlatives suggest how the *Donna Angelicata* in her love for a man will appear as "Aire" to his sensory perception; and how a man, unsatisfied with such material representation, is compelled to rarefy his love by accommodation to angelic purity.

But the last two lines may reflect a chiastic arrangement: "Aire" is linked with "mens" love, and "Angells puritie" with "womens love." A man's love is drawn to the more materialistic representation of the angelic woman, whose presence he strives to embody all the more, whereas a woman's love counteracts that impulse in men by projecting an aura of antidotal sublimation. Whether correlative or chiastic, the range of tensions, interactions and transactions suggested by the last two lines recapitulates how and why men's love and women's love may potentially or actually be antithetical, and how and why they may not only mutually coexist but also potentially or actually achieve accommodation, if not integration.

6 • Male Lesbian Voices
Ronsard, Tyard and Donne Play Sappho

Anne Lake Prescott

John Donne's "Sapho to Philænis" is a startling poem, an erotic "lesbian" epistolary elegy by one of English literature's most famous male heterosexual love poets (if, to be sure, one also able in his younger days to write a male friend with a fervor that may go beyond ordinary male bonding).[1] In very recent years, after long neglect punctuated by snorts of disgust or chaste refusals to think that Donne could have written such a poem, it has won attention from a number of Donne scholars. I will not engage current debates over what "lesbian" meant in the early modern period, whether it was visible or invisible, how it related to dildos and cross-dressing, or how women's cooler anatomy was understood as a reversed and undeveloped version of the male. It might be wise to recall, though, that in those days dildos and cross-dressing sometimes seemed less "Sapphic" than more generally transgressive. The crime was not same-sex love so much as the inversion of hierarchy and confusion of gender. Women wielding dildos, puffing pipes, prancing around the capital in doublet and hose, or — an extreme instance — playing the husband in a supposed marriage, are pretending to be men. And that was all the more dangerously criminal because women, should they increase their vital heat or grow into their disguise, might actually become male and so produce little eddies of social chaos.[2] By "lesbian" I mean a woman's passionate fondness for another woman with feelings that transcend even a generous definition of friendship, that take precedence over attachments to men, and that may hint at physical desire.

In these terms, Donne's poem sounds "lesbian."[3] In his elegy, my readers will recall, Sappho addresses her beloved Philaenis, celebrating their now broken love for each other as the love of like for like, so different from the more penetrating "tillage" by a "harsh rough man." At least, nearly everybody assumes that Sappho is the speaker and that Philaenis, a lascivious courtesan and possibly fictional author of a how-to-do-it book on sex who figures in several ancient texts, is the reluctant beloved who has deserted Sappho for heterosexual companionship and the pleasures of sexual difference.[4] We assume this because of the poem's title and because of a fleeting reference to Phaon, the faithless ferryman whom, said a late and dubious legend, Sappho loved so dearly that she killed herself when he failed to reciprocate and to whom, in Ovid's *Heroides*, she writes a pleading letter. (Phaon was younger than Sappho; the introduction to a paperback edition of Sappho's verse quotes one scholar's irritating remark that she had reached "woman's most tragic age, when beauty wanes but longing is not gone.")[5] Yet nobody knows who first gave the poem its title as it is found in the 1633 edition of Donne's poetry. Without this clue, as George Klawitter has pointed out, and even with the mention of "Phao," the poem would be homoerotic but need not specify Sappho herself as its speaker.[6] And, I would add, the poem would not so insistently claim Ovid's heroic epistle from Sappho to Phaon as its chief intertext. For Klawitter, in fact, the lines suggest male-to-male passion. I do not find the claim plausible, although one modern critic has wittily noted "an ongoing tendency among Renaissance authors to slip from femininity to effeminacy — from Rosalind to Ganymede."[7] Klawitter's argument, though, is a helpful warning not simply to assume that Donne means his reader to think hard about Ovid or to read this poem against what little was then known of Sappho's poetry.

Here I will, though, assume that the title is, if not Donne's, then a probable index of how the poem was read in 1633 and follow that early edition in taking the speaker as Sappho and her friend as Philaenis, whose name indeed means "friend." Much as a human body has bilateral symmetry, thinks Donne's Sappho, so the love of two women for each other has erotic symmetry. Philaenis is perfect, a "naturall Paradise," just as she is, and needs no masculine attention, no Adamic digging and plowing — and hence, Donne may suggest, no need for that other curse, the labor of childbirth. The two women's dalliance, moreover, leaves no criminal trace behind it. No footsteps in the snow to mark the thief, no more signs than fish leave in water or birds in the air. Not only safe sex, one might say, but hardly sex at all — sex without consequence in every sense, if presumably offering a little pallid pleasure, for Renaissance writers tended to assume that lesbian sex was mere imitation of the real thing and thus neither truly satisfying nor to be counted as fornication or adultery. Then, in lines that some critics have found disturbing (for squeamishness is not dead in Renaissance studies, even when it takes the curious form of arguing that Donne makes autoeroticism into a symptom of verbal failure), Sappho asserts that the two women mirror each other to such a degree that in touching herself it seems to her that she is touching Philaenis. Oh may Philaenis return to her, she begs, and thus keep sickness and change far away.

Reaction to Donne's "Sapho" has provoked both admiration and cold dislike, even irritation. Does it subtly denigrate a narcissist claustrophobia that diverts love to autoeroticism? Or is the poem, rather, a sympathetic experiment in imagining an alien sexuality, and a safer sexuality, too, with no scratchy beard to hurt one's soft skin and no trace left on the body of what one has been doing, if indeed it counts as "doing" at all? Like many poets, Donne was probably intrigued by imagining other voices, other rooms, other stanzas, other stances. But some find his Sappho's self-speculating image of sex without trace or sign a deliberate comment on the failure or inadequacy of poetry that literally does not signify. Lesbianism as Donne constructs it is inert, its egalitarian mirroring parallel to a flat, onanistic and repetitive language that means only itself. (I might add, although I am reluctant to take too solemn an approach to Donne's exploration of sameness and erotic identity, that if he *is* commenting on masturbatory, unpregnant and unsignifying language, then what he says is relevant to post-Reformation arguments over the Eucharist and over how signs relate to the things they point at in, whose nature they participate.[8])

Despite occasional statements to the contrary, Donne was not the first Renaissance male poet to imagine love from a lesbian perspective, although he is the first I know of to do so sensuously and (probably) to make his lesbian speaker Sappho herself.[9] At least three French elegies written between 1565 and 1585, two by Pierre de Ronsard (1524–1585) and one by Pontus de Tyard (1522–1605), an aristocratic cleric with Neoplatonic leanings best known for his *Erreurs Amoureuses* (1549) and *Solitaire Premier* (1552), adopt the voice of a female speaker who yearns erotically, or at least passionately, for another woman. None mentions Sappho, perhaps because the authors were still under the sway of Sappho's Ovidian reconstruction as a heterosexual poet, a merely partial reconstruction, however, thanks to a medieval tradition of commentary on Ovid, and the myth that there had been two Sapphos: one a fine and decent poet, the other a degraded courtesan. (True, Jean Dorat, who taught Ronsard Greek, wrote a sweet poem to his newborn daughter hoping she would use the pen as well as the needle and vowing that although Sappho was "depraved" his child would be "better behaved.")[10] In an essay on "Sapho to Philænis," Janel Mueller does very briefly note the elegy by Tyard and its relevance to Donne.[11] So far as I know, however, Ronsard's more ambiguously "lesbian" poems, epistles that could, with a little nudging and coaching and historicizing, be read as expressing more *philia* than *eros*, have gone unnoticed by those who write about Donne. For that matter, the few *seizièmistes* who mention even one of these French poems ignore "Sapho."

For the rest of this essay I will set Donne's "Sapho" next to these "lesbian" — at a minimum equivocal — precedents. The context, the cultural forcefield surrounding and sustaining the poem, should include Continental verse that Donne could have known, and that, even if he did not know, was part of the world in which he wrote. I beg my reader's indulgence for devoting so much space to paraphrase: early modern representations of female same-sex desire are sufficiently rare to make any instance worth getting to know better, and none has been translated.[12]

The first pseudo-lesbian poem is an elegy by Ronsard, whose love poetry I am sure Donne knew and to whose taste for green-eyed girls he refers.[13] It first appeared in Ronsard's *Elegies, mascarades et bergerie* (1565), a collection that also addresses Elizabeth I, gives Merlin a rapturous prophecy of her future grandeur, and in very fancy language praises Lord Burleigh, who must have been amused and perhaps mildly flattered to see himself called the "Docte Cecille, à qui la Pieride / A fait gouster de l'onde Aganippide."[14] (Some years later, angered by England's treatment of Mary Stuart, Ronsard revised the poem so that the English "Cecille" becomes a nameless "Sicilian.")

The "Elegie" in question supposedly accompanies the gift of a portrait sent by one lady to another. Since the speaker describes the image and its setting in detail, interpreting its little allegories as she goes, the elegy should interest those concerned with Renaissance portraiture and how pictures might be "read." Whatever is the case in Donne's Sappho's pleading epistle, moreover, *this* poem imagines a crowd of signs and signifiers, with no suggestion that same-sex affection might put meaning and language at risk. The ladies are Anne and Diane; the speaker points out that "Anne" lives "in" "Diane," but they are otherwise unidentified). In a pinch — a strong pinch — we could read the lines as the expression of powerful friendship: Cicero's *De amicitia* for girls. Even some decades ago, however, Ronsard's editor Paul Laumonier did not scruple to call the speaker's effusions "lesbien" or to associate them with rumors circulating at the court of Catherine de Medici about the tribades and dildo-happy goings-on among her ladies-in-waiting.[15] Perhaps thanks to a belated worry about the change in cultural tone under the bisexual but showily pious Henri III, Ronsard withdrew it from the 1584 edition of his works; or perhaps he came to regret its uncharacteristically flat and repetitive language. It was, though, posthumously reprinted in 1609 and thereafter.

I offer a condensed paraphrase with some running commentary. My "you" translates the speaker's more formal "vous," not an intimate "tu." "Vous" preserves a slight difference in social position, although its use is also common in French Renaissance love poetry.

"This portrait is a sign of how much I wish to serve you." Note that there is nothing here of Donne's ambivalent interest in female erotic equality or similarity; rather we find the old system of erotic service merged with the more egalitarian custom of exchanging portraits among friends. "The impression on the gold setting that shines like the faith kindled in me by your holy flame parallels the love for you that your virtue has imprinted on me," a telling detail, in this age of print, and a metaphor usually applied to the impress of masculine form on female matter; Ronsard maintains a sort of gender difference for his two female friends.

> On each side is a temple; one, to Apollo, shows Corœbus dying of love for Cassandra.[16] Oh happy death! May I die yours! Nothing shall part us: not storm, war, or the envious. And around the image is some Latin that means "My love and yours so chaste / Shall overgo loves past."

Ronsard gives only the French translation, a decision worth considering in terms of the two languages' social meanings. Did he think, despite imagining a lady who appreciates and understands Latin posies, that quoting one would make her seem too "learned," too "masculine"?

> The other Temple is for Diana, where we see Orestes and Pylades, the pair that won fame for the blood each shed for the other. Such friendship, although perfect, is surpassed by mine, for I would die for you a hundred and a hundred thousand times. So I have used a Latin verse showing that there is no parallel to our love and that Orestes and Pylades yield place to our fidelity, which can surmount them ["les peut surmonter"]. Below the temple is the altar on which the Greeks vowed to die for one another and kill the youth of Troy. On this altar I swear to serve you, Mistress, for whom I would shed my blood in immortal sacrifice. In the raised center is my image: pale, silent, grieving at your absence. Alas that it is mute and cannot tell you of my pain.

As in much elegy, and certainly in Donne, love-longing, absence, and the threat of silence are connected: love torments us into poetry but also into inarticulate grief.

> It would tell you at leisure my anguish when apart from you, my all. I live only on memory and on your reputation, written on my soul. But what need of a picture when you are the mistress of my body and spirit? So that you will at least grieve for me as I languish because I cannot see your face before me, for I can have no greater pleasure than to serve and see you.

Because I so much wish to be within you ["dedans vous"], I
have put this Roman verse around the portrait: "Anne lives
fervently in her Diane, Diane in Anne, and Time, which breaks
empires and kings and subjects everything, cannot untie two
such lovely names."[17] The greatest good God can give us here
below is a friendship that effaces all else. Without friendship, a
person would die, unable to live whole in the world, for blood
and heart do not make one live as much as faithful friendship
when one has found again one's other half.

Having experienced this love in me, Mistress, you have found
me sure within your love, for you and I are one; and if we share
one common body, then your thought is mine and my life entirely follows yours. We have one blood, one soul, one faith; I
am in you and you are in me with a knot so tightly made that
you can never forget me without forgetting yourself; and thus
I have no fear, so much do I find myself wholly in you, Madame,
and my soul is utterly in your soul.

This good comes to me, as I acknowledge, without illusion,
from the favor it has pleased you to show me, knowing myself
to be much less than you. For you deign to join your greatness
to me, most lowly, and such honor makes me equal to you
through good fortune: that is why I dedicate to you my blood,
my heart, my picture, and my life.

Catherine Yandell has noted that despite Ronsard's attempt
to express close female friendship or erotic affection (French
amitié can slide into either meaning), he cannot escape the
dominant — and dominating — heterosexual tradition in
which he worked: for example, this lady's love will "sur-
mount" all others. Indeed so: the speaker's love, like her
portrait, dazzles, glitters, deserves fame, recalls lovers of old,
defeats the jealous, conquers, outdoes. The old competitive
paradigm, the laurel-grabbing, temple-building, race-winning,
my-lady-is-better-than-other-ladies swagger, still shapes the
poet's attitudes even when he plays the almost-lesbian. This
poem, unlike Donne's, could be fairly easily heterosexualized
by shifting the pronouns and unfeminizing some parts of
speech while leaving the poetic and erotic assumptions in-
tact. Nobly born women can of course serve even nobler

women, and the social context for the poem is the hierarchi-
cal Valois court in which many a lady waited on those yet
higher on the social pyramid, even when mutual love, as in
this poem, partly overcame social difference. The stress on
self-sacrificing bloodshed and service unto death, however, is
more male and feudal than Sapphic, more Loire valley than
ancient Lesbos. True, for all we know, court ladies did imitate
feudal love service when doing whatever it was that court ladies did when generating the rumors of tribadism that Ronsard
(and, later, Tyard) may have been exploiting.

The second "lesbian" poem is an extraordinary elegy that
Donne could not have read unless he had access, which it is
not beyond possibility, to the often risqué poetry circulating
in late Renaissance French manuscripts. It comes from a seventeenth century collection that ascribes it, not implausibly,
to Ronsard, whose most recent editors make room for it at
the end of his *Oeuvres*. In several regards it is worth juxtapos-
ing with Donne's "Sapho."

The elegy records an energetic if longwinded lament by a
widowed female dove, moping on a dry tree and mourning
the loss of her female mate, snatched away by a young male
fowler and now held captive in a dark cage. Ronsard presumably chooses doves to allegorize parted friends because those
birds are said to be faithful lovers and because Venus favors
the dove. But there may be a further implication in this context: what modern Americans call "French kissing," something that Brantôme quotes Lucian as saying lesbians enjoy,
in Ronsard's France was called kissing "en pigeonne."[18] The
fowler might represent a father or brother and the cage simply
some chateau, but it seems likely that he is meant specifically to suggest a husband and that the cage is an avian equivalent of what Blake was to call a "marriage hearse." (True, the
dove's status as a "widow" makes marriage in this poem a
puzzle; evidently, in these woods, forest laws permit same-
sex marriage, at least for birds.)[19] Her day is now night, weeps

the widowed bird, the streams keep harmony with her plaints, and even the flowers are tainted by her grief. The poet then turns to a human addressee, switching from "tu" to the more respectful "vous," and imagines for her an equally impassioned complaint to be said to that lady's female friend, with whom she had shared both a body and a soul, as the latter leaves for the Alps and marriage. She will lament, says the poet, that she feels eviscerated, paralyzed, lifeless, sustained only by memory. May the new husband receive only a very cold kiss while in thought the two women still enjoy amorous heat, games and pleasures, and the bereft lady, even as she curses the man who has taken her beloved (may rocks and brigands trouble his journey), anticipates nocturnal visions in which she will hold her friend in her arms, consoled by her empty image.

Donne's Sappho would sympathize: two women, once sharing an identity, have been torn asunder, although in this case by male force, not by one woman's sexual reorientation. Then, at the very end, in a sudden swerve to a heterosexual economy and rhetoric, the speaker tells the desolate recipient of his poem that as consolation for her loss she can reflect that she has gained a servant — the poet himself. He will drink one of her tears, make room in his heart for her sighs, and his unfeigned love will assuage her anguish. We are back to the normal course of things: male poet bowing gallantly to a lady and the lady's friend destined for marriage, babies and the upward pointing Alps. I do not know who these ladies are: nobody in Pierre de Brantôme's gossipy stories of French court life and ladies quite fits. The poem nevertheless reads less like Donne's gendered thought experiment than an ingratiating intervention in an actual lady's grief over a separation entailing marriage in another country.

Ronsard, if indeed he is the author, again shows a genuine sympathy for a female erotic bonding that is more than *philia*. And again same-sex passion is interrupted by and absorbed into the ordinary world. Has the world once more been made safe for patriarchy? Perhaps. But Ronsard, it is worth stressing, is at no pains whatsoever to make that world appealing. Nor does he offer either birds or ladies any alternative. Perhaps he agreed with Shakespeare's Benedick that the world must be peopled, although being in minor orders himself he could not himself help people it, or not legitimately. And, yes, the poem relies on explicit ventriloquizing. That is, although within the poem's fiction the sad dove has her own elegiac language, the sad woman has only the words given her by the poet as he scripts her complaint. With what has to me come to seem an endearing arrogance (not everyone agrees), Ronsard plays the voluble dove's audience, the so far silent lady's speechwriter, and her talented and faithful servant.

Ronsard was a great writer, one who, it has been observed, adopts female voices to access a part of his own psyche or verbal capacity otherwise subdued or even mute.[20] Seldom in the poetry he wrote in a male voice, not even in his love poetry, and not even at his most powerfully moving, does he show the sheer passion, the overt emotionality, of — for example — the lovesick prophetess in his *Franciade*, that incomplete epic with a twit of a hero and two compelling women. Perhaps he thought, and he would not have been alone, that unrestrained tears and storms of affect are womanish, diagnosable as a touch of the mother, perhaps. In a strange reversal of anatomy, when it comes to emotion men keep everything tucked in and women let it all hang out. For whatever reason, Ronsard's empathy for the voluble dove and bereft lady seems worth sustained pondering. As witness his frequent excuses for failing to finish his epic, he too had seen his desires and preferences blocked or deflected by those more powerful than he. Getting very far outside his own head, though, was not among Ronsard's talents. His reversion to a traditional stance — humbly wheedling but *au fond* imperative — is not astonishing.

Tyard's "Elegie pour une dame enamouree d'une autre dame" is more explicitly homoerotic. Although mentioned briefly by several scholars writing on homosexuality in early modern France and by at least one Donne scholar, it deserves more attention even from English professors (it is getting somewhat more from the French). Tyard published it in his *Oeuvres poètiques* (1573). It was possibly written considerably earlier, and in any case seems mystifyingly unlike his other poems.[21] Like Donne's "Sapho," a poem of seduction, it shares with that elegy some entertainingly sophistical logic concerning desire and honor. It also shares with "The Canonization" the dream of a love that might live on in story as an example to the nation, although I suspect that a closer parallel is with a poem by Ronsard.[22] Janel Mueller, one of the very few Donne scholars even to mention the poem, remarks that its "lesbian longings are altogether checked in the implied plot" because the "beloved lady is disdainful and unresponsive." True, yet more precisely it is not the lesbian longings but the lesbian hopes that are "checked." It is also the case, moreover, that much compelling love poetry by poets of whatever sexual orientation expresses loss, not gain, and frustration, not enjoyment. Few poets have had their desires so "checked" as Petrarch. In "The Tower," Yeats asks, "Does the imagination dwell the most / Upon the woman won or woman lost?" and never quite gives an answer. Experienced readers can supply it for him. That is why, I think, one should not make too much of the speaker's failure, like that of Donne's Sappho, to win back her lady. Although one can think of many exceptions, especially in real life, lovers of any gender are especially interesting when vexed into poetry by pain, desire, betrayal, distance and memory. Happy lovers, if not all alike, are often too busy *doing* something to grope around for pen and paper.

Tyard's lovelorn speaker, perhaps thinking that unhappy lovers should all be unhappy in their own way, calls her desire for another woman unprecedented. Nobody, she claims, has written like this before or loved like this before — common claim in love poetry, of course, and almost always false. Indeed, Tyard is here more or less paraphrasing a passage from Ariosto's *Orlando furioso* in which Fiordispina expresses her supposedly unheard-of love for Bradamante.[23] Does Tyard hope we will remember this precedent — or forget it? Maybe his lady's insistence on novelty is the reason Tyard avoids naming Sappho, unless he so tightly associated that now famous name with Ovid's heterosexual poetess that he forgot, or (despite the evidence that other Renaissance poets were well aware of her proclivities) did not want to know, that Sappho's passion had preceded his speaker's, and Ariosto's, by two millennia. A unique passion, moreover, makes the love in question more "monstrous" — "queer," but not in any good sense. Indeed, monstrosity is just what many thought tribadism must imply, for a discouraging number of medical authorities, including the great Fallopius himself, supposed that women given to lesbian sex must have enlarged clitorises (for them, apparently, the answer is yes — size matters).[24] Tyard is not unsympathetic, certainly not denunciatory, but it is hard to find in his poem the sort of imaginative empathy that Ronsard and Donne could intermittently sustain, whatever their lapses into a more traditionally "masculine" poetics.

What follows is a somewhat condensed paraphrase. I apologize for the convoluted language: like Donne, Tyard had a taste for curly syntax and compressed logic. It is impossible in English, moreover, exactly to replicate the impact of the gendered adjectives and participles: one can hide a speaker's gender in French, but doing so takes effort and attention.

> I had always believed that Love and honor, the only two flames that burn my heart, would kindle so beautiful a blaze that nothing lovelier would shine in the soul. But I was unable to think how one should light these two fires together: for however much beauty might be matter for Love, and utter beauty be in utter honor, it did not seem to me that the same beauty should

pertain to both Love and Honesty. I said, "My honor's beauty is in myself, but not so the beauty that I must love: because to judge beauty by myself would be only to love my honor, and a [female] lover must seek outside herself for the beauty that Love claims as a conquest. Will honor's flame find place only in me? Must I flee the other god's flame?

"Alas! I will choose Love's beauty from men! Wait — no. Nowadays a man loves beauty and scoffs at honor; the more beauty pleases him, the more honor perishes." Thus dearly caring only for honor I scorned all amorous flame until Love, offended by my liberty, spreads for me a subtle trap. He enriches thy wit; he sugars thy mouth and eloquent speech; he lurks in thine eyes; in thy hair he coils an unprecedented knot that binds me to thee. He makes burn a flame (alas, who will believe me?) of such a novel fire that he enamors me of a woman — alas, of another woman.

Never more softly had Love glided into a heart: for un-wounded honor retained its beauty unspoiled and Love enjoyed a beloved beauty in the same person. Ah, what happiness! If only, light one, it had pleased thee not to love lightly. But cruel Love, having seen me wounded to the quick has breathed all himself into me and left thee empty. . . . Where are thy promised faith and thy proffered vows? Where are the beautifully devised words of thy speeches? Like a counterfeit and persuasive Py-thia[25] thou has known how to chain me, captivated, by the ear.

Alas that I have vainly poured out my speech! That I have vainly fled all other loves! That vainly I have chosen thee, disdainful one, as my only joy! That vainly I had believed that in times to come we would be thought a miracle down the long centuries and that, as a unique exemplum, we would live in memory to prove that a woman's love for a woman can snatch the prize from male loves. A Damon for Pythius, an Aeneas for Achates, a Hercules for Nestor, Chairephon for Socrates, a Hopleus for Dymas,[26] have shown that the love of a man for a man has been known: and proof that men can love women is so ample that there is no need for an example.

The male couples are provocatively chosen. Tyard's lovelorn speaker implies that Aeneas and his "fidus Achates," as Virgil calls him, are a loving couple, not just good friends; perhaps she was not alone in Renaissance France. But why link Socrates to Chairephon? Figuring in several Platonic dialogues, he reported that the oracle at Delphi had called Socrates the wisest man in the world; but it was Alcibiades who, according to the *Symposium*, attempted to seduce Socrates. Hercules and Nestor make an odd couple, not least because Hercules killed Nestor's brothers. Does Tyard laugh a little at the lady's way with classical example, winking at his male readers? Or does he, rather, grant her a share of classical learning and please his female ones?

> But as for love of a woman for a woman, there has not yet been seen so rich a treasure in Love's empire, oh too light one, since in return for my faith thine has proven a liar. For never was there such great purity in Heaven, greater ardor in fire, more sweetness in honey, greater goodness in the rest of nature than in my heart, where Love is nourished. But thine is harder than a rock in the sea; crueler than a Scythian barbarian; and the Bear Callisto [that is, Ursa Major, that compliant nymph who was first ursified, then stellified, and lastly condemned to paw her way around the North Pole] does not see so much ice as thou hast in thy breast; nor has the mobile face of Morpheus so many forms as your inconstant spirit has variable thoughts.
>
> Alas! Desire transports me far from myself! Open thou to Love, thankless one. Allow the sweet shaft that pierced our hearts once more to pierce thine; let thy language show the old feeling; retie the sweet knot laced together by common liking, and rejoin these hands that swore inviolable faith. But if Love enflames thee with a new fire, I pray Anteros that before my heart's pain can change me so that only my sad voice remains as I wander the forest or my anguish distills into a flower or flows as a spring, and while alone in this dense forest I tell the deer of thy disdain, that thou, consumed by passion for someone unworthy, languish in love and never be loved.

As an exercise in queering Cupid this poem has problems, if only because the speaker's desire is merely what Tyard can but suppose a woman's might feel like. Granted the psychological effect of literary and cultural traditions and the flexibility of the human spirit, it seems reasonable to assume that somewhere a woman has experienced just such feelings as

Tyard imagines. Nevertheless, the emotions and their expression seem too familiar for a supposedly novel sort of passion. Generic expectations, the resort to the usual personifications and imagery, and the magnetic tug of traditionally male attitudes, inherent or cultural, make for familiar rhetorical moves that enter the poem like old friends knowing where to hang their hats and find the whiskey: I love you but you betray me; make things as they used to be or I will be an echo, flower or running water (see Ovid), and if you *won't* love me, may you suffer. Some readers will remember, among many other poets, the most unlesbian Wyatt threatening his reluctant lady with her future sexual frustration under the cold moon of old age.

What might be the use of these three poems to Donne scholarship? First, very simply, remembering more often and more attentively that other early modern poets, although for any number of reasons not naming Sappho herself, had also adopted a passionate and, in the case of Tyard, an unabashedly homo-erotic female voice. Donne (maybe) stars Sappho and Philaenis, but his plot — girl loves girl, girl loses girl to boy — parallels that of Ronsard's unpublished elegy and, although only if we take the beloved's infidelity as implying a new love for a man, that of Tyard's elegy as well. In Donne's London, Ronsard and Tyard were not obscure poets, and if in his day the height of their vogue was passing or past in France, in England they still enjoyed fame and prestige. Their poems allow us to see near contemporary male poets, one a writer of international fame whose career seemed stellar to the outward eye (although given to gloomy laments that he was underappreciated by rich magnates and underfunded by his several kings), experimented with adopting the voice of an "other" who for once loves the "same." That is to say, a male poet imagines a female "other" writing not in response to some male like the poet's self but to yet another female "other."

Questions that Donne scholars raise concerning "Sapho to Philænis" can be raised about Ronsard and Tyard as well. To what extent do their poems escape a male subjectivity, granted that anatomy probably ensures that there is such a thing? Are not their voices, perhaps in spite of their authors' efforts, still "masculine," as their culture tended to define "masculine"? If so, then it is here that Donne's originality shows most clearly, for there is little in his "Sapho" that parallels Ronsard's and Tyard's lapses into quasi feudal hand-kissing service on the one hand or bragging competition with other lovers on the other. To be sure, Ronsard and Tyard might argue, everybody knows that lesbian love must entail masculine behavior on one lady's part, which is why a tribade must use a dildo, when not equipped with an enlarged clitoris, so as to imitate heterosexual intercourse.[27] A woman who makes love to another woman must be pseudo-manly. Donne's Sappho, then, fails to follow standard expectations inherited from centuries of (male) assumptions concerning lesbian sexuality. The self-mirroring symmetry, the literal *homo*sexuality, that so disturbs some readers, and is perhaps meant to do so, is unsurprising in recent times but could have seemed a striking departure in Donne's own culture. Sappho wants only to love Philaenis, not to serve her, and although she prefers a lovely self-resembling and unplowed woman to any hairy and trace-leaving man, she nowhere boasts that her passion outdoes that of famous lovers past.

Should we, moreover, perceive in these French poems the "anxiety" that so many now see in — or, I suspect, often project onto — Renaissance male writers? Do they appear sympathetic to same-sex love between women in part so as to sidle quietly up to same-sex "sodomitical" love between men? Neither Ronsard nor Tyard seems to have been drawn to male homo-erotic poetry, but their social and personal circumstances — literary, ecclesiastical, academic — encouraged masculine ca-maraderie quite as much as court life encouraged the wooing or flattery of women. Do the three French elegies, that is, serve male homosociality? Is the sparkling group of poets called "The

Pléiade" further constellated, so to speak, by Ronsard's and Tyard's slightly naughty flirtation with lesbianism? After all, Donne's fancied Sappho, more truly Sapphic than Ovid's epistolary ferryman-lover, may have helped a young man-about-Lincoln's Inn look urbane, and doubtless all the more jauntily urbane if he could also look somewhat French, somewhat proto-*libertin* as well.[28]

Do the French poems, beneath their show of empathy, satirize the tribade bonding taking place in the closed chambers of Catherine de Medici's ladies? Or is Ronsard trying to *please* court ladies named Anne and Diane and one other whose dearest friend had been caught, caged and transported to the snowy mountains? How do all four poems, three by unmarried Catholics well inside the church and one by a Catholic somewhere near its exit ("Sapho to Philænis" is undated, so it is hard to know just how near), relate to shifts in attitudes toward marriage? Would scholars who claim, in a pleasantly Donnean paradox, that Sappho's lesbian autoeroticism signifies failed signs as well as narcissist flaccidity say the same of Ronsard's and Tyard's "lesbian" poems? Is Ronsard's lady's imagined portrait a sort of narcissist looking glass? Or, as Lacan might ask, is he reflecting on an extended mirror stage? Compared to the poets' other works, moreover, Ronsard's 1565 elegy and Tyard's "Elegie pour une dame" can seem insipid, with uncharacteristic verbal repetition. Is this an effort to sound feminine? Or an indication that the poets' hearts are not really in what they write? Does such flatness hint at condemnation?

If critical response to Donne's poem is any guide, a consensus on answers to such questions is unlikely. The topic itself is likely to provoke a more than ordinarily subjective reaction, consciously or not, and the texts in question are more than ordinarily unstable and ambiguous. In thinking about Donne's "Sapho," however, it is well to remember that although the first in England to write in the person of the famous lesbian poet and to insist on her lesbianism he was not the first to impersonate a woman loving — and in the case of Ronsard's moping dove married to — another woman. Does this matter? Yes, because the French poems can help us more accurately to disentangle what is unique and what merely unusual in Donne's poem, to set his elegy in one more literary and cultural context. To read him simply as attempting to rival, undo, overgo, imitate, revise Ovid is useful, although without its title the poem might seem less insistent in soliciting such a reading. But Donne may also have hoped, although I cannot prove this, to show his friends that an English wit could rival, overgo, imitate or otherwise equal the risqué French. The map of his social world included the Continental literary scene as well as that of ancient Rome and, more faintly drawn, Sappho's Lesbos.

At the very least these French analogues can reinforce our awareness that good poets, like good people, can envision, inadequately or with mixed motives, more possibilities than they wish to or could act out, more lives than they can live. "He do humanity in different voices" is not the only way to be a fine poet, to be sure, and, like Ronsard, Donne was too much himself to range through as many octaves as, say, Browning, let alone Shakespeare. Negative capability was not his strong suit. Nevertheless, and taste in such matters is of course very personal — anything to do with gender and sex must be — many might prefer these three poets' treatment of women's same-sex desire to the sniggering of the slightly later *libertins* who wrote about tribadism, with or without dildos, sometimes noting its supposed effects on the health (no hair on the palms, one gathers, but pallor, sunken eyes, bad breath, and lassitude).

Those displeased by Ronsard's and Tyard's efforts to appropriate or "ventriloquize" lesbian voices, and I assume that those who distrust Donne would distrust the French poets as well, might compare these sixteenth century poems to a sonnet by Denis Sanguin de Saint-Pavin (1595–1670), a distinguished cleric and reputed atheist, which says that

> Two belles love each other tenderly, one drawn to the other, and each suffering equally from the same arrow-wound. Without complaining of their torment, both sigh ceaselessly: sometimes the lover ["amant," the masculine form] is the mistress, sometimes the mistress is the lover. Whatever they do to please themselves, they cannot satisfy their hearts and lose their best time of life. In such sort of love, these "innocent" [naive, that is] ladies who abuse themselves ["abusent" also means delude, fool] vainly seek the pleasures that they refuse to us [that is, us men].[29]

The tribades themselves might retort that it is likewise surprisingly *innocent* on the part of a libertine poet, hardly a promoter of family values, to assume that their mutual pleasure is unreal, but such innocence was (among men) common. Donne, had he lived to read this poem, might have been intrigued by the ease with which the ladies reverse roles: this behavior is not quite Sappho-in-the-mirror, but it does have symmetry. Historians of sexuality and gender will note that these "belles" evidently must include one "amant" and one mistress, not two female "amantes." And any reader can detect the hostility behind the speaker's mock resentment at the denial of sexual favors to the appropriate sex.

Ronsard could also snigger at times, as witness his sonnet on a woman who, to preserve a purely notional virtue, prefers fooling around with a dildo to going to bed with men — not even bed with Ronsard, who, if the lady really is Hélène de Surgères, had asked for it so prettily and so often.[30] But whatever their moments of misogyny, of accusatory cynicism, Ronsard, Tyard and Donne could also imagine, or try to imagine, or think they were imagining, a sexual subjectivity other than their own and to do so with what strikes some readers as real if limited sympathy. Their poems, moreover, perform a love that was culturally subversive, however we take it. If such love is physically sexual, it may not be adulterous but it is at least ostensibly repugnant to respectable early modern imaginations. If it is intense but purely emotional, with no dildos or genital monstrosity, no *doing*, it proves that whatever Platonic tradition holds to be the case, even women (anatomically too cool for perfection, mentally too hot for rationality) are capable of a love that transcends the body. Even those who perceive these poems' limitations, then, or catch the verse's negative overtones and biases could, in a generous mood, find it moving to hear Ronsard and Donne — those imperiously masculine poets — and the less cocksure Tyard attempting to up their vocal register, if momentarily, from commanding baritone to melting soprano.

7 • Reading Donne
Old and New
His- and Her-storicisms

Stanley Stewart

1

Literary critics attentive to sea changes in career opportunities know that it is better to hoist the banner of "new" than of "old." "Old" criticism implies "used" in the pejorative sense of "worn out," rather than used, as in "utilized" or *really useful.*" We don't invest pension funds in manufacturers of buggy whips, not because Western methods of production proved faulty or were outstripped by cheaper foreign competition. New modes of travel simply narrowed the market for even the best buggy whips to curators of special interest showplaces, like the Roy Rogers Museum in Victorville, California. For good or ill, consumerist trends indicate that literary history has waxed "old" in the antiquarian sense of "quaint" and "outmoded." Like "age" in Lear's troubled reckoning, archival research "is unnecessary." Although rechristened with a mind to intellectual respectability, methodologically, "New

Historicism" is "but [New Criticism] writ [race-class-and-gender] Large." So New Historicists say that "[i]n the past few years . . . explorations of gender, ideology, power, and language in the Renaissance have not only provided radically new understandings of familiar texts but have also forced us to reexamine the critical, historical, and cultural presuppositions on which our readings are based."[1] The idea is to link "New" with "radical" (that is, left-leaning) change: "'New philosophy calls all in doubt,' wrote John Donne in 1611, and many of his critics in the 1980s could say the same about the effect of recent literary theory upon their own interpretive practices" (ibid.).

There is more bravado than bravura here, since New Historicists seldom call the "interpretive practices" of New Historicists into question. On the contrary, they celebrate their "radically new understandings of familiar texts." Hence, "[w]hat is 'new' about the 'new historicism' is not so much the fact that it is historicist," that is, that it implies a connection with history, "as the fact that it conceives the relationship between literature and history in a new way" (x). Note that the persuasive definition of "historicism" here does not imply that New Historicists have uncovered historical evidence overlooked by "New Critics" whose method of textual analysis they employ, but only that "[m]any recent critics have been redefining the kinds of history that might be important for a reader to know." We can see that the tangential reference to the concept of knowledge ("to know") deflects attention from the normative crux of the sentence, namely, identification of the "kinds of history that might be important for a reader to know." In this context, the concepts of "kinds of history" and of "knowledge" are, at best, murky. One could even infer that, in practice, beliefs held prior to historical investigation seem to be the New Historicists' important "tool for counteracting an ideological system that uses aestheticism or spirituality to conceal politically oppressive tactics." That is, political desire determines what counts as "redefining the

kinds of history that might be important for a reader to know."
Hence, as they impose their mentors' technique of "close reading" of texts — historical documents as well as the usual literary warhorses — New Historicists celebrate a "new way"
of *declining* to celebrate the values represented in the established canon. In so doing, they aim to flout "an ideological
system that uses aestheticism or spirituality to conceal politically oppressive tactics" (x), which explains why they admire William Empson for daring not to "mince words" about
Donne "'gradually killing his wife by giving her a child every
year.'"[2] In the apocryphal words of Nietzsche, whom New
Historicists never tire of misquoting, "There are no facts, only
interpretations."[3] For them, historical facts are "problematic"
and a bore, since their assertion depends on a naive faith in
objectivity. In fact, feelings precede and determine construc-
tions of the past. Subjectivity — *interest* — rules. So it is not
the precise number of children that Donne forced Anne to
bear, nor even her actual desires with respect to having any or
all of them, but the all-encompassing imputation made by New
Historicists that counts in New Historicism.

It would not distort literary history, then, to nickname New
Historicists "New Empsonians." They are the incarnation of
just such practitioners of the "Old" "New Criticism." Take
the claim that New Historicists are "deeply skeptical . . . [of]
established modes of interpretation" (xxi), for instance. In this
pose, they share Empson's disdain for the use of Renaissance
archives in the pursuit of knowledge about the Renaissance.
So even while celebrating their strategic departure from their
New Critic mentors (xi), they emulate Empson: "But whereas
the New Critics tended to take paradox as the expression of a
necessarily contradictory but eternal human truth — the
simultaneity of death and life, disorder and harmony, sensuality and spirituality, weakness and strength, and so forth —
their successors are likely to see paradox or contradiction as

the site of some unresolved conflict, a strategy of management and containment as well as revelatory expression" (Harvey, xi).

Actually, this remark is unfair to Empson, since New Historicist efforts at "demystification rather than celebration" (xi) of the values expressed by the Metaphysical poets, if ever "New" in the twentieth century, was a staple of Empson's rhetoric 50 years ago. When New Historicists follow Freud, they follow Empson away from Renaissance archives. "Thus," write apologists of "New Historicism," "while quite eclectic in their use of theoretical models, many recent critics find most consistently helpful those writers who can help articulate those strategies [of management and containment]: Marx, Althusser, Foucault, Freud, Derrida, Lacan, Irigaray" (xi). Here, we should recall that Tuve's most strenuous objection to Empson's remarks concerned his casual assumption that Freudian assumptions and practices were relevant to interpretation of Herbert's poetry.

So "New Empsonians" are quite open in their adulation of their critical ancestor, characterizing him as their "critical guide," and therefore understandably as "ingenious," "brilliant," "most brilliant" — no less than the literary equivalent of Albert Einstein and Werner Heisenberg combined. (If talk like this is "skeptical," it must be so in a very odd sense of that term.) Let me give an example of how the admiration of Empson fits with the method and manner of "New" as distinct from "Old" literary history. Since all printed matter was written in the past, then all remarks about literature are "historical." Thus, when critics bring reading of one text into play in interpreting another, they are, by definition, citing historical evidence. But then there are works written in the relatively distant as distinct from the more recent past, and these might answer in very different ways than do later ones to the criterion of relevance. Literary history drawn on sources that

Donne and Herbert had read or could have read exert different claims to relevance in discussions of their works than do those that draw on writings of "Marx, Althusser, Foucault, Freud, Derrida, Lacan, Irigaray," and Empson.

On the surface, it may seem that "Old" and "New" applications of history do pretty much the same work. Thus, when "Old" and New Historicists talk about Donne's poetry, they often quote from "the same text" in the Grierson edition. And their remarks do not (perhaps cannot) proceed from a hermetically sealed experience of the text — "the thing itself." Let us say that critics have read widely, and been exposed to a variety of different experiences. Focus on these differences to the exclusion of much else is nowadays often fetishized as "subjectivity" talk. Naturally (or "unnaturally," say, by a process of "social construction," whatever that may be), critics bring themselves — their whole past, readings included — to bear on Donne's poetry. But the differences between the effects of these readings on the propositions that critics generate on Donne and his writings are at least as interesting as the fact that both "New" and "Old" literary historians display footnotes and lists of works cited. We could say the same of Empson's famous clash with Tuve. He thought that clever Herbert critics should read Sigmund Freud and Sir James Frazer. She assumed that interpreters of "The Sacrifice" should saturate themselves in Medieval and Renaissance religious literature and art. For to her, Herbert was, like Donne, a seventeenth century Anglican priest, not a late nineteenth century psychoanalyst of upperclass women in Vienna.

There is a matter of substance in this tension between "Old" and New Historicism. When Edward W. Tayler approaches the Grierson text of Donne's *Anniversaries*, presenting a history of the Platonic locution *eidos*, he assumes that this information might be relevant to Donne's "Idea of a Woman." Critical work in this mode proceeds as if literary history were a branch of the history of language. What is "important . . . to know" here is the history of language, especially of its various expressions in the period in which Donne and his audience shared a common idiom, and lived in certain common ways. When discussing "The Canonization," then, Tayler likewise assumes the relevance of literary, linguistic and ecclesiastical history. So he notes the convergence of Donne's expression and historical practice: "The linear structure of the five stanzas also coincides ... with the topical (and linear) 'structure' of the ecclesiastical *processus* of canonization: (1) proof of personal sanctity urged against a Devil's Advocate, (2) practice of virtue in heroic degree, (3) examination of alleged miracles, (4) consideration of writings and remains, and (5) canonization."[4] As the discussion proceeds, it is clear that, for him, historical understanding of "The Canonization" requires familiarity with procedures of canonization in the period, as well as with the writings of Petrarch, Shakespeare, Spenser, Digby, Browne, Ascham, Augustine and Aristotle, all of which were part of the world in which Donne's expression "lived and moved and had its being." In his effort to frame Donne's expression in terms of Renaissance ways of thinking about and doing such things, Tayler posits a contextual claim of relevance for the various literary and cultural practices encompassed by his argument.

In contrast, New Historicists finesse archival research in favor of theoretical proclamations like this: "We need to remember that the authorial voice always reaches us through a process of mediation."[5] With the momentous tone of the pronouncement here, imposed on the argument so unobtrusively that its relevance is presumed to be self-evident, they aim to obscure their failure to advance archival evidence in support of specific assertions about specific works. Even if the proposition about "mediated voices" were true (by what means would we determine *that*?), and even if it could be shown that we remembered it, the question of the relevance of that "truth" to the Donne question at hand would remain. But if critics have never learned "that the authorial voice always reaches us through a process of mediation," it makes no more sense to insist that they remember than that they forget it. More to the point, if it is important to remember this utterance, we must be able to understand the contrast between voices that reach us "through a process of mediation" and those that do so by some other mechanism. This means that critics inclined to mediation talk must show that they analyze literary and nonliterary texts in ways significantly different from those of other observers. For instance, how do we distinguish mediation from nonmediation in this sentence: "Shortly before she died in 1558, England's Catholic queen, Mary Tudor, reluctantly designated her Protestant half-sister Elizabeth as her successor"?[6] Here Louis Montrose, whose method Corthell emulates, insists that, since all consciousness of the past is mediated, statements which mediate consciousness of the past must also be so. But even if this proposition makes sense, how does mediation or nonmediation alter the significance or truth of the statement that "[s]hortly before she died in 1558, England's Catholic queen, Mary Tudor, reluctantly designated her Protestant half-sister Elizabeth as her successor"? Suppose I agree or disagree with the proposition that this sentence, like the language of Mary Tudor's will and Donne's "The Canonization," is mediated or unmmmediated. I claim that my understanding is necessarily mediated or unmediated, and point to these artifacts as evidence to support my hypothesis. Would a decision in the matter weigh on a proper understanding of the critic's statement, Mary Tudor's will, or Donne's poem?[7]

2

Even more important than "mediation" and "ideology" talk, I think, is the almost universal sense in which New Historicists take such talk seriously. For instance, Ronald Corthell begins his discussion of Donne's *Anniversaries* with a diatribe against Tayler, whom he accuses of a polemic against "new historicism, deconstruction, Geertzian 'thick description,' and Victor Turner's concept of liminality, perhaps to inoculate readers against new historicist and other ideological interpretations that have yet to be written" (108). I'm not qualified to judge whether this characterization of Tayler's critique is accurate, but I am puzzled by the tone of "inoculation" talk here. Corthell implies that, if Tayler *were* trying to "inoculate readers against new historicist and other ideological interpretations yet to be written," he would be doing something wrong, offending against "ideological interpretations," as if these should be held sacrosanct. But why would anyone think *that*? Citing Anthony Easthope, Corthell claims that critics are "compelled to read [Donne's poem] through a palimpsest of other interpretations." Again — and typically — the general proposition holds sway, as if it were not only relevant and true, but (Corthell's term) "important." For who can argue against necessity? Critics can't choose, because they are compelled. Freedom of choice here, and maybe everywhere, is an illusion. Why? Because Corthell is "compelled" to say so. But, less dramatically, we can will to set compulsion talk aside as an irrelevant concept, and say, contrariwise, that an unwarranted assumption emerges from this picture of *n* interpretations imposed and wiped clean from a palimpsest. The relevant picture in the mind holds that all citations are equal in their inevitable "passage through these looms" of endless inscription and erasure. Accordingly, Corthell cites Freud's "On Narcissism: An Introduction" and Freud's "Mourning and Melancholia," proffering his mediation of a psychoanalytic approach, with a host of writings by Freud and Freudians like Luce Irigaray, Julia Kristeva, Jacques Lacan and New Historicist scions of these twentieth century followers of Freud.

Critics need to develop and to extend their critical — and

by that I mean their skeptical — capacity, and in the process to jettison their credulity. Let me elaborate on what might seem to be a gratuitously polemical remark. In his introduction to *Ideology and Desire in Renaissance Poetry*, Corthell summarizes what he takes to be the "ideological" situation in Donne studies. Focusing on pronouncements of Elizabeth D. Harvey and Katherine Eisaman Maus in *Soliciting Interpretation*, and seconding Richard Strier's admiration of William Empson as the "model critic" (13), Corthell tackles notions of history and literature as bedeviled by New Historicism in a "post-Althusserian" context, namely, the challenge to "disinterestedness" (14). Assuming that terms like "interpellation" work in Donne criticism by exposing "contradiction and negativity" (15), Corthell cites Stephen Greenblatt and Louis Montrose on the assumption that billboards and Wonder Woman comics help, in the same way as do Freud and Empson, to explain Donne (15). For Corthell, this seems to be so because Arthur Marotti's work is so "conventional" (18) that it is not sufficiently "decisive." So turning to "conventional" "subversion and containment" talk (18), Corthell is justified in agreeing with Stanley Fish that Donne isn't in control of himself.

This is how Corthell's defense of psychoanalysis works (20). He claims that psychoanalysis fits Donne's "formalist practice" (21). While fitting Donne's satires into Montrose's notion of "equivocal process," he admits that the result might be to collapse the difference between the Renaissance and the present time (25), which, of course, is the crux of Tayler's thesis. Ahistorical procedures lead to anachronistic understandings. Choosing to confuse "now" with "then," Corthell proceeds to formal analysis of Donne's satires with the aim of rescuing Donne from "conservative or cynical critics" (29). He does this in a manner reminiscent of Thomas Docherty, whom he cites, as well as of George Klawitter, whom he does not.[8] Docherty and Klawitter would also rescue Donne from "conservative or cynical critics." But what is the method of this salvific undertaking? Corthell employs the tried and true way of New Critics: by "close reading" of texts, without the support of *contemporary* evidence. That is, he proceeds as if evidence from Renaissance archives were a crutch employed by "conservative or cynical" critics like Tayler. Through "close reading," Corthell knows when a Donne poem is "autoerotic" (68), and when it is a hymn to the vulva, which "can only be seen as the [*sic*] penis" (69–70). And all of this because, enabled by Jacques Lacan, Corthell thinks Donne feared "turning into a woman" (65).

But don't such perceptions require evidence that someone in the seventeenth century understood the language of Donne's poems in this way? This figure was construed as a vulva in that work; and yes, in such and such a manuscript, we find evidence that someone in the period, even if not Donne, used this kind of expression to indicate fear that he would turn into a woman. If Corthell's assertions are relevant, aren't they so for reasons that pass skeptical scrutiny? Which is to ask: *Did* Donne fear turning into a woman? What would evidence that Donne feared turning into a woman look like? In fact, Corthell proffers not a shred of evidence that Donne feared turning into a woman, even temporarily, let alone for any length of time. Considering that Corthell sets out to rebut what he characterizes as Tayler's "grumpy version of T. S. Eliot's 1931 disclaimer of his earlier views on Donne" (191 n. 1), and that "[a] great deal seems to be at stake in Tayler's book" (108), critical assumptions, including New Historicist "ideological" methodology, would appear to be at least one of the issues "at stake" in deciding whether or not Donne feared turning into a woman. For even if, in the Alice in Wonderland world of New Historicism, "silly" trumps "grumpy," it does not follow from protestations of "subjectivity," however buttressed by such secondary sources as Freud and Lacan, that we have grounds to believe that Donne feared turning into a woman. In literary studies, Gresham's law does not *necessarily* apply.

Perhaps New Historicists do not consider Freud, Lacan and Irigaray as secondary sources, and some might think the term derogatory. But historical critics write and use secondary sources all the time. So the term is not intrinsically derogatory. The use to which a secondary source is put is what matters. Is the secondary source relevant to the historical question asked? So we return to the question: *Did* John Donne fear turning into a woman? Well, who or what, in that time, had the power to turn men into women, or women into men, even temporarily? Perhaps Corthell means that Donne feared being convinced, say, by a magician like Simon Forman, that he had been turned into a woman. (Did Forman give him a mind-altering drug like laudanum, rendering him fearful of turning into a woman?) That is not what Corthell says, but such an event might be documented, perhaps, by consulting Forman's diary, or some other contemporary document for evidence that the two men met, conversed, drank together. Even more to the point would be evidence that Forman, who was often at loggerheads with the College of Physicians over his credentials as a healer, treated Donne or members of his family, or even distant relatives. Theoretically, *n* documents residing in rare book libraries all over the world *could* bear on the assertion that Donne feared turning into a woman. Why depend on the text of Donne's "The Indifferent" as scaffolding for the proposition that Donne was afraid "of women and of turning into a woman"? (65) The problem with this way of talking is not, I think, that Corthell and critics like him talk like this, but that they take talk like this as if it were about Donne. I am suggesting that what really interests Corthell is the true subject of subjectivity talk, and the implicit subject of that branch of New Criticism called "Affective Stylistics," namely, himself. To Corthell, "Donne's play of wit [in 'The Indifferent'] is not subversive in the sense of directly challenging any ideology, but neither is it orthodox in the sense of reflecting an ideology" (63). Instead, Donne seeks an ironic truce with the tensions "of sexual relations," which he finds in "irony, a literary language that makes it easier to live with contradictions." This much seems like straightforward formal analysis, in the manner of New Criticism. But, significantly, Corthell adds, "Or does it?" Does the poem *do* this, as it has all the other things that Corthell says it does? Answer: "'The Indifferent' does not put [him] completely at ease" (63). That is, he invokes the criterion of "complete" personal "ease" as the standard by which "The Indifferent" is measured. Oddly, the poem "discloses our culture's tendency to construct love or sexuality around oppositions like promiscuity and fidelity, sex and love, male and female" (64). This leads to "its chief effect . . . of discomfiture" (64).

Note that the poem's chief effect arises from the power of a "tendency" exerted by something called "culture" to create such opposites as "promiscuity and fidelity, sex and love, male and female." Truly, this "discomfiture" does not seem to me to be a historically viable option in Donne's time. Culture at that time didn't express a tendency to construct a difference between promiscuity and fidelity. It had institutions well equipped to clarify the difference between the two, to correct the intellectually challenged of the time who were unable to perceive demarcation between the two. But Donne depends on perception of that very contrast for the poem's power to amuse some (like me) and discomfit others (like Corthell). For if all young women were faithful, the subject of the poem, which is the difficulty presented about the exception to the rule of promiscuity, would not make sense, and the world would be bereft of the implicit comic material. The same can be said for the difference between love and sex. But then most of us have read book 2 of *The Faerie Queene*, not to mention book 9 of *Paradise Lost*, so we know that for Spenser and Milton the distinction does not in and of itself "discomfit."

As for this opposition of male and female, it was more or less, in Donne's time, considered a fact of nature, which is why Webster's or Overbury's or Overbury-Webster's "faire and happy Milke-mayd" goes early in the morning, "deckt in *innocence*,"[9] to milk cows instead of bulls. The telling question is: Why should a distinction so long established in the phylum, and such a source of amusement in Donne's time, "discomfit" a critic like Corthell today? It seems to me that Corthell deflects the answer: "Again Freud's meditations seem pertinent" (64).

Again, I would suggest, the fact that "Freud's meditations seem pertinent" is the source of the critic's "discomfiture," not Donne's witty poem. Look at the subtitle of *Ideology and Desire in Renaissance Poetry: The Subject of Donne*. With the best will in the world, this designation is misleading. For Corthell has little to say about Donne, because his real subject is "subjectivity" talk, scaffolded on summaries of arguments drawn from Freud and Freudians like Lacan and Irigaray. This explains why he can say, with no hint of irony or humor, that Donne feared "turning into a woman," and that he had this or that sexual desire, or this or that poetic conflict.[10] And it explains, too, the absence in Corthell's New Historicist account of any sense of obligation that his assertions be supported by evidence that these poems were read, or could have been read, by anyone in the period in this way. By focusing instead on the "subject" of how twentieth century critics talk about subjectivity, Corthell "inoculates" himself against the demand that argument pertaining to *The Subject of Donne* proffer relevant evidence about Donne or his historical context.

3

Donne critics also need to ponder the normative stuff. For instance, Docherty says of "The Canonization," "Such love, of course, is always being seen from an exclusively male point

of view; the central element in the identification is the notion of rising, of erection,"[11] in the sexual sense. Setting aside
the incisiveness or absurdity of this assertion, notice the tone.
It is as if, if the assertion were true, Donne *erred* in articulat-
ing a "male point of view." How so? Well, by his "exclusive-
ness" in doing so. The concept here is not difficult to grasp.
The term "male" suggests the opposition between the sexes.
And Donne's poem excludes the female point of view. Of
course it does. How, without excluding what is female, could
Donne present a male point of view? Is Docherty suggesting
that Donne was congenitally unable to appreciate and represent a female viewpoint? His "Sapho to Philænis" serves as
the counterinstance to that misapprehension. So what justifies the tone of indignation? The critical issue now is that of
advocacy, which in practice amounts to name-calling (and in
its most pernicious form, slander). In the interests of "demystification," New Historicists have traduced the character of
Renaissance authors, including John Donne, George Herbert,
Sir Thomas More, Shakespeare, Jonson and Milton, to mention only a notable few, whom they accuse of offenses ranging
from misogyny and racism to incest. And all of this on the
basis of "close reading" of texts, and in the absence of what
responsible prosecutors and critics would consider forensic
evidence. To my knowledge, New Historicists accuse Donne
of only the one serious felony of murdering his wife (by seri-
ally impregnating her). But his wife's forebear, Thomas More,
hasn't been so lucky. Jonathan Crewe insinuates the case
against him for incest.[12] (Remember More's daughter washing
his shirt, and him kissing her before ascending the scaffold?)
Mostly, the charges against Donne are misdemeanor thought
crimes. He is an "absolutist" and a "misogynist."

Not that New Historicists take such charges lightly. New
Historicist gender studies make misogyny a hate crime, even
if nobody connected to it is technically guilty of overt criminal acts. (Remember Nietzsche? "Words are deeds." When

misogynists speak, rape is imminent.) For New Historicists, sex "is the spur" to critical calumny. And everywhere they look they see penises and vulvas, armed as they are with the demystifying license of psychoanalytic theory.

Consider the case of the phoenix as phallus in Donne's "The Canonization." In typical New Historicist talk, Docherty argues that the phoenix rising has something to do with sexual arousal "from an exclusively male point of view":

> Call us what you will, wee are made such by love;
>   Call her one, mee another flye,
> We're Tapers too, and at our owne cost die,
>   And wee in us finde the' Eagle and the Dove.
>   The Phoenix ridle hath more wit
>   By us, we two being one, are it.
> So to one neutrall thing both sexes fit,
>   Wee dye and rise the same, and prove
>   Mysterious by this love.
>
> (19–27)[13]

Most readers will not find the assertion that the speaker here is male particularly controversial, surely not sufficient grounds for moral indignation. But the inference that the rising of the phoenix has something to do with an erection of the male organ has less claim to credulity. The idea is that copulation wipes out differences between the lovers, who experience the metaphoric death of ecstasy, which is (to coin a phrase) gender neutral. Resurrection follows death, of course, as, unlike Gandhi, most lovers do not literally expire in the act, never to be revived. This is not the hard part of interpreting stanza 3, unless we take such remarks as Docherty's seriously, in which case we must reverse the sense that Donne implies here. In "The Canonization," as in "The Exstasie" (51–52), the mystery of love is in the alchemy of blending two souls into one. The "beast with two backs" is still one body, if only for the moment of "[t]his exstasie." Tayler's remarks point in the right direction, toward the link between the language of sexual union and that of religious mysticism, which found its way into canon procedures of beatification:

> But as all severall soules containe
>   Mixture of things, they know not what,
> Love, these mixt soules, doth mixe againe,
>   And makes both one, each this and that.

(33–36)

"Defects of loneliness" are controlled through change, which is not perceptible from the outside, and to the uninitiated, not at all. So in "The Canonization," it is not the male point of view that justifies canonization, nor an untimely erection from the male point of view, *after* the unifying ecstasy. The lovers merit veneration for what they, in their mysterious union, come to "epitomize," to lovers who pray to them for "[a] pattern of [their] love." So the Renaissance records of the institution of canonization provide a better fit with the text of Donne's poem than do general speculations of twentieth century Freudians. To put this thought another way, unlike Tayler, Docherty offers no contemporary evidence that Donne, or readers in Donne's time, construed the phoenix rising, in the manner of precoital erection. So the question is, do all risings imply erection perceived "from an exclusively male point of view"?

Corthell and Docherty are not isolated examples of this species of gender talk. Far from it, New Historicism has been justly described as the dominant mode in literary studies to-day.[14] I am talking now about another aspect of the tone of this kind of criticism. I think it is undeniable that New Historicists would rather read Lacan and Foucault than invest their time in archival research in rare book libraries, and their work is often imbued with a sense of indignation directed toward what they call "traditional" historical scholarship. Tayler is only one of the targets of Donne critics. New Historicists routinely lambast the usual suspects, critics like Grierson, Eliot, Gardner, Simpson, Bald and Tuve.

Tension between "Old" and "New" literary historians exposes an odd connection between literary studies and science. New Historicists often refer to "traditional" literary historians as "positivists," in the disparaging sense of throwbacks to the era of Auguste Comte. (More dubiously, some critics label their archival counterparts "logical positivists.") At the same time, New Historicists associate themselves with softer versions of the soft sciences: sociology (as ethnic studies), psychology (in its confessional mode of psychoanalysis — Freud, Lacan), anthropology (in its imaginative mode — Geertz, Greenblatt), and political theory (in its normative mode of Marxist race, class and gender advocacy). Accordingly, various trends of identity politics come together in the dispensation of government and foundation supplicants and government bursars. The intellectual effects of this symbiotic relationship appear in such documents as the 1996–1997 National Endowment for the Humanities sponsored Program, announced by the Newberry Library's Center for Renaissance Studies' Interdisciplinary Programs, on the topic of "Teaching Gender in the Middle Ages and the Renaissance Center for Renaissance Studies." Nowadays, the locution "interdisciplinary" serves as the mantra for upwardly mobile deans of humanities and social sciences colleges, and can be considered as something like a synonym for "fundable" (in the sense of "important" or "relevant" or "politically correct"), in the larger world of grants and conferences:

> Gender, the Economy, and the Law
> Gender and Race/Ethnicity
> Genders (*sic*) and Sexualities (*sic*)
> Gender and Institutions: The Family, Property and the State.

These topics indicate only the general headings of the Newberry Library Center's program sessions, which, in turn, register ten lectures or workshops with such titles or subtitles as "Gender and the Economy in the Middle Ages," "Gender,

Catholicism, and the Law in Seventeenth-Century England,"
"Gender, Honor, and Law in Early Modern England," "Dia-
spora and the Gendered Politics of Resistance," "Literary
Whiteness in Shakespeare's Sonnets," "Shakespeare's Sexual
Politics," "State Violence and Gender Ideology in English
Renaissance Drama" and "Shakespearean Reconstructions
of Gender."

I am not making this up, nor do I mean to pillory the Newberry Library Center's program as worse than any of the
hundreds of like-sounding symposia announced in slick, tax-
subsidized brochures throughout the country over the past
several decades. But whether it is worse or better than most,
its announcement is unerringly true to the norms of this
ultranormative genre. By this I mean that, no matter how it is
trussed up with pseudoscientific vocabulary imported from
the social sciences, these New "His-" and "Her-storicisms"
are in fact thinly disguised forms of social preachments. While
ostensibly advocating a relativist stance appropriate to a thor-
oughgoing multiculturalism, New Historicists confusedly lac-
erate the old, archival, white, male, heterosexualist, objectivist,
elitist, scientistic, hegemonist defense of knowledge, which
their secularist "construction" of reality rejects as illegitimate.
But whence comes the indignation? How can "social con-
structivist" programs, fattened on government largesse, end
up with the generic requirement of the Puritan sermon,
namely, moral zeal?

"What," a critic asked not long ago, "brought us to the pass
where an honorable profession seemed to surrender with very
few shots fired."[15] And why, in my recent book, had I not addressed the question of how it came about that so much of
what passes for professional criticism lacks intellectual weight
and philosophical discipline? The critic was right, of course.
In *"Renaissance" Talk*, I "investigate," in Wittgenstein's sense
of that term, critical statements and assumptions about seemingly intractable critical problems endemic to the interpretive

project. Investigation follows odd assertions back to their source, which, in critical theory and philosophy (in practice, the two often coincide), begins in odd ways of talking when we "do" theory or philosophy. As for the "how" in "how did we come to this pass?" of the general lack of interest in knowledge about literary history, and in archival research that powers the engine of historical knowledge, well, I more or less ignore that question.

This does not mean that I consider the question of intellectual provenance uninteresting or unimportant. On the contrary, humanistic studies came to doubt its contribution to knowledge as an end in itself, the desideratum of post-Enlightenment thought, at just the time when scientific inquiry overcame entrenched superstitions of the past, by the simple perpetuation of the the applicable literary genre: the homily. For note: while pretending to adhere scrupulously to the true sense of the scientific nomenclature cribbed from sociology and anthropology, New Historicisms routinely end up hectoring colleagues, students, neighbors, business, labor, politicians and society as a whole with moral preachments on a wide range of issues. Under the guise of literary discussion, New Historicists take explicit or implied positions on everything from abortion and bilingual education to Proposition 13, and from the graduated income tax to the caliber of handguns allowed in K-12 classrooms. As if this were not in and of itself a travesty, they insist that on every one of their issues, one and only one attitude fits the given article of belief articulated by New "His-" and "Her-storicisms."

For "His-" and "Her-storicisms," knowledge is neither an end in itself, nor power to accomplish ends of human conquest over nature, but a "construction" — that is, an imaginative, verbal creation — of interested groups striving to augment their power, prestige and wealth. Accordingly, interest trumps evidence, and, therefore, history, which these worldviews reduce to self-serving fictions. Here, feelings are what count — and what is more, only *certain* feelings. For instance, it is okay to exhaust students with canned diatribes against the traditional canon, but *infra dig* to suggest that many of the works assigned to student victims of race-class-and-gender studies are subliterary in quality. Nor is it thought collegial to point out that the criticism of "pop culture," aka "cultural studies," seldom rises above the already plunging standards of journalism. In some cases, in fact, it is an offense to suggest that literary quality exists at all, for such a term does little more than hypostasize oppressive standards of the elite, dominant, white, male, heterosexual, European, hegemonist culture. It goes without saying that these intensifiers characterize pernicious elements in traditional academic discourse, which the "New" evangelists of political correctness are in the process of ferreting out, as had their predecessors in the seventeenth century England, "Root and Branch."

In the seventeenth century, Puritan precursors of pop culture critics today, had a go at their elitist, high culture adversaries. And like the "New" homiletists of "His-" and "Her-storicisms," Puritans of the Revolutionary and Civil War period, then often connected with Cambridge University movements, held that literary artifice militated against the plain, unvarnished, scientific truth. For them, it followed that artifice frustrated the plain, moral purpose of the pulpit. Thus, writes Joseph Glanvill, one of the original fellows of the Royal Society: "Plainness is a Character of great latitude, and stands in opposition, First to *hard words.* Secondly, to *deep* and *mysterious notions.* Thirdly, to *affected Rhetoriciations,* and Fourthly, to *Phantastical Phrases*" (353).[16] "The Preacher," Glanvill argues, "should use *plain words,*" because "the end" of the practice is "*Edification.*" Nowadays, New Historicists claim that they "demystify." Similarly, Glanvill protests, the preacher who uses "*hard words*" doesn't connect with "his Auditors." His elitist posturing is "contemptible," not just in preaching, "but in all matters of solemn discourse and ordinary conversation." If only abstract questions of philosophy were at stake, such flourishes would be of negligible "concernment." But when values of the highest order are at issue, pretentious "terms of art" hinder the purpose at hand: "These [hard words] are strong meat, babes must have milk, and simpler diet" (354).

Like their New Historicist scions, Puritan divines campaigned against their "art for art's sake" contemporaries, who were "metaphysical" tricksters like John Donne, playing with words, entertaining their congregations with noisome subtleties of expression, jokes, puns, outlandish comparisons. For Glanvill, their high church "mysterious notions" and "conceits" and "matters fit for the schools of learning" were a waste of air — "proud, phantasticall, and troublesome" (355). Plainness — today's Puritans would "demystify" — requires "seriousness and gravity," which "relate[s] to man's present and future well being" (355). The target of Glanvill's rhetoric is, of course, high church, elitist artistry in the pulpit. Prose stylists like Donne and Lancelot Andrewes drew attention, not to immutable, moral truths, but to their own conceits:

> There are some that place the power, and spirituality of Preaching in these [phantastical phrases]; and reckon that there is something of extraordinary grace, and force in them: so that if a man represents the truths of the Gospel in simplicity and plainness, that shall go for dull morality; but the same things set off by conceited, fashionable phrases shall be most rare, and spiritual Divinity. Thus if you teach men to believe *Christ's* Doctrines, to obey his Laws, to trust to his promises, and to conform to his Example; these shall be counted dull, dry, and unedifying things that no-ways affect or move: but if you tell the people, that they must roll upon *Christ*, close with *Christ*, get into *Christ*, get a saving interest in the Lord *Christ*: O, this is savoury, this precious, this is spiritual teaching indeed; whereas if any thing more be meant by those phrases, than what the other plain expressions intend, it is either falshood, or non-sense. (356)

Glanvill thinks the witty, intellectual preacher falsifies the meaning of the sacred text with metaphorical flourishes, when what is needed are "clear and distinct ideas." There is no mystery to the connection between Puritanism, science, and the "plain style." Frivolous artifice smacked of Romish corruption. Forget the fact that Donne and Herbert sought the middle way between nakedness and pompous show (Satyr 3 and "The British Church"). Glanvill thinks it is time to separate sheep from goats; temporizing is not an option. By renovating prose of its stylistic flourishes, Glanvill means to sweep "falshood" and "non-sense" away. Hence, there is no stylistic *via media*. There is plainness and truth, and there is artifice and obfuscation. Writing after mid-century, Glanvill expresses a proto-Augustan admiration of clarity, and an equal and opposite disdain for "fancy." We are not far here from the dubiety of Dryden for poets and poetry that "affects the metaphysics."

In comparison with the obfuscation and hypocrisy of the way critics handle "the normative stuff" today, Glanvill's frank and open disdain for the "high style" sounds admirably forthright. The Newberry conference is just one example of the way in which normative imperatives have assumed the guise of New Historicism. With ersatz scholarship in this mode, the aim is not to disseminate, much less to advance, knowledge about the Renaissance, but to purge discussion of the period of any pretense that such knowledge exists, or could exist. We should — we must, if we want to read on the Program at the Newberry — feel a certain way about whatever we read; and what we read, or ask others to read, must be vetted of all but the right moral values, which are nominated by the interest groups dominating the current political landscape (Third World-Afrocentric-Marxist-feminist-lesbian-gay-queer-transsexual-marginalized-dysfunctional-unemployed-homeless-undocumented — the list goes on.).

Wittgenstein remarked that the appearance of similarity between "descriptive" and "absolute" normative statements

("The best way from here to Laguna Beach is . . . The best way to treat abortionists is . . .") has something to do with their grammatical structure. In practice, the former turns out to be more like a shorthand version of a description of comparative routes, involving such factual concerns as road conditions, detours, tolls, traffic problems and so on. In this case, not much hangs on shared perceptions of what constitutes criteria of judgment. The new six-lane freeway will probably get you there faster and with greater ease than the old, winding route through the Cleveland National Forest. In contrast, no description of the medical circumstances of an abortion, or of a number of abortions, or of abortions in general, using "New" or "Old" techniques, is likely to circumvent difficulties surrounding communication, much less agreement, on characterizations of the subject. Even the vocabulary involved ("abortion" versus "a woman's right to choose") is part of the characterization. The point is that normative language in the latter case will seldom, if ever, be reducible to a more detailed description of factual conditions because the judgment involved does not concern facts, but how facts should be regarded. How should we characterize agreed-upon facts? Thus, we have Wittgenstein's contrast between knowing one plays tennis badly and knowing one has treated another person badly, and yet saying, in both cases, "I don't want to do any better." In the one case, moral indignation would seem out of place; in the other, lacking it would appear pathological.

When they are finished, and unobstructed by local conditions, such as auto accidents or sporting events, "New" freeways are likely to get one from Los Angeles to Laguna Beach faster than "Old" surface streets. But does "New," with its implied contrast to "Old," work the same way in literary criticism? (*Check one*: Yes __; No __; No Opinion __)

8 • Plague Writing, 1603
Jonson's "On My First Sonne"

Ernest B. Gilman

> There wends the fainting Son with his dead Sire
> On his sole shoulders borne, him to interre;
> Here goes a father with the like desire
> And to the graue alone, his Sonne doth beare'
> — John Davies, *Humours Heau'n on Earth*

For Jonson scholars, *The Alchemist* has always figured as the richest imaginative document of the Jacobean plague years — a period that supplies a woeful chapter in the history of epidemic disease in early modern England, but one that has until recently been noted in literary histories as scarcely more than a footnote to explain the closing of the theaters whenever an outbreak loomed. The plague also establishes a context for understanding Jonson's nondramatic verse, especially the epigram "On My First Sonne."[1] Seven-year-old Benjamin Jonson died of the disease, we know, during the epidemic of 1603; and we know, too, that whether by design or happenstance, the elder Jonson managed to evade the likelihood of a similar fate. Like *The Alchemist's* Lovewit, he had quit the city, and was staying at Robert Cotton's country house in Huntingdonshire at the height of the epidemic.

Jonson's Oxford editors, and following them, nearly all scholars who have commented on the poem since, call attention to the account by Drummond of Hawthornden of the father's uncanny premonition of his son's death. The night before the fatal news arrived from London, Jonson had a dream in which the boy appeared to him with the "Marke of a bloodie crosse on his forehead" — a mark like the "red Crosses set vpon dores" of plague houses by the municipal authorities (HS 1:139–40).[2] Yet most readings tend to overlook the specific cause of the boy's death, which is to be sure never mentioned directly in the epigram, or else to regard it as incidental information. Despite the attention paid to Jonson as a plague playwright, no one has fully considered the meaning of this poem in relation to the lived experience of the pestilence in the early seventeenth century — to the ways in which the successive waves of bubonic plague were endured and imagined by the survivors and the bereaved, and recorded in contemporary accounts.

Plays and Plagues

The sheer numbers tell the tale. According to the official bills of mortality, there were at least 225,000 deaths from the bubonic plague in London and its environs between 1570 and 1670. (The figure for England as a whole is around 750,000.) Mortality tables for London in the same century can be graphed as a series of sharp spikes indicating the number of plague deaths during the epidemic years of 1593, 1603, 1625 and 1665. In 1593 more than 15,000 people died — one out of every eight Londoners, given a total estimated population of 123,000. More than 30,000 died in 1603, Benjamin Jonson among them.

Thomas Dekker, Jonson's fellow playwright and an indefatigable chronicler of the pestilence in London, gives an exact figure of 30,578 in that year, and notes that in its worst week the plague claimed 3,035 individuals (143). Another 40,000 died in 1625, followed by at least 50,000 during the "great" plague of 1665.[3] In the dormant periods between these peaks, the plague never really disappeared, nor did the constant fear that when the warmer weather returned, so might another devastation. Plague historian Paul Slack observes that "even if we ignore years in which less than 100 casualties were notified, plague was present [in London] in 28 of 64 years between 1603 and 1666"; overall, "at least a fifth of all deaths from 1603 to 1665 can be attributed to it" (147).

In its production history, *The Alchemist* mirrors the disruption of city life brought on by visitations of this dread disease. For most of Jonson's career, plague, or the threat of it, closed the theaters for longer or shorter periods of time. During the late summer of 1610, with the sickness "hot" in London as in the plot of Jonson's new play, the King's Men were forced to withdraw to Oxford, taking *The Alchemist* with them.[4] Audiences who were warned by the authorities that they risked infection by crowding into public playhouses might see their own vulnerability reflected in Jonson's "Argument." The master having "quit" the city "for feare" (and, significantly, because he could afford to), the little world of Lovewit's house is turned upside down by the charlatans to whom he has abandoned his authority (HS 5:293).[5] In effect, for the course of the play, the audience finds itself crowded together in quarantine, the playhouse having become a virtual (and perhaps a real) pesthouse.

Meanwhile, the greater world outside the playhouse might be transformed at any moment into a carnivalesque theater of death, London echoing to "the loude grones of rauing sicke men" careening through the streets in their final agony, and to the voices of wives crying out "for husbands, parents for children" (Dekker, 27). Corpses would be thrown higgledy-piggledy into carts destined for open pits, and Jonsonian mountebanks would hawk their posies and elixirs to the desperate. The "Plague doth rage," wrote John Davies during the epidemic of 1603, "Making our Troy-nouant a tragicke Stage / Whereon to shew Death's power, with slaughter sore."[6]

Underscoring the connection between plays and plagues, antitheatrical writers such as "I. H." were quick to charge that the licentiousness of the theater itself had brought down the wrath of God upon London, and so to conclude that His "pestilential arrows, which fly among us by day, & lethally wound us by night" will not be "quivered up, till these menstruous rags be torn off (by the hand of authority) from the city's skirts."[7] A 1577 sermon had more succinctly argued the same point in a compelling (if logically questionable) syllogism: "[T]he issue of plagues is sin, if you look to it well; and the cause of sin are plays: therefore the cause of plagues are plays."[8] The master's absence from *The Alchemist*, as well as "I. H"'s call for the "hand of authority" to take strong action against the corruptions of the theater, also remind us that, for Jonson's age, plays represented the potential for — if they did not actually cause — the kind of civil disorder reported in accounts of urban epidemics going back to Thucydides and Boccaccio. Sin on such a scale required divine retribution to be seconded by official vigilance. In the response of the court and the city, a Foucauldian plague politics is unveiled. Benign measures for improving sanitation, for the removal of the dead and for the systematic compilation of bills of mortality went hand in hand with more repressive policies for increasing surveillance, quarantining infected houses under guard (for six weeks, by longstanding orders of the Privy Council), restricting travel, banning public assemblies, and closing theaters. In 1603, the "iust day" on which Jonson's son was "exacted" by his fate was also a day when it was the fate of London to fall under the sternest exactions of the law.

When we turn to "On My First Sonne" (the poem is re-printed below) we find, in addition to the antitheatrical texts often brought into discussions of the drama, a substantial body of writing in the form of sermons, pamphlets, religious tracts and medical treatises spawned during the plague years. These documents allow us to recover a sense of the shared social trauma resonating through Jonson's very private grief. In 1603–1604 alone, the years with which we are specifically concerned, 28 books dealing with the plague were published in London (Slack, 23–24). The medical writers, Thomas Lodge among them, debated the various causes of the pestilence: bad air, contaminated water, crowded conditions, malign astral influences.[9] Divines were reluctant to rule out such natural factors but tended to regard them as heaven's "pestilential arrows," the second causes through which the Lord worked his vengeance on the wicked. If "the Ayre does (round about) / In flakes of poyson drop on all," why were not all afflicted (Dekker, 83)? Perhaps "corrupt and rotten humours" in the bodies of some individuals made them more apt than others to "receiue the effects of a venomous ayre."[10] More likely God's arrows, directed by his hidden will, were aimed only at those he wished to chastise. But why, on that "iust day," were children and godly preachers struck down, and the wicked often as not spared? Why were some parishes or households visited with "slaughter sore" and other barely touched?[11] And even if the poison should be spread from one person to another, "then who breath'd vpon the first" (Dekker 84)? In the course of these debates Scripture was scoured for plague references that might unlock the mysteries of wholesale human suffering.[12]

There was, of course, no possibility of grasping the true nature of the disease. Lodge noted that "any increase of such creatures as are engendred by putrefaction" (worms, flies, serpents) is a sign that the plague is near (C2v). Still, the exact role of rats and fleas, let alone of the bacterium *Pastuerella pestis* and the complex vectors of its transmission, were inconceivable, although plague was (with some dissenting opinion) recognized as a "contagion" that could somehow be spread from one person to the next, as it indeed can be in its pneumonic form. There was no cure for the disease once its telltale "tokens" appeared in the form of "buboes," or hard, swollen lumps in the armpits and the groin. The horrible way plague could reduce a healthy person to a pustulant corpse in a matter of hours left few means by which the victim's anguish could be lessened, but for a penny there was no shortage of receipts for surefire nostrums guaranteed to ward off infection — typically, sweet-smelling (or, occasionally, foul-smelling) concoctions to be burned for their vapors or worn in pouches around the neck.

The most notable of all these plague publications from a literary point of view are two pamphlets by Dekker, *The Wonderfull Yeare* (1603) and *Newes from Graves-end* (1604), along with the later *A Rod for Run-awaies* (1625), which looks back at the earlier outbreak and treats the crucial question of flight, to which we shall return. Jonson's poem can be read as a plague poem, as itself a response and a contribution to this larger body of plague writing.

Jonson's Roman Frame of Mind

Given these inescapably stark realities of life and death in Jonson's London, it might seem all the more surprising that the plague and its contemporary accounts have not figured more importantly in readings of Jonson's valediction for a plague victim. Two reasons, it seems to me, lie behind this omission. First, only in the past 30 years have historians such as Alfred Crosby, William McNeill, and Sheldon Watts begun the task of reassessing the systemic impact of infectious disease on a global scale in such fields as migration, colonization and urban history — a project undertaken out of an awareness of the new dangers posed by old microbial foes once thought to have been "conquered" by the triumphs of modern medicine.[13] In the age of AIDS (not to mention Ebola, Marburg, Lassa Fever, drug-resistant tuberculosis and other "super germs," as well as perhaps a host of other apocalyptic pathogens destined to "emerge" from their disturbed ecological niches, or to make the "species jump" from animals to people, or to be disseminated by the frightening technologies of biowarfare), understanding the profound effects of disease on human culture has taken on a new urgency.[14] In this endeavor, however, literary historians — with the exception of those medievalists who have written extensively on the literature and art of the Black Death of the fourteenth century — have for the most part lagged behind their colleagues in the social sciences.

Second, in the case of Jonson's "On His First Sonne," contextualizing the poem within what Katharine Maus has called the poet's "Roman frame of mind" has seemed sufficient to explain the grave and understated tone admired as its distinctive excellence. Thus Maus observes that the Roman moralists "regard with awe those who can accept the death of a child with relative equanimity"; and that Tacitus, as Jonson would have known, "cites Agricola's restraint upon the death of his son as a proof of his sound character."[15] Jonson's paradoxical resolve at the end of the poem, that "hence-forth, all his vowes be such, / As what he loues may neuer like too much," directly renders the final line of Martial's epigram 6.19, on the death of a boy "worthy of his master's true love" [quidquid ames, cupias non placuisse nimis].[16] The comment by Martial's Loeb translator — that "Excessive excellence or good fortune, and the praise of it, was supposed to rouse the jealousy of the gods" (374–75) — may plausibly be taken to explain both the Latin sentiment and, in the English version, the father's "too much hope" for the son. Reading Jonson's verb "to like" in "the active seventeenth century sense of 'to please,'" Wesley Trimpi concludes: "It is precisely because a

child should not delight us as a pastime but rather be loved as
a human being," with the tempered fatherly affection recommended by Aristotle, that "Jonson borrows Martial's caution
that what he loves should never please him too much."[17] Similarly, Maus sees the father's obscure wish, in line 5, to "loose
all father now" as adumbrating the "Roman idea" of a necessary detachment of feeling from the son to whom, in death,
Jonson begins to grant "some separate identity" (122).

The Plague Context

Yet if Drummond's memory is to be trusted, Jonson's frame
of mind at the news of his son's death had little in it of the
Roman father's decorous restraint — which, as it appears in
the finished poem, may strike us less as a stoic victory over
the passions than as a failure of those same venerable ges-
tures in the face of an inconsolable loss. Here emotion is recollected, but not in tranquility. In light of the terrible events
of 1603, the poem as a document in the history of human
mourning is better understood as a Roman reframing of the
father's very English, peculiarly tangled feelings of grief, anger
and guilt as a plague survivor.[18] If the cause of the child's death
is not mentioned in Jonson's poem, neither is that of the boy
in Martial's original. But the omission, or suppression, of the
plague as a fact in the English poem does not remove its
influence on Jonson's language and emotion.

The account of Jonson's extraordinary dream is brief
enough to quote in full, from Drummond's *Conversations*
(HS 1:139–40):

> When the King came jn England, at that tyme the Pest was jn
> London, he being jn the Country at Sr Robert Cottons house
> with old Cambden, he saw jn a vision his eldest sone (yn a
> child and at London) appear to him wt ye Marke of a bloodie
> crosse on his forehead as if it had been cutted wt a suord, at

which amazed he prayed unto God, and jn ye morning he came to Mr. Cambdens chamber to tell him, who persuaded him it was but ane appreehension of his fantasie at which he should not be desjected[.] jn ye mean tyme comes yr letters from his wife of ye death of yt Boy jn ye plague. He appeared to him he said of a Manlie shape & of yt Grouth that he thinks he shall be at the resurrection.

Elizabeth having died on March 24, 1603, her successor literally "came into England" on April 6, when he crossed the Scottish border (Riggs, 93), but his entry into London at the beginning of May coincided with the arrival of the plague. The old queen's funeral was "but the dumb shew," writes Dekker: "the Tragicall Act hath bin playing euer since" (13).

Drummond's linking of the accession with the pestilence is thus more than coincidental, especially since just at that crucial moment of political transition opinion was sharply divided on how the plague should be read. Henoch Clapham, working off the familiar triad of war, famine and pestilence as the three scourges of God, wrote at the time of the outbreak that "Famine was threatned vpon the death of our late souveraigne Elizabeth." A blessing in disguise, the plague fells us quickly under the blow of "a mercifull Father," thus "leauing us not to lingring Deaths, whereby we might be more pained" (B3r). Dekker concurs that "Of Euils, tis the lighter broode, / a dearth of people, then of food" (102). Still he believes that the pestilence cannot be interpreted but as a sign of God's anger. Although the punishment may fall indifferently upon lowly individuals, even on seven-year-old children, the crime deserving of such a terrible judgment must be found in the highest councils of state: "Sure tis some Capitall offence," Dekker insists, "Some high, high Treason doth incense / Th'Eternall King, that we are / Arraign'd at Deaths most dreadfull barre" (86). Catholic propagandists charged that James's accession had called down the divine wrath on the kingdom.[19] Dekker argues instead that the plague will "cleere" the debt of sin accumulated by the English during the long reign of Elizabeth: "Iehouah lookes / But now

> vpon those Audit-Bookes
> Of 45. Yeares husht account,
> For houres mispent . . . and there
> Finding our grieuous debts, doth cleere
> And crosse them vnder his owne hand,
> Being paid with Liues, through all the land. (88)

Far from being the harbinger of the pestilence, James is its beneficiary, espousing a realm with a clean moral slate: "Heauen meanes to giue him (as his bride) / A Nation new, and purified" (88).

The language of audit books, accounts and grievous debts paid with lives recalls the judicial language of Jonson's poem: "Seuen yeares tho'wert lent to me, and I thee pay, / Exacted by thy fate on the iust day." Jonson's wavering sympathies between the old and the new religion may also have led him to wonder whether, in preparing James's bridal bed, heaven meant to purify the nation by killing his own son. But for what particular "sinne" of the father must the death of the son be "exacted" from him in recompense? What debt was crossed out by the same divine hand which, in Jonson's dream, had marked the forehead of his son with a "bloodie crosse"? Apart from a vaguely shared sense of some accumulated national debt, plague writers point to other sins — hours misspent in drunkenness, gluttony, even the "Schollers enuy" (Dekker, 86) — that may have struck closer to home in Jonson's case.

In the context of the plague theodicies of 1603, Jonson's self-diagnosed, puzzling "sinne" of "too much hope" has a more specifically Christian than Roman resonance. It may be foolhardy to tempt the gods, as Niobe did, by immoderate pride in one's children, but it was Augustine who taught that we should regard all earthly possessions, even those most dear to us, as only on temporary loan. Thus, Jonson vows that what he loves, he may never "like too much" in the sense of being too much attached to one who belongs to God, one whose innocence may not protect him from a judgment after all, and one whose loss would otherwise break a father's heart. (That he *will* continue despite all — as the final emphasis of the line implies — to like such a boy as Ben *too much* for his own good hints at the futility of "all his vowes.")[20] Such resolve, however difficult to sustain, made hard practical sense in a year when plague deaths (on top of the alarming rate of child mortality that characterizes the early modern period) rendered it unlikely that any child would live to attain the "Manlie shape" Jonson imagined for young Ben in his dream. Jonson's "too much hope," then, may have been to hope too much that his son would simply survive.

Flight

The one sin unspoken in the poem but strongly suggested in the setting of Jonson's dream — "he being in the Country at Sr Robert Cottons house" — is that of fleeing the city in an attempt to protect oneself from the plague. In contemporary plague writing the prominence of the debate about the morality of flight cannot be ignored. Luther and Calvin had each pondered this vexed question, and English divines from the mid-sixteenth century onward carried the contention into Jonson's time (see Slack, 40–44). In favor of flight it might be argued prudentially that nowhere does Scripture deny the right of self-preservation — although a recognition that most Londoners had no means of travel and nowhere to go made it difficult to argue that the titled and the wealthy should be able to ride out to their country houses with a clear conscience. But in any event, were God's people not enjoined to flee from evil-doing as from flood and fire, or from the pestilence which, in Egypt, had claimed the lives of first sons?

Yet surely the fond hope, or the arrogant conviction, that flight would guarantee one's safety — no less than the hope (Jonson's "hope"?) that those one left behind would somehow remain untouched — flew in the face of Providence. Clapham cautions against the abuse of Proverbs 22:3 and 27:12 ("A *prudent* man seeth the plague and hideth himself"): safety is assured only "to him that coucheth vnder the Lords wings," so that "If thou were with *Ionah* vnder the hatches, and after with the Whale in the bottome of the Sea, he will finde thee out" (A4v–B1r). In *The Alchemist* Lovewit betrays his own insensitivity on this point when he speaks blandly of his "knowne auersion / From any air o' the towne, while there was sicknesse" (HS 5:403.34–35). Surely it was a blasphemy to limit the power of God to smite or protect whomever he pleased without regard to geography.

In 1625, another plague year (and another year of royal transition fraught with the same anxieties about the divine intention at such a climacteric moment), Dekker published *A Rod for Run-awaies*. Here he speaks scornfully to those who are "merry" in their "Country houses" and warns that "Gods arme, like a Girdle, going round about the world" has no limit to its reach (145, 169–70). Whatever the subtleties of the debate, however, the strong consensus in 1603, as in all plague years, is that flight is always sinful on the part of magistrates, ministers and the fathers of families who thereby betray their obligations to those under their care. In his pamphlet of 1604 Dekker bluntly admonishes those who abandon such vital responsibilities: "you do erre / In flying from your charge so far . . . so Lambes do perish, / So you kill those, y'are bound to cherish" (96). Seen from this unforgiving vantage point, the absentee father's unspoken "sinne" is the sin of murder. One may feel that Lovewit's reappearance in London at the end of the play — including his relief at finding his household healthy and fortunate, and his forgiveness of all their childish truancies while he was away — fulfills a Jonsonian fantasy: the return of the prodigal father.[21]

In another passage Dekker imagines a far darker scene, of a father fleeing into the country with his son under the illusion that he has put a safe distance between himself and the plague:

> Now is thy soule iocund, and thy sences merry. But open thine eyes thou Foole! And behold that darling of thine eye, (thy sonne) turnde suddeinly into a lumpe of clay; the hand of pestilence hath smote him euen under thy wing: Now doest thou rent thine haire, blaspheme thy Creator, cursest thy creation, and basely descendest thou into bruitish & unmanly passions, threatning in despite of death & his Plague, to maintaine the memory of thy childe, in the euerlasting brest of Marble. (30)

It might have offered some small, if ironic, solace to Jonson to reflect, on the evidence of such an anecdote, that Benjamin (dead, in London, under the Lord's wing) would not have been safe even under his father's wing in Huntingdonshire. But knowing that he had, even if inadvertently, left him behind and in harm's way could only have sharpened his remorse. Dekker's passage may serve as a kind of urtext for Jonson's poem. Here we see in raw form the anger, the self-reproach, the open blasphemy, the unconstrained passion, and the desire to cling to the memory of the child — to turn the "lumpe of clay" into marble — that will be (incompletely) subdued by the Roman decorum of Jonson's polished epigram.

The Speech of the Dead

That the child is said, in commemoration, to be Jonson's "best piece of *poetrie*" — the father's masterpiece — evokes the Greek sense of the poet as a "maker" and thus, as Riggs notes, "links the vocations of fatherhood and art" (96). It will now be the work of this grieving father to turn his own lump of clay into a "piece" of verse that will keep the memory of the child alive. The dead child is furthermore empowered, through the father's poetry, to speak his own commemoration, and in the course of the child's speech it appears momentarily that it is the *father* who lies in the grave (students always "misread" the line "here doth lye / BEN. IONSON"). Such confusion of the dead and the living suggests other links to the plague writing of 1603.

The dead, we are told, pile up so quickly that they can only be shoveled indistinguishably into pits where "twentie shall but haue one roome"; there "friend, and foe, and yong and old, / The freezing coward, and the bold" find a common end (Dekker, 94). Whole families are buried together, "husbands, wiues & children, being lead as ordinarily to one graue, as if they had gone to one bed" (Dekker, 33–34). One (in the) grave, one (in) bed: not so far in apprehension from Jonson's bed in Huntingdonshire, the churchyards of London resound with an antiphonal chorus of wailing: "Here cry the parents for their childrens death; / There howle the children for their parents losse" (Davies, 230). Death makes all his messengers "to fetch both one and the other out of life: the Sire doth fetch the Sonne, the Sonne the Sire" (Davies, 237). The biblical Benjamin received a blessing from his dying father, but in time of the plague, the "Father dares not come neere the infected Son, nor the Son come to take a blessing from the Father, lest hee bee poysoned by it" (Dekker, 144). If the errant father kills the child in effect by his absence, the child in turn has the power to kill the parent in fact if he comes too close: "The trembling father is vndone, / Being once but breath'd on by his sonne" (Dekker, 92). Often one will follow the other into the same grave.

Less often, people thought to be dead speak from the grave. Dekker tells of the drunkard who topples into a pit of plague victims one night, and whose oaths in the morning terrify the sexton who disturbs his sleep: the sexton "beleeued verily, some of the coarses spake to him, vpon which, feeling himselfe in a cold sweat, tooke to his heeles" (53). When Jonson's dead child, having been "ask'd," will "say" who "doth lye" here, the chilling shadow of this *danse macabre* of the living and dead on the lip of the grave falls over the poem.

As the presiding deity of plague poetry, Apollo has a double role as "both Poesies Soueraigne King, / And God of medicine" (Dekker, 100). When Apollo "bids vs sing" of the pestilence, the poet both speaks of the dead as their "Souueraigne King" — speaks for the dead, on behalf of the dead, and so makes them speak through his power. Through the power of the "God of medicine," his speech is at once life-giving and yet, like the breath of the diseased father who would pronounce a lethal blessing on his son, poisonous. When young Ben (whose name in the poem is given only indirectly in its Hebrew meaning as the "child of my right hand") declares "here doth lye / BEN. IONSON," we hear the sovereign voice of the dead, and we think first of the father as the occupant of the grave. Father and son have changed places: the mourner becomes the mourned. For this moment, it is the child who has lost "all father, now" and the father who has revived the son — paying, as he willingly would, the price of his own life in the exchange. And it is the child, his voice restored as at the resurrection, who relieves the father of the painful burden of saying the words "here doth lye," in effect, since the son can speak, giving the "lye" to those very words. The "soft peace" denied to Jonson in his grief is granted him in an apprehension of his fantasy: a glimpse of his own death as commemorated by his "best piece" of poetry. In this sense, the notional graveside scene in the epigram recalls the symbolism of Jonson's dream, since a bloody cross on the door, like the son just emerged from death's door, says to all passersby that a plague victim lies within.

Two related meanings, Greek and Hebrew, are adduced from Scripture to explain the meaning of the word "plague" itself. In the New Testament, "The word *Plague* is originally a Greeke word: for *plegè* it is termed in Revel 16:17," that is to say, a "blowe or stripe" — the "stroke of God" delivered "for sinne"

(Clapham, A4r). Thus, to speak the word is to inflict the stroke: the cause and the effect, *verbum* and *res*, are one. In the Hebrew of the Old Testament, the word for plague is said to derive from the word for speech itself: "The language of God & Adam in the old Testament, doth terme it [the pestilence] Deber . . . of Dabar to speake, whether it be a speech of life or death." Pestilence is an "effect of the Lords Word for sinne," not only the consequence of the divine rebuke threatened in Scripture (Clapham refers to Deut. 28:21) but the word itself: that which is spoken, the "speech . . . of death" (Clapham, A4r). Taking the role of "all father" on himself, Jonson utters the speech of death — "Farewell, thou child" — but in remaining silent about the pestilence he refrains from speaking the killing word itself. Instead he puts the "speech of life" into the mouth of his son, reviving him briefly as a kind of prelude to the vision Jonson saw in his dream of Ben as he would appear "at the resurrection." It is then given to the undead son to bespeak the father's death in his own concise epitaph on "BEN. IONSON." Just as for Robert Burton writing is both a cause and a cure of melancholy, the plague text has the same double nature of the *pharmakon*.[22]

Old Camden, Young Ben

The persistence of Jonson's dream takes us back to the role of "old Cambden," who was "with" Jonson "jn the Country at Sr Robert Cottons house," and who according to Drummond reassured the poet that his foreboding was "but ane appreehension of his fantasie at which he should not be disjected." Although, in the *Epigrammes*, "On My First Sonne" is quite naturally paired with "On My First Davghter," the strongest and most intimate bond in Jonson's poetry is (to borrow a phrase from Jonson's poem on Shakespeare that hovers between poetry and paternity) the "liuing line" connecting fathers and sons (HS 8:392.59). Camden's paternal presence at the creation of the "fantasie" that would issue in the poem (with its own fantasy that young Ben can speak from the grave, that he lives after all, just as Camden had said) suggests what we might regard, speculatively, as a psychogenetic affiliation between "On My First Sonne" and the epigram "To William Camden." (HS 8:31).

In 1603 William Camden was "all" the "father" Jonson had. It is to this surrogate father and former master at Westminster School that Jonson owes "All that I am in arts, all that I know" (The poem is reprinted below). This obligation is repaid by a poem to Camden; in the plague year, Jonson's debt to his heavenly Father is repaid by a son, his best piece of poetry. Jonson's obscure wish to "loose all father, now" may be read as a desire now to be free of all the pain of fatherhood, and perhaps to lose the exacting Father who had taken his son. Behind this thought may loom an even more shadowy desire to loosen his obligation to Camden, whose voice carried all the weight of paternal authority for Jonson, and who had only given him false hope by dismissing Jonson's ominous dream. It is nonetheless from the "authoritie" of Camden's "speech" that Jonson inherits his own voice as an author, and which he lends to the son, making him however briefly and posthumously a poet. Camden has the godlike power of conferring names: it is to his magisterial book, the *Britannia*, that "my countrey owes / The great renowne, and name wherewith shee goes." The hallmark of Jonson's poetic authority in the *Epigrammes* is his own power to honor the names of the virtuous and rename the vicious according to their moral nature. That power is in turn conferred upon the son, who names the occupant(s) of his own grave.

Still, the knowledge that young Ben can only speak through his father's lines, that the dead son will never be able to offer his own father the "pietie" that Jonson offers Camden in repayment of his filial obligation, underscores the poignancy of the comparison. Jonson's *pietas* is Virgilian. With Camden figured as Jonson's "reuerend head" (perhaps transposed, in the dream, into the "forehead" on which the bloody mark of the Father is inscribed) and the son as the "child of my right hand," it is as if the three are part of the same body. As the plague writers emphasize, national destinies are bound up in the affliction of individuals. The very survival of "our Troy-nouant" is imperiled by a pestilence that threatens to bring to a tragic end the epic project of civilization-building fathered by Aeneas, and, in the case of Britannia, celebrated by Camden as the English Virgil. More intimately, the filial line connecting Camden, Jonson and — until the summer of 1603 — young Ben, ultimately runs back to Anchises, Aeneas and young Ascanius. In the Virgilian vision of patrilineal responsibility, a burden both personal and political, it is the fate of father Aeneas to lead the past into the future. Surviving Roman images show him shouldering his own aged father while leading his son by the hand out of the burning city. But Jonson's "right hand" is severed, buried in the city. In the Aeneid the father rises from the grave to speak to the son. With the encounter of the living and the dead in Jonson's poem, the Virgilian roles are sadly reversed.

Furthermore, the Latin sources of Jonson's poem on "old Cambden" (the scholar was 52 in 1603) reveal a preoccupation with the "miserie" of age — the very grief (so Jonson would console himself) that young Ben had "so soone scap'd." Jonson's praise of Camden's gravity — "Then thee the age sees not that thing more graue, / More high, more holy, that shee more would crave" — renders a line from a letter by the younger Pliny (4.17.4) in which the Roman writer speaks of his late mentor, Corellius Rufus. Pliny here recalls that Corellius "displayed the vigour of youth, despite his failing health and advancing age," and that as Corellius lay dying he spoke of his close friendship with his younger colleague (292–95).[23] In another letter (1.12), Pliny meditates on Corellius's long years of suffering from the gout, which spread from his feet through all his limbs: "He bore up through sheer strength of mind, even when cruelly tortured by unbelievable agony" [eum quiden incredibiles cruciatus et indignissima tormenta pateretur] (36–37). In the end, having "suffered so long from such painful affliction that his reasons for dying outweighed everything that life could give him," Corellius committed suicide. "When we see men die of disease," Pliny writes, "at least we can find consolation in the knowledge that it is inevitable, but when their end is self-sought, our grief is inconsolable because we feel that their lives could have been long" (34–37).

Pliny also supplies Jonson with the "authoritie" of Camden's "speech," and with the latter's "faith . . . in things" [Iam quanta sermonibus eius fides, quanta auctoritas, quam pressa et decora eunctatio], as well as with the beautiful line, "Man scarse can make that doubt, but thou canst teach" [Nihil est quod discere velis quod ille docere non posit], this time from a letter (1.12.2–3) in which Pliny lets his correspondent know that he is "exceedingly worried about Titius Aristo, a man I particularly love and admire, who has been seriously ill for some time" (68–69). Unlike Corellius Rufus, Titius Aristo — a noted jurist and mentor of Pliny in the law — resists the temptation of suicide despite his almost unbearable suffering: "His patience throughout this illness, if you could only see it, would fill you with admiration; he fights against pain, resists thirst, and endures the unbelievable heat of his fever without moving or throwing off his covers" (70–71).[24]

Of these prolonged agonies there is no hint in the language Jonson culls from Pliny's letters. And yet it is surely significant that, of all the classical sources Jonson might have consulted for descriptions of learned and generous men, the ones he chose focus precisely and at length on the "miserie" of age. Corellius Rufus and Titius Aristo provide the pattern for William Camden, Pliny's tone the decorum of Jonson's reverence for his teacher. But the suffering of these Roman progenitors is written out of Jonson's account — just as, in the poem on his first son, the horror of a bubonic death (on which other plague writers dwell in gruesome detail) is never acknowledged. These miseries will return in Jonson's "To Heaven," a poem burdened with "feare," "horror," "griefs," and "sinne," in which Jonson — as if he were caught between the tenacious clinging to life of Titius and the suicide of Corellius — dares not "wish for death" (HS 8:122).

Even if Jonson's teacher may have been in perfect health in 1603 (we have no way of knowing), the poem to Camden conceals a substrate only hinted at in Jonson's crucial rhyme of "graue" and "craue" in lines five and six — a craving for the grave heard both in the buried reference to the Roman fathers' weariness of life, and in the ambiguous epitaph put into the mouth of the English son. Jonson's poetry here as elsewhere calls for a kind of critical archaeology if the foreconceit of his invention is to be fully disclosed. On this level — a subsurface marked by the themes of disease, of the broken ties between fathers and sons, of early death and long suffering, of suicide and endurance — the two poems on Camden and on his first son find their common ground.

Epilogue: Plague Texts

The discussion above assumes that it will be productive to consider all literary texts written during plague times as plague texts. It would perhaps be more prudent to qualify this assertion by saying that such literary texts may be seen as responding more or less directly to the constant threat of biological meltdown in which their authors lived. I prefer to let the claim stand in its stronger form, however, if only to test its limits. In other periods of literary study, analogous assumptions have yielded important insights. We have seen that the cultural tremors of the French Revolution and its aftermath echo everywhere in English writing after 1789, loudly in Wordsworth and Blake, and more softly, though with no less telling effect, in the novels of Jane Austen.[25] For the Victorian period, Edward Said and others have traced the strands of Britain's preoccupation with empire not only in the novels of Conrad, where they form the very material of his fiction, but in other works where their partial concealment or even their attempted suppression is itself a crucial feature of their design.[26] And what novel or poem written in the United States between, say, 1965 and 1975 can be understood apart from the war in Vietnam, or what postwar Jewish-American (or Israeli, or Palestinian) writing apart from the Holocaust?

As the dilemmas of Holocaust writing have shown, one way of addressing the "unspeakable" — an enormity so great that language is said to fail in the attempt — is not to speak of it. But the trope of refusing to speak of what for that reason takes on an even greater significance is as old as rhetoric itself. Apotropaic figures of demarcation or sequestration such as *occupatio* enforce distinctions within the literary system parallel to those enforced by health authorities to separate the well from the sick. Renaissance pastoral defines its boundaries by a kind of generic quarantine against the squalor and sophisticated corruption of city life. Utopias (which tend to be salubrious places) are, as More's title suggests, "noplaces" that establish themselves as much by what they are determined not to be as by any positive constitution. Significantly, Utopia came to be when King Utopus cut the isthmus that had until then connected his realm with the mainland, and since then the well-being of the Commonwealth has depended upon its isolation — on a kind of perpetual quarantine within a political *cordon sanitaire*. Utopia itself serves less as the blueprint of a possible society than as an antipathetic cure to the ills of England.

Imagining the ideal country house as a blend of the utopian and the pastoral, Jonson begins his greatest poem by emphasizing the power of such an exclusionary poetics: "Thou art *not*, PENSHURST, built to enuious show" (HS 8:93). The "walkes for health" open to the visitor in the gardens of Penshurst do not speak of the sewers of London. But Jonson's urban mock-epic "The Fantastic Voyage," which I would want to see as a companion piece to the country house poem, does, taking us on an extended tour of the pestilential effluvia under the streets of the city. As I have tried to suggest above, much of the pathos of the epigram on his first son comes from the father's refusal or inability to speak the unspeakable.

In the same vein, looking ahead from 1603 to Defoe's latter-day account of the epidemic of 1666, *A Journal of the Plague Year*, I would argue that Robinson Crusoe's island utopia, a little England reconstructed through the effort of an incredibly hardy, solitary survivor, should be read against the blighted city of the *Journal*. If *Crusoe* is about new beginnings (and itself marks the beginning of the "new" genre of the English novel), the *Journal* marks off the diseased ground from which the novel takes flight. An event of such destructive magnitude as the plague will be registered broadly, both early and late, and by various means, in the writing of the host culture. The perspectives opened onto the literary history of the period by such a notion of plague writing have yet to be explored

Texts of The Poems

Epigram XLV: On my First Sonne

Farewell, thou child of my right hand, and ioy;
  My sinne was too much hope of thee, lou'd boy,
Seuen yeeres tho'wert lent to me, and I thee pay,
  Exacted by thy fate, on the iust day.
O' could I loose all father, now. For why
  Will man lament the state he should enuie?
To haue so soone scap'd world, and fleshes rage,
  And, if no other miserie, yet age?

Rest in soft peace, and ask'd, say here doth lye
    BEN. IONSON his best piece of *poetrie*.
For whose sake, hence-forth, all his vowes be such,
    As what he loues may neuer like too much.

Epigram XIII: To William Camden

CAMDEN, most reuerend head, to whom I owe
    All that I am in arts, all that I know,
(How nothing's that?) to whom my country owes
    The great renowne, and name wherewith shee goes.
Then thee the age sees not that thing more graue,
    More high, more holy, that shee more would craue.
What name, what skill, what faith hast thou in things!
    What sight in searching the most antique springs!
What weight, and what authoritie in thy speech!
    Man scarce can make that doubt, but thou canst teach.
Pardon free truth, and let thy modestie,
    Which conquers all, be once ouer-come by thee.
Many of thine this better could, then I,
    But for their powers, accept my pietie.

9 • Erich Auerbach's *Seltsamkeit*

The Seventeenth Century and the History of Feelings

Martin Elsky

While vacationing in Rome in September 1935, Erich Auerbach was bracing himself against his impending dismissal from the University of Marburg by the Nazis. Writing to Walter Benjamin that he would probably not be able to teach again in Marburg, he comments: "it is impossible to give a picture of the strangeness of my situation" [von der Seltsamkeit meiner Lage eine Vorstellung zu geben ist unmöglich]. He was referring to the uncertainties to which he was subjected: "In any case, it [my situation], with all its advantages, yet has no prospect of certainty and daily becomes more and more senseless" [Jedenfalls hat sie, bei manchen Vorzügen, doch kaum Aussicht auf Bestand und wird täglich sinnloser].[1] But perhaps *Seltsamkeit* is also the word that aptly describes the situation of a Jewish intellectual who strongly insisted on the relationship between Europe and Christendom. There were, after all, other choices, other possible historical narratives that Auerbach did not choose. In retrospect, to have defined one's inhabited culture to be opposite to one's own history, and then to be defined as alien to that culture, must have indeed seemed *seltsam*.

A kind of *Seltsamkeit* is also the condition that some critics have attributed to Auerbach's position during the writing of his most widely read book, *Mimesis*, first published in German in 1946.[2] Edward Said's observation on this topic is perhaps the most widely known. Said suggested that Auerbach's "homelessness," his exile in Istanbul, provided him a particular position of "alienation" to look back on European culture. However, the very choice of Romance philology suggests a more oblique relationship to German *Heimat* even before the war and the Nazi regime than is suggested in Said's remark. In Auerbach's case, his Romance essays seek the heart of European culture in that part of Europe where he was *not*, in the countries that are heir to Latin language and civilization, in that part of Europe that is heir to the Roman empire through the Roman Catholic Church. Auerbach's earlier essays suggest a sense of distance from the European center, a sense of distance which, intellectually and culturally, if not personally, may be on a different point of the same spectrum as actual exile in Turkey. His ambiguous attitude toward the geographical location of identity even before his exile implicates his cultural identification as a German, a Jew and a European.

I would like to pursue this issue by examining a theme in Auerbach's work that rarely if ever receives attention, namely the history of feelings. Moreover, I would like to pursue this theme in works of Auerbach that receive little attention, his early untranslated essays written from before the Nazi rise to power up to and during the Second World War, before *Mimesis* that is.[3] Many of these essays highlight seventeenth century literature, whose importance for Auerbach has largely gone unnoticed because it has been overshadowed by issues stemming from *Mimesis* and the history of realism. Also little discussed in critical treatments of Auerbach is a topic that runs throughout these early essays: the history of emotions. These essays supply nothing less than fragments of a history of what it means to *have feelings* in the European West, how the structure of feeling, we might say today, is culturally fashioned, or perhaps more accurately, how the words we use to categorize our feelings have been historically shaped. We emote the way we do, Auerbach would have it, because of what the seventeenth century did to Latin Christianity's medieval interpretation of what was for Auerbach the central experience of the West, the earthly life of Christ between the Incarnation and the Passion.

Auerbach gave the emotions a location not only in the psyche, but also in the topography of Europe. He located the emotional impact of the gospel narrative in the Romance tradition outside his own cultural location as either German or Jew. Germany played no significant role in the history of the European inner life that constituted modern European identity. The important figures were Bernard of Clairvaux and Dante, Montaigne and Racine. Indeed, Auerbach suggests that Germany has to overcome its anti-French prejudice to see the importance of France as the crucible of emotions, as the location where one began to feel like a European feels. Auerbach never says so explicitly, but his position is that of the transnational, cosmopolitan intellectual asking his German audience to look beyond their national boundaries to become Europeans. This sense of mastery of European culture through philology took on a new urgency when Auerbach himself was both literally and culturally excluded from Europe, and found himself yet further removed from the centers of European civilization when he arrived in Istanbul. In the essays I will discuss below, the seventeenth century transformation of medieval into modern emotion was the issue around which

Auerbach negotiated his identity first as a German and then as a Jew.

Auerbach's attitude toward France may be gleaned in his essays on Racine, one written in Germany in 1927, the other during the war in Istanbul in 1941. In the earlier essay, "Racine and the Passions," we see Auerbach trying to puzzle out his relation to France in one of his first attempts to treat the history of emotions.[4] Most readers know of Auerbach's negative judgment of Racine in *Mimesis*, where his separation of styles makes him an almost reactionary bulwark against the possibility of an emerging realism.[5] In contrast, in the 1927 essay France is designated at the originating location of modern emotion. Most interesting, Auerbach here explicitly positions himself as a German writing about France. The essay begins with praise of his intellectual mentor, Karl Vossler, who, in his 1926 book, is the first German of rank since Schlegel, Auerbach observes with pride, to undertake a serious study of Racine. Auerbach congratulates Vossler for breaking through the German prejudice against French classicism (which he admits is felt by the French as well), but more generally for overcoming the *Spannungsverhältnisse*, the tense relations, between French and German poetic cultures evidenced by Schlegel's treatment of Racine. This tension, Auerbach comments, still exists today.[6] He points to Germany when he decries the lack of interest in Racine as the result of "the undeniable lack of culture in the taste of our time" [die unleugbare Unbildung unseres Zeitgeschmacks] (196). He recommends Vossler's suggestion that we read Racine out loud to become familiar with the work of this master, especially "if one feels the lack of understanding of a great poet as a shameful lack of culture and would like to do something about it" [wenn man die eigene Verständnislosigkeit für einem grossen Dichter als eine beschämende Unbildung empfindet und ihr anhelfen möchte] (197). He further laments that even in the best days of German culture Racine was greeted with indifference and worse by the Sturm und Drang, by the Romantics, indeed by Schiller and Goethe themselves.

Auerbach's main point is that Racine poetically articulated an emotional sensibility directly antithetical to Christianity. Auerbach sees in Racine "one of the first documents" of the conflict between Christianity and worldly art. Racine raises desire to a self-sufficient, principled, autonomous state of feeling (*selbstständigen, prinzipiellen und autonomen Seeleninhalt*) (199), a lofty and sublime mental state worthy of admiration, a state that was, in fact, perceived as a threat to Christianity and indeed any pious humility. Even though, as Auerbach reminds us, erotic passion as a cultural practice has its origins in the Middle Ages, it was freed from its religious origins in seventeenth century France, where the emotions began to fill themselves with their own contents. Racine's success in presenting the emotions in this way depended on social conditions that produced an audience that would respond sympathetically. This audience was part of a new social class whose elevated position did not depend on either intellect or birth, but on a common material base. Auerbach does not explain in any detail, except to suggest that this audience and the conditions that produced it were unique to France. It was there, then, that a public existed that saw in both the novel and in the drama the value of grand earthly passion, which they regarded as the mark of highest and the most sublime humanity. By completely removing the passions from any religious mooring that had anything to do with either virtue or piety, Auerbach explains, Racine continued what Corneille began, and drove to completion the expansion and unfolding to its fullest flowering of the worldly in the context of the personal (*Racine vollends treibt die Expansion und Entfaltung des Weltlich-Persönlich . . . zur strahlendsten Blüte*) (200). In representing the passions, Racine portrays the new autonomy of the human personality. Individual worth resides purely in an overwhelming vitality, the source, for Racine, of *sinnliche Individualität* (203).

Auerbach nevertheless reveals a good deal of ambivalence toward Racine's representation of the passions. His ambivalence is evident, for example, in his critical remark that Racine's new audience distanced itself from the life of ordinary people — *das Volk* — even more than the feudal upper classes did. He may speak of Racine's passions in honorific terms, extolling his appreciation of the contents of the human personality, but counterbalancing such judgments is his sense that Racine's characters are not only un-Christian, but also inhuman, as he observes about *Athalie*, which he singles out for special attention: "the purity and measured decorum of his diction" [die Reinheit und den massvollen Anstand der Diktion] only thinly masks Racine's conjuring of "the entire gruesome tribal conflict of primordial times" [das ganze Grauen eines Stammeskampfes in Urzeiten] and "the dull, terrifying sound of the overpowering bloodthirsty Demiurge" [der dumpfe, schreckliche Ton des übermächtigen, blutdürstigen Demiurgen], which he locates "here in France, around 1700" [hier, um 1700 und in Frankreich] (202). Auerbach goes so far as to say that the primitive gruesome quality of Racine's passion makes it un-European.

In the final sentences of the essay, Auerbach returns to Germany's relation to Racine. Since the awakening of national feeling in Germany, he comments, Racine has remained misunderstood and unloved. He is alien to us in his good as in his bad qualities. We Germans, he remarks, do not have a history that allows us to share the conditions in which his representation of the passions flourished: "We have no monarchical age; we never experienced the century of Louis XIV" [Wir haben kein königliches Zeitalter, kein Jahrhundert Ludwigs des Vierzehnten erlebt], but most important, "we never had a social class, which, released from the demands of daily life, could freely display and enjoy desire" [und haben keine Gesellschaftsschicht besessen, die, gelöst von den Bindungen des täglichen Laufs, ihre Begierden frei darstellen und geniessen konnte] (203). Auerbach's final word complicates his attitude toward Racine. On the one hand, one has to lament that Germany did not have the opportunity to experience the transformation of personal feeling and the expansion of human personality that Racine provided for France. France is the European location where the *Gemüter*, the *Leidenschaften*, had the historical capacity to develop. On the other hand, Germany missed out on this stage of the development of the emotions not only because it was preoccupied with its own national development, but also because it did not experience a national monarchy with an extravagant king at its head that promoted the interests of an indulgent leisure class with nothing else to do but revel in the imagination of sublime, near-monstrous emotions. We see Auerbach poised here between the *Gute und Böse* not only of Racine, as he puts it, but also of German culture and German history.

Auerbach's position here is consistent with Martin Chalmers's observation about Victor Klemperer's work, and by implication the interwar project of Romanistik itself, as "a contribution to Franco-German understanding" as well as "a critique of the German academy's dominant francophobia." One may add Auerbach's name to the list of figures Chalmers names, like Siegfried Kracauer and Walter Benjamin, who "challenge[d] the opposition postulated between supposed German 'depth' and French 'superficiality.'"[7]

In the concluding paragraph of the essay, Auerbach expresses his regret that he cannot spend more time on the historical origins of Racine's representation of the passions. He fleetingly suggests that the same Christian countercurrents which oppose Racine's metaphysic of the passions are in fact the basis of its inner structure. That France was the location where modern emotions developed out of medieval religion in the seventeenth — and late sixteenth — century is a theme that would occupy Auerbach in several of the essays that were to follow. He returned to this issue at some length in his later essay on Racine. However, before he did, he first addressed the theme in his 1932 essay "Montaigne the Writer."[8] Here the relation between religion and secular emotion takes on a different hue, while at the same time his ambiguous attitude to France disappears. Whatever his lack of religious faith, Auerbach argues, Montaigne could unveil his inner self because religious sentiment in France, through whatever unspecified historical process, was transformed into a secularized sensibility. In Montaigne, France produced the modern intellectual, the man of letters, who was to lead Europe in replacing the intellectual leadership of the clergy. The wars of religion provided the conditions for the emergence of such a figure; they inclined Montaigne toward outer conformism while moving him to a process of eccentric selfdiscovery, thus creating a sense of inner being as the basis of individual existence. The feeling expressed in this individuated self-portrait, while totally secular, Auerbach here argues, would have been impossible without prior historical developments in the Catholic Middle Ages, without, that is, the preparation through the cultural impact of the gospel story, particularly the Incarnation and Passion. Auerbach thus offers a fuller explanation of his passing suggestion in his 1927 Racine essay that there is a fundamental continuity underlying the apparent opposition between religious and secular emotion. Most important, Montaigne represents the modern intellectual who created a sensibility that replaced religious intellectual authority, but that very sensibility was made possible by, and inevitably stretched back to, medieval Catholicism.

Nearly a decade later, Auerbach returned to this issue in Racine once again in "*Passio* as Passion," this time at great length, frontally addressing the question he had briefly posed in his 1927 essay on Racine.[9] This later essay suggests a pattern in Auerbach's thought: the modern psychology of the emotions, however devoid of religion, is derived from religious structures of feeling developed in the medieval history of countries of Romance language and Catholic religion. With few exceptions, including Schlegel, Vossler, and himself, this history, he suggests, has not been understood by Germans. The German deficit, that is, may be religious as well as emotional. Writing before the Nazi regime about the Catholic heritage of secular France to a German audience is a way of engaging that deficit. While it may be too much to say these pre-1933 essays reveal a sense of "homelessness," they do evoke a sense of being written from a periphery within Europe itself. "*Passio* as Passion," however, was in fact written in a state of homelessness. There is a 14-year span between it and "Racine and the Passions." The latter essay was written in 1941 when Auerbach's relationship to Germany had radically changed. On this occasion, he was to applaud France, through Racine, as the crucible of noble feeling, while he was an exile and while Germany was occupying France. Most worthy of notice from our perspective is Auerbach's forceful claim in this essay to cultural authority about Europe when he was furthest removed from Europe, the only place it could have meant anything. The concerns in the smaller literary portraits of Montaigne and Racine now grow into an article of monumental proportions in "*Passio* as Passion." It was written in Turkey and published in the United States in *PMLA*, circumventing Europe altogether. But if the place of writing and publication evaded Europe, the article did in another sense encompass it in subject and scope.

"*Passio* as Passion" is written in a genre most readers of Auerbach would know from "Figura," which was written a few years earlier. Both are classical exemplars of Romance philology, the very models of philological practice. They are based on the belief that cultural change can be measured in the semantic change traceable in the key words of a culture. Here, however, Auerbach does not choose a technical word of biblical hermeneutics, but a common word that appears in both our daily and literary vocabulary, with the understanding that our everyday usage is ultimately derived from how words are used by great writers and thinkers. Auerbach the philologist guides us on a semantic narrative that travels tellingly through key historical moments of Western culture, which for him usually means classical and late antiquity, early Christianity and the high Middle Ages, and finally modernity. In the case of this essay modernity means the seventeenth century, looked at with occasional glances to the present moment, *"bis heute,"* to today.

The essay is an investigation of how the Greek word *pathos* and the Latin *passio* were transformed in meaning from *Leiden* (suffering), associated with *Gefühl* (feeling) and *Empfindung* (sensation), into *Leidenschaft* with its current meaning of passion, as first used by Racine. Auerbach's treatment of the subject is a continuation and modification of an article by the important Romance philologist Eugen Lerch, who originally raised the issue in 1938, and proposed that the distinction between the Greco-Roman *pathos-passio-Leiden* and *passion-Leidenschaft* has to do with a change from a passive to an active concept of emotion.[10] Auerbach will further develop and will qualify Lerch's attempt to show how *pathos-passio* went from a deformation of feeling to a dimension of inner life that would take its place next to thought and will as a worthy activity of the mind. Its overall theme is the poverty of the emotional contents signified by the word in antiquity compared to the emotional plenitude it acquired in Catholic Christianity, a plenitude passed on to its modern secular meaning. What is at stake is our ability to feel now in the present. Auerbach's argument is more complex and more subtle than I have space to recount. I will rehearse it only in broad outline.

He begins with the basic meaning of the Greek *pathos* as something that happens from the outside *to* the person who feels it, as an attack or affliction, a sensation or a suffering (*ein*

Befallen- oder Behaftetsein, eine Empfindung oder Erleiden)
(161). In Aristotelian terminology this can apply to plants and
animals and even material objects as well. It can also signify
perception, experience, feeling (*Wahrnehmung, Erfahrung,
Erlebnis, Empfindung, Gefühl*) (162). Finally, in colloquial
usage it can signify pain, sickness, suffering, misfortune
(*Schmerz, Krankheit, Leiden, Unglück*) (161).

An important change in the meaning of the word was made
by the Stoics. Whereas for Aristotle *pathos* was ethically neutral, for them, passion signified the inner turmoil that destroys
the tranquility of the wise man. The term thus takes on a
sharply pejorative meaning. The original contrast of *passio* to
actio is now replaced by the opposition to *ratio*. The pejorative Stoic meaning of the word became much more widespread
than the Aristotelian meaning and lives on today in the moral
imagination of the most varied groups of people, Auerbach
observes. It appeared in all later ethical systems.

The Stoic meaning of *passio* gained wide usage because of
its influence on late antique Christian authors, as in Augustine. Nevertheless, there is a fundamental difference between
Stoic and Christian uses of the word. The difference becomes
increasingly apparent as the word becomes radically altered
in a way that reflects a new sensibility inconceivable before
Christianity. The intention of the Christian is not to withdraw from the world in order to avoid suffering and passion
(*Leiden und Leidenschaft*), but to suffer in the world in order
to prevail over it. The object of Christian enmity to the world
is not to attain the absence of passion outside the world, but
to attain a countersuffering (*ein Gegenleiden*), a passionate
suffering in the world and through that, a suffering against the
world (*das leidenschaftliche Leiden in der Welt und damit
gegen die Welt*) (164). Against the evils of the flesh and of the
world, Christians set neither reason, nor Stoic apathy, nor the
Aristotelian golden mean. Christians instead engaged in entirely new emotions, hitherto unheard of. They opposed the

world and the flesh in order to achieve "the *gloriosa passio* through burning love of God" [die *gloriosa passio* aus glühender Gottesliebe] (164). In this Christian usage, the difference between *Leiden* and *Leidenschaften* has become blurred. God's love, which moved him to take *Leiden* upon himself for the sake of man is a *motus animi* without measure or boundary. *Leiden* becomes *Leidenschaft* in the *Passio*(n). The Crucifixion thus establishes a crucial turning point. Through it, the Christian redefinition of the word establishes a major transformation in the history of feelings, a transformation of the same magnitude Auerbach attributed to Augustine's conversion in *Mimesis*. It marks the beginning of a new culture, a new structure of mind and emotion. Pre-Christian classical culture is cold and emotionless by comparison.

For Auerbach, the gospel events remain largely placeless and without historical inflection until their significance emerges in medieval France. Untroubled by huge chronological gaps in the transmission of the emotional values of the gospel, Auerbach characteristically sees the significance of the Gospel events as coming to cultural fruition over centuries that ultimately take us to Catholic France, where, we are told, it reemerged in the twelfth century when the incarnate Christ (*der menschengewordene Christus*) (165) once again begins to overshadow the *rex gloriae*. Bernard of Clairvaux's *Passionsmystik* is Auerbach's main source. It was through Bernard, Auerbach suggests, that the Christian meaning of *passio* was to be transmitted in the coming centuries. Through difficult but exalted mystical, allegorical and figurative readings of Canticles and Psalms, Bernard connects the suffering of Christ on the cross to the *passio* of the Christian. He particularly points to Bernard's typological connection between a passage in Canticles that foreshadows passages in Mark and thus connects both the bitterness of Christ's suffering and the healing power of his crucified body, available to the Christian through the mystical body of the Church. Moreover, in the classical mysticism of Bernard, the themes connected with passion, or the suffering of the Christian, are treated as love motives, so that *passio* comes close to meaning "a creative, ecstatic love passion" [eine schöpferische, ekstatische Liebesleidenschaft] (167). The passion of love (*die Leidenschaft der Liebe*) leads to an *excessus mentis* through suffering and union with Christ. In the centuries that followed, the meaning of *passio* as used by Bernard endured and was strengthened, especially under the influence of the Franciscans, among whom, he declares, will be found the perfection of the Passion and the inner closeness of the meaning of *Leiden* and *Leidenschaft*, passion and fervor. Unlike anything in antiquity, *passio* is therefore something one should strive for. Whoever has no *passio* has no grace. Whoever does not partake of the *passio* of the savior lives with hardness of heart, and mystical treatises teach how to overcome it, though in the end identification with the *passio* of Christ is a gift of grace.

Once again skipping over several centuries to reach another set of cultural milestones in France, Auerbach lands in the sixteenth century, when, he argues, the word *passio* begins to take on the meaning of *Leidenschaft* in the modern sense. But first it had to overcome the continuing influence of its lingering classical meanings (still persistent in Montaigne, Bèze, Garnier and Lecoq), and linguistic competition from another word that threatened to appropriate the modern sense of *passion*, namely *affectus/affection*. In love treatises from France and Italy *affectus* rivals *passio-Leidenschaft; affection* as we know it begins to appear in Boiardo and Lorenzo de'Medici, and in France in Marguerite de Navarre.

By the seventeenth century, the process is complete. As *passion* fully enters the sphere of literary culture, the word clearly and conclusively takes on its modern meaning as *Leidenschaft*, mostly in connection with *Liebesleidenschaft*, but also with the self-love and self-assertion (*Selbstliebe und*

Selbstbehauptung) associated with *ambition* and *gloire*. Auerbach credits Corneille, Racine and Pascal with the decisive
change in usage. In seventeenth century France, the *passions*
are the grand human desires (*die grossen menschlichen Be-
gierde*) (173), and they are characteristically regarded as tragic,
heroic, exalted, and worthy of admiration. This attitude is
palpable in Corneille and in Pascal, and even in Descartes,
but it reaches its high point in the tragedies of Racine, whose
goal is to excite and glorify the passions, the *Leidenschaften*.
For the sensitive reader capable of real feeling, the torment
and delight of *Leidenschaft* become the highest form of life.[11]
The narrowness of the emotional life inherent in the vocabulary of Aristotle and the Stoics has finally been put to rest.
This second major semantic shift is also accompanied by a
reorientation away from Catholic Christian culture. Seventeenth century *passion* bore within it the polemic of a new
culture that threatened the Church. As he had mentioned in
his earlier article on Racine, Auerbach's treatment of the transformation from the Christian to the secular suggests not only
antithetical cultures in antithetical uses of the same word; it
suggests that we simply could not experience an emotion we
still value as ennobling without the historical experience of
the twelfth century. Feelings we assume to be part of our
psychic repertoire are unthinkable without the cultural assimilation of the meaning of the Passion, of an incarnate God
who took on a body to suffer for humans, so that humans
could experience the same suffering, which was both exalting
and saving.

It is equally important, as I have been suggesting, that for
Auerbach the full modern meaning of the word *passion* was
actualized in France. The passage from the classical to the
Christian to the secular takes place on French soil within the
context of the history of the Church in France. That Auerbach's
philological narrative is so firmly set in France is not without

implications. To write about Racine in 1927 as the origina-
tor of the ennobling passions, an experience denied to Germans and acquired by Germans from the French; to write of
Montaigne in 1932 that he taught us to think of ourselves as
having an inner life and that in the process he created the
figure of the modern literary intellectual; to return to Racine
(as well as Corneille, and Pascal), as the culmination of some
2,000 years of history — all this is to recognize France as the
European cultural center during a period when intense anti-
French feeling in Germany would finally be expressed in war.
It is also of some significance that Auerbach completed a
project in 1941 first conceived in 1927 about the Christian
sources of Racine's passions, and hence the Christian basis of
the European psyche, at the time when Auerbach was in exile
as a Jew.

Auerbach's nascent or implicit opposition to German nationalism in his early essays extolling France as the land of
exalted and exalting passion could of course only have been
more intense during the German occupation of France. That
"*Passio* as Passion" was written in Istanbul in exile only adds
to the unspoken intensity about its subject, an intensity further enhanced when reference to dislocation is made in the
essay itself. In his discussion about the role of the Franciscans
in the *Passionsmystik*, he self-consciously apologizes for having too few texts to demonstrate his case. Since the publication of his "Epilogomena to Mimesis," Auerbach's work in
Istanbul has been famously associated with this lack of resources.[12] In this earlier essay, too, the scarcity of scholarly
resources, and the identification of Istanbul as the location of
writing, are marks of exile, especially in contrast to Lerch's
"excellently documented" [ausgezeichnet documentierte]
(161) article.[13] These are all part of a complex gesture of both
loss and persistence of mastery and cultural authority. No
longer in a place where European sources are easily available,
no longer in a Europe that heeds his judgments about European

culture,[14] no longer in a Europe where he is considered European, Auerbach pronounces on which European writers contributed to the establishment of the European psyche, to the establishment of Europeanness of the mind: Aristotle, the Stoics, Augustine, Early Christianity, Bernard, Bonaventure, Suso, Aquinas, Boiardo, Lorenzo de'Medici, Ariosto, Tasso, Marguerite de Navarre, Montaigne, Bèze, Garnier, Lecoq, Hardy, d'Urfé, Corneille, Racine, Pascal. Perhaps not surprisingly, except for Suso, Germans are conspicuously absent.

Behind this gesture of simultaneous loss and mastery of a sense of Europeanness stands Auerbach's experience in Turkey. Commentators on Auerbach have no more than speculated about what this experience was like, or they have simply mentioned it in passing. As far as I can tell, no one has commented on the one piece of evidence written by Auerbach himself about that experience, namely a letter to Benjamin about his position at the university in Istanbul. The letter provides an indispensable guide to Auerbach's writing during this period. The great irony that emerges from the letter is that in Turkey the exiled European is treated as the consummate European. In letters of 1936 and 1937, he tells Benjamin about his academic contribution to the Europeanization of Turkish academic culture. Among the newly hired Europeans at the university, he is responsible for instruction in all European languages. In a broader sense, he is one of the faculty responsible for the academic, and by implication, the cultural transformation of Turkey. Not only do he and his European colleagues teach all European philologies, Romanistik, Anglistik, ancient philology, and Germanistik, but they are charged with Europeanizing everything from pedagogy and library usage to the organization of filing cabinets.[15]

His academic post was part of what he termed Ataturk's larger *"fanatischer antitraditioneller Nationalismus"* that fuels a cultural and political transformation which opposes both pan-Islamicism and Turkey's Sultanic past. By rejecting

Islamic culture and adopting European technical moderniza-
tion, Ataturk throws all tradition overboard in order to build
a thoroughly rationalized state after the European model. As
a result, European teachers are much in demand, especially
because they come without hostile European propaganda.
However, to accomplish its cultural goals, he tells Benjamin,
Turkey has rewritten its history by looking back to a fantasial
ur-Turkish past. The combination of this invented past and
the use of European cultural weapons to be used against a hated
Europe has resulted in "nationalism in the superlative" at the
expense of distorting Turkey's real historical national character. One consequence, Auerbach laments, has been that
traditional Turkish texts are becoming incomprehensible
because of language reforms, including the adoption of the
Roman alphabet. No one under 25 can any longer understand
religious, literary and philosophical texts that are more than
ten years old.

Auerbach is struck by both the absurdity of his personal
situation and its portent for the condition of world culture.
His stay in Turkey, he remarks, has convinced him of the en-
croachment of a worldwide decline of cultural authenticity
whose most heinous example is "the horrible inauthenticity
of [Nazi] Blubo propaganda" [(die) grauenvollen Unechtheit
der Blubopropaganda], "Blood and Soil" propaganda.[16] Witnessing Turkey's exchange of its historical past for a fabricated
past has helped him understand this phenomenon.

For Auerbach, Turkey also became an emblem of this
inauthenticity, made visible in the modern quarter of Istanbul,
Pera, which he describes as both a "caricature and perfection
of a nineteenth century European colony now in complete
decline" [Karikatur und Vollendung einer europäischen Sied-
lung des 19. Jahrh(underts), nun in völligem Verfall].[17] There
is a gap of some four years between this letter and "*Passio* as
Passion," but the letter supplies the larger context for the full
impact of the cultural displacement behind Auerbach's demure

apology that he does not have access to the texts he needs to demonstrate his argument. The essay can be understood as an attempt to overcome that displacement. It is in this condition of inauthentic Europeanness that Europeanness is both attributed to, and claimed by, him.

That it was on vacation in Italy, in the months before he left for Istanbul, that Auerbach realized his inescapable distance from his colleagues, the inevitability of his dismissal, his uncertain future, and his *seltsam* situation, is another irony.[18] For, as a Romanist, he also considered Catholic Rome as the center of the European culture with which he so strongly identified. With somewhat different emphases than his treatment of France, he also attributed to Dante's Rome an important role in the history of the European psyche. This is an issue that has often gone unappreciated by Renaissance scholars, for whom Auerbach's reading of Dante principally exemplified his exposition of biblical typology, which, through his influence, played a powerful role in the interpretation of Renaissance literature. As much as any French writer, Dante, according to Auerbach, created the possibility of emotions that could be called European. In his discussions of Dante, he turns to the great medieval shift in European culture in a more specifically transnational European context. For Auerbach, Dante remains the central figure of European civilization, a figure far more significant than either Montaigne or Racine. Auerbach expresses palpable affection for Dante, who, one surmises, is central to his own sense of European identity.[19] Dante's role in the transformation of feeling is important for Auerbach precisely because it is attached to empire. Dante is Auerbach's guide to what it means to be a European, to what it means to feel emotions that grow from European soil. Perhaps as a retort to Burckhardt's identification of the Italian city-state as the location of the Renaissance and the birth of the modern individual, Auerbach argues that Dante prepared the way for the emotions we regard as modern by establishing the integral unity of the individual in a Catholic Middle Ages centered in empire, the very political arrangement whose disappearance is generally regarded as the enabling condition of the Italian Renaissance.

Auerbach's early essays on Dante are often devoted to retrieving Dante from prejudices, not the least of which are German, that have obstructed a full understanding of his poetry. It is perhaps not so startling that in the course of doing so, while exploring the origins of the integral modern European individual, Auerbach expresses strong feeling for a surprising example of the incomplete European who qualifies his notion of European authenticity, and which, I will argue, stands for the European Jew. Auerbach's 1929 essay "The Romantic Discovery of Dante" brings us back to Auerbach's prewar years, when he counted German Romantics as among those who posed the strongest obstacles to an understanding of Dante's role in representing the unitary personality, the necessary condition of expressing strong emotion.[20] Germans were not alone in this. Italians lost sight of Dante's true significance because they read him too narrowly within Italian national aspirations. In general, though, the Romantics distorted Dante because they saw the didactic and doctrinal elements in the *Comedy* as a deviation from its true poetic value; its dogmatic content was unfortunate, they lamented, but should be forgiven and overlooked because of its great poetic passages. This was true in France as well, but Auerbach is particularly harsh on Germany by decrying its greatest literary figure. In critical tones, he observes that Goethe had no real appreciation of Dante. The author of the *Italienische Reise* had no notion of the full meaning of the *Comedy* as a codification of either European or Mediterranean culture. The judgment amounts to a charge of German provincialism embodied in the most hallowed German literary giant. Just as Germany could not appreciate Racine, even at the pinnacle of its literary culture, Auerbach contends, Germany was not attuned to the center of European literary culture.

Nevertheless, there were eighteenth and nineteenth century German Romantics who reached the highest understanding of Dante's poetry. They recognized in Dante's work the most powerful unified poetic structure of our time. They understood that religion and poetry could not be separated in Dante, that the *Comedy* contained the entirety of its culture, and, most important, that Dante was the prophetic precursor of the modern world of the individual. These thinkers saw that the central meaning of the *Comedy* was that our particular earthly and historical existence is revealed in its true and eternal form by the divine judgment rendered after death. The structure of the work as a whole subordinates the individual to a divinely ordained end point of damnation, purgation or salvation. But while the individual is thus seen from the perspective of the eternal and the immutable, the essence of individual character is also eternized by translating the individual's earthly essence into its immortal essence in the afterlife. It was the eternal perspective of life after death that rooted the life of individuals in the specific circumstances of the earthly world through their inner drives, intentions and sufferings, which together formed their characteristic inner being. The individual's earthly essence was the sum of these drives and feelings expressed in the corresponding sum of his or her actions. Schelling, Auerbach remarks, was the first thinker to understand this about Dante since the collapse of Catholic ideology in the Middle Ages. Auerbach implies that Schelling cut a path through German anti-Catholic sentiment expressed in the dismissive remarks of German writers.[21] Herder, the Schlegels and Hegel walked this path, as did their twentieth century follower, Vossler, and after him, Auerbach himself.

However, while Germans not hostile to Catholicism rediscovered the Mediterranean poet's foundational insight that an individual's passions and drives add up to a coherent, unitary whole expressed in a coherent, unitary set of actions, they unfortunately did not exert enough influence to overcome Romantic distortions of the *Comedy*. Only more recently,

Auerbach suggests, has Vossler been able to overcome these distortions.[22] One senses Auerbach's strong identification with German intellectuals who understood the importance of the Mediterranean world as the center of European culture. Auerbach would clearly like to place the German critic at the center of Europe and thus contribute to the cure of German parochialism. Given that Dante is the object of a German desire for a personal wholeness to be found in Mediterranean empire, Auerbach's compassion for — even attraction to — Virgil as the incomplete individual is especially interesting. Auerbach returned to Dante in several later essays, but I refer here to his 1931 "Dante and Virgil."[23]

Here, unlike many other essays, Virgil occupies a central position in Auerbach's analysis. Virgil is Auerbach's great exception to his view of the emotional dearth of classical culture, but Auerbach's Virgil is laden with emotion for unusual reasons. At the center of the essay is the very basic question: Why should Beatrice choose a pagan poet to be Dante's rescuer? Why should she choose a heathen to prepare him for the vision of God? The answer, Auerbach proposes, lies in the medieval view of Virgil as a figure of legend, a *Sagenfigur*, improbably preserved in his much maligned medieval image as a sorcerer, an image sustained in Mediterranean lore. Much of what Auerbach has to say about Virgil has become the standard explanation for the position of Virgil in the poem. As poet of the fourth eclogue, Virgil was regarded in medieval lore as a *Magier*; he was a prophet of the Incarnation; he understood the connection between the *Pax Romana* and the birth of Christ. This folkloric Virgil, Auerbach argues, was connected to his role as the poet of Roman world empire, the poet who created the myth of a Roman ur-history directed by a providential, divine force that found its fullest culmination in the *Pax Romana* under imperial rule.[24] Tied to both imperial and papal Rome, the medieval Virgil remained the legitimizer of the idea of *sacrum imperium* and the literary guarantor of the continuity of European history. The medieval Virgil was a heathen prophet who was either a secret Christian or an unconscious herald of divine truth. Virgil is thus the appropriate choice to guide Dante on his ascent to Paradise because of his celebration of universal peace under universal monarchy, a divinely ordained peace in a historical scheme that prepared the world for the appearance of Christ.

There is nevertheless a sense of pathos in this praise of Virgil, for Virgil himself can never enter Paradise. In Auerbach's concluding description of Dante's resurrection of Virgil, perhaps the most moving passage in all his early work, he calls special attention to Beatrice's use of the word *cortese* when she addresses him, "O anima cortese montovana." *Cortesia* was the great virtue valued by the followers of the *stil nuova*, the Florentine school of love poetry out of which Dante's poetry developed. Here Dante uses the word not to characterize an emotion he feels for Beatrice, but one Beatrice feels for Virgil, as Auerbach points out. As applied to Virgil, *cortesia* is not a love term, but an attribute that inheres in an inner worth which leaves Virgil always prepared for good, even if he is prevented from enjoying the fruits of his own goodness. For Virgil is forever excluded from the kingdom of God. Whatever he does for Dante and for the heavenly kingdom he does selflessly, out of greatness of heart, fully knowing he will receive no reward. He wishes for no recompense other than the consciousness of doing good. That is his *cortesia*, nourished by *Einsicht* and *Bescheidenheit*, intelligence and modesty. Virgil represents "the simplicity of a man who has reached the highest stage of human culture" [die Einfachheit eines Menschen, der die höchste Stufe menschlicher Bildung erreicht hat] (122), *purely* human culture one might add, without benefit of full spiritual enlightenment. He can never be fully part of the world he announces, the world he inaugurates, the world to which he leads those who are permitted to cross the threshold. If the medieval lore of the Mediterranean *Volk* kept

Virgil the *Magier* alive, what is the lore that fashioned him into this figure of a human achievement that could never be complete, never fulfilled in itself? and why is it that Auerbach waxes poetic over it? It is precisely Virgil's incompleteness that gives him his dignity and his humanity: "Mut and Milde des Herzens, Mass und Festigkeit des Urteils, königliche und zugleich demütige Weisheit bilden in ihm eine in jedem Wort und jeder Geste neu sich offenbarende väterliche Humanität." (122). [Courage and mildness of heart, moderation and firmness of judgment, kingly and at the same time humble wisdom form in him a fatherly humanity revealed anew in his every word and gesture.]

Auerbach's own palpable but sad affection for Virgil here becomes apparent. Virgil may be Dante's instrument for the representation of the integral individual, but Auerbach implicitly questions whether Dante can reveal Virgil as a complete individual. Virgil is an object of emotion, not because he achieves integral fullness of personhood, but just because he does not. He may be the *father* of the new world he foreshadows, but Virgil is forever the unsaved; he is forever the outsider. In emphasizing the truth of the medieval view of the prophetic *Sagenfigur*, Auerbach stressed Virgil as a pagan prefiguration of the Christian, but unspoken in the essay is that Dante also placed Virgil in the same position vis à vis Christianity as the Jews. In using German sources like Schelling and Hegel to correct the (German) Romantic reading of Dante, Auerbach points to Dante's emphasis on the Roman Empire rather than the Davidic kingdom as the historical, prophetic prenarrative of the Incarnation, but the depth of feeling that Auerbach expresses for Virgil, I would contend, may have more to do with the descendants of David than with those of Aeneas. Dare one say that Virgil is Auerbach's Jew? Auerbach's positive cultural identification with a transnational Europe embodied in Dante is here complemented with an empathy for those who are not permitted full membership in it. Auerbach's tribute to Virgil, I would suggest, is not unrelated to the feelings of an intellectual German Jew who, in a Protestant Germany, located the core of Europe in Catholic France and Italy.

Perhaps Auerbach's most telling word in his portrait of Virgil is *Bildung*, for he uses it both to praise Virgil and to characterize his incompleteness. The word asks that we consider Auerbach's work not only in the context of the German practice of Romance philology, but also in the context of German-Jewish assimilation and acculturation, particularly its role in what Paul Mendes-Flohr has called the dual identity of German Jews.[25] *Bildung* broadly connotes a German educational ideal derived from the French Enlightenment. It is also much discussed as the ideal through which Germans and Jews connected culturally, the ideal through which Jews entered into German society from their once separatist communities. From their first moves toward either assimilation or acculturation during the Enlightenment, Jews struggled with two ways of defining *Deutschtum*: affiliation by *Kultur*, and by what we would now call ethnicity. *Deutschtum* as *Kultur* could accommodate the inclusion of Jews; *Deutschtum* as ethnicity could not.

Mendes-Flohr has recently summed up the role of *Bildung* in bringing Jews into German society. From the start, he explains, Jews embraced this "educational ideal of self-cultivation" (2), and clung to it to the end. Jews believed that *Bildung* represented "an inclusive, cosmopolitan ethos" (9) that presupposed a "neutral society" (15) in which religion and ethnicity were irrelevant and could be placed in the background. Over the course of the nineteenth century, Mendes-Flohr continues, the meaning and status of *Bildung* changed among Germans; the concept lost its cosmopolitan character, as Germans, in deliberate contrast to the French, sought a distinctly German form of *Bildung*. Increasingly, Germans cultivated their identity through the idea of a *Volksnation*, in which Jews could only play a problematic role. There were public debates over the issue in Auerbach's youth before the Great War. In his letters, Auerbach's correspondent-to-be, Walter Benjamin, commented extensively on these debates. As Flohr-Mendes puts it, "The one group not to compromise the liberal, cosmopolitan image of Bildung . . . was the Jews. Indeed the Jews were 'the last guardians of the original German idea of Bildung'" (12).[26] A palpable change occurred during and after the Great War. Jews thought their patriotism would win them an assured place in German society, but the resurgence of anti-Semitism led to widespread disillusion. The value of *Bildung* was reevaluated even before the war ended. Hermann Cohen, the neo-Kantian Marburg philosopher, known for his promotion of German Jewish acculturation, expressed pessimism about the future of German-Jewish relations.[27] Writing between the wars, his disciple, Franz Rosenzweig, having considered conversion to Christianity, advocated a form of dual identity. He argued that Jews be Jewish by nationality, and German by culture, through *Bildung*, that is.

The foregoing account is necessarily schematic, but helps us understand Auerbach from a perspective not often applied to him. As a World War I veteran, Auerbach reacted against German nationalism by appealing to European transnationalism, but he also must have been aware of the anti-Semitic atmosphere to which Cohen, Rosenzweig and Benjamin reacted. Perhaps his attribution of *Bildung* to only a transitional historical figure like Virgil is an indication that he, too, could not accept *Bildung* as an ideal complete in itself. But unlike Cohen and Rosenzweig, who turned to Judaism as a form of national identity alongside *Bildung*, Auerbach turned to the Roman Church as the source of cultural cosmopolitanism. In his "Epilogemona to Mimesis," published in 1954 when he was settled at Yale, but presumably addressed to a German audience, he took the occasion to look back upon some of these issues. Most suggestive are his comments about his relationship to Germany and Europe (13–15). He was particularly

sensitive to the charge that his emphasis on Romance, especially French, literature and the near absence of German
literature in *Mimesis* were signs of an anti-German bias, presumably, though he never says so, the result of an assumed
hostility to Germany stemming from his exile. Auerbach re-
sponded that the charge was based on a misunderstanding he
wanted to correct. "As a consequence of world history," he
reflected, "someone in my situation can hardly comment on
this subject without hurting somebody's feelings" [Die
Weltgeschichte hat es mit sich gebracht, dass man sich in
meiner Lage zu diesem Thema kaum äussern kann, ohne
irgendjemandes Gefühle zu verletzen] (13). He concentrated
on Romance literature in *Mimesis*, he explains, because the
Romance literatures are more representative of Europe than
German literature is, and it is European culture, he implies,
that is important. From the twelfth to the nineteenth century, he goes on, European cultural leadership passed back and
forth from France to Italy and back to France. This is very
much the inference I have drawn from Auerbach's earlier essays. However politely, he quietly maintains the view that
German culture is marginal in European history. This is perhaps the insult he tries to avoid. Nevertheless, it would be a
mistake, he warns, to read any personal aversion to, or estrangement from (*Abneigung oder Fremdheit*), German literature or culture in these omissions. He assures his readers,
almost comically, that, for all the historical importance he
ascribes to French novelists, he prefers Goethe, Stifter and
Keller when it comes to personal pleasure.

This assertion, however, is couched in a complex set of ges-
tures. His affirmation of personal German identity shades into
the intellectual and the professional. He bristles at the suggestion, made in hostile German reviews, that *Mimesis* is primarily read and praised outside Germany, "im Ausland," a
phrase that suggests his appeal to "foreigners." He reminds
readers of "Epilogomena to Mimesis" that more than half the

reviews have come from Germany and German Switzerland, and that in France, the book is barely known (15 n. 16). It speaks more to Germans about France than it does to the French. He insists that *Mimesis* is a thoroughly German book even though its subject is a Europe in which Germany hardly figures. *Mimesis*, he maintains, emerged from the themes and methods of German *Geistesgeschichte* and German philology. "It is unthinkable except in the tradition of Hegel and German romanticism" [es wäre in keiner anderen Tradition denkbar als in der deutschen Romantik und Hegels], (though we have seen that Auerbach is far more circumspect about the role of German *Romantik* in his work than he concedes here). And his professional and intellectual interests are tied to his prewar German education in a way that suggests a personal context: *Mimesis* "could never have been written without the influences that I experienced in my youth in Germany" [es wäre nie geschrieben worden ohne die Einwirkungen, die ich in meiner Jugend in Deutschland erfahren habe]. In the course of refuting his German detractors with a resounding affirmation of his own German identity, he manages to maintain his view of German provincialism, and to portray himself as having practiced a scholarship that transcends that provincialism.

Auerbach, too, thus chooses a kind of dual identity, both German and European. In an essay that in part explains the conditions of writing *Mimesis* in Istanbul, he is silent on Jewish identity. Years earlier, when he wrote to Benjamin describing his situation in Marburg after his dismissal, he could refer to himself as a Jew only by distinguishing himself from his colleagues, "who are not of our origin" [die nicht unserer Herkunft sind].[28] In contrast, Auerbach's rival, Victor Klemperer, in his diary entries during the years that the Nazis came to power and Auerbach left Germany, speaks of himself alternately as a Jew and a Protestant, alternately affirms his German identity and castigates himself for falling for such an illusion. We do not have such a diary for Auerbach, and there is no way we can know his personal feelings about his identity, but at one point Klemperer refers to himself in a way that Auerbach would have concurred: he calls himself a "German European."[29] Klemperer maintained this German European identity by writing on Enlightenment France; his record of his work on his book on the eighteenth century is a refrain that runs throughout his diary, counterpointing the increasing Nazi stranglehold, and in this he is close to the pattern enunciated by Mendes-Flohr whereby Jews sought universalism in the French Enlightenment.

For Auerbach, in stark contrast, it was the universalism of the Catholic Church, the successor of the pre-Christian Roman Empire whether in France or in Italy, where the foundations of the modern European psyche were laid, where the sources of the integrated personality and cultural, personal wholeness were to be found, and hence the capacity to feel — to feel like an authentic European, that is, an authenticity that Auerbach did not always seem to assume easily. In 1941, the figure of Virgil may have been a gesture in that direction. He is the figure who stands between the Christian and pre-Christian world, the figure who creates the bridge between them. Whereas in "Figura" Auerbach sought a model of typological fulfillment that did not exclude its own foreshadowing, Virgil poses instead the opposite problem — that of the figural foreshadowing who cannot partake of the fulfillment of his own prophecy. He is a figure of deep cultural anxiety, a surrogate for Jewish cultural anxiety. He is proof that *Bildung* is not enough. He is proof that even those who articulate the advent of a new world in which human emotion reaches new possibilities of richness may themselves not be allowed to participate in it. He is the powerful counterexample of the modern integral individual, a counterexample whose importance is discovered in the very process of delineating the triumphal historical emergence of his healthier opposite. Those of us who so assiduously applied Auerbach's method to the study of the Renaissance devotional lyric had little idea of the troubled history and tangled identities that lay behind it.

10 • The Fall into Subjectivity

Milton's "Paradise Within" and "Abyss of Fears and Horrors"

Anthony Low

The drive inward toward individuality, self-examination and subjectivity in *Paradise Lost* is a major feature of the poem. In his book *The Paradise Within*, Louis Martz argues that the whole epic may be conceived of as taking place within the mind of the poet — and by sympathetic extension (we may presume) in the minds of fit readers willing to follow him: "[T]his poem is an action of thoughts within a central, controlling intelligence that moves with inward eyes toward a recovery of Paradise." Martz rightly stresses the importance of the inward journey of the mind toward salvation, reminding us, as we draw toward the close of both the poem and his essay on it, that "the promised redemption consists primarily in the renewal of man's inner powers: those powers of the

soul by which the bard has just pursued his triumphant journey of the mind toward Paradise."[1] Although salvation occurs
objectively in history through the life and atonement of Jesus,
it operates effectually upon each separate individual by taking
an inward turn within his heart, mind and soul by his response
to grace. Michael instructs Adam, as he goes forth into exile
in the fallen world, that above all he and Eve must cultivate
the inward, spiritual virtues and perform deeds that flow from
and are enabled by those virtues. Earlier in the poem Milton
briefly summarizes the relation of the inward soul to outward
deeds in his synecdochic phrase "Faith and faithful works"
(11.64).[2] Milton subscribes broadly, but not strictly, to Luther's
doctrine of salvation sola fides. To faith, Michael tells Adam
to add patience, temperance, love and the other virtues. These
are the means by which faithful and virtuous deeds, enabled
by grace, will issue from within the regenerate soul.

In his famous promise, Michael assures Adam that if he
properly cultivates what many spiritual writers, drawing upon
biblical imagery, have called the inward garden, "Then wilt
thou not be loath / To leave this Paradise, but shalt possess /
A paradise within thee, happier far" (12.585–87). So, instead
of spending their days tending a physical garden filled with
paradisal fruits and flowers, which, as Eve laments, they must
abandon forever because such prelapsarian plants "never will
in other Climate grow" (11.274), Adam and Eve shall learn
henceforth to tend the gardens of their souls, to cultivate inward fruits and flowers of "Faith, /. . . vertue, Patience, Temperance [and] Love" (12.582–83). God will enable them to
do so by his promised gift of grace, which he offers not mediated through churches, congregations, priests or prelates but
directly to individuals, specifically by means of his "Umpire
Conscience," through which he will speak to and empower
them from "within" the very centers of their minds and selves
(3.194–95).

The importance of this inward turn in the journey toward

salvation cannot be overestimated. *Paradise Lost* is, ultimately, a hopeful and consoling poem, a divine comedy that
anticipates a happy ending as time nears its close, when mankind will cross to the far side of the abyss that separates time
from eternity. Nonetheless it also tells and shows us that just
as the world will "tend from bad to worse" (12.106), so will
the Church, even the reformed churches, human institutions
that are inextricably parts of the world. From the death of the
last apostle until the Last Judgment, "carnal power shall force
/ On every conscience" (12.521–22). The churches will im-
pair rather than help their members. "[S]o shall the World go
on, / To good malignant, to bad men benign / . . . till the day /
Appear of respiration to the just" (12.537–40). The Reformation
provided Milton with much of his theology, as it provided him
earlier with hopes of earthly reform, but in *Paradise Lost* he
no longer finds its ameliorating effect on the churches worth
mentioning. There will be no truly reformed church until the
Last Judgment.[3] As Michael explains, even in the time of the
apostles the Holy Spirit does not inspire and work through
the seven Churches or prelates but through individual con-
verts: "His Spirit within them, and the Law of Faith / Working through love, upon thir hearts shall write, / To guide them
in all truth" (12.488–90). Similarly, Jesus tells us in *Paradise
Regained* that his chosen way is not conquest, prescription,
or worldly rule, but "By winning words to conquer willing
hearts, / And make persuasion do the work of fear" (1.222–
23). Therefore, when history reaches its happy ending, as the
Son of God rises into heaven "with the multitude of my
redeem'd" (3.260), he will bring with him not organized
churches, or even those within particular churches who are
loyal and responsive to the graces they claim to channel, but
elect individuals. Those who follow the guidance of men will
at best end up in the Paradise of Fools. Milton does not speak
of election in the strict Calvinist sense but refers to those who
respond internally with faith, love, patience and the other

virtues Michael enumerates to the grace that God offers to all: "The rest shall hear me call" (3.185).[4] Under the guidance of "Umpire *Conscience*" (3.195), they will cultivate the "paradise within [them] happier far" (12.587).

Nonetheless, although the promised ending of the tale of history will be happy for those who respond to grace and cultivate the virtues of the mind, throughout the poem another, darker process of internalization works counter to grace and virtue. Milton first and often associates the journey into the mind, the growth of self-consciousness and subjectivity, not with the blissful journey to heaven but with the tragic double Fall of Satan and Adam. Internalization may lead to heaven, but it begins with the fall and may lead down into hell. The Fall brings in its train, together with Sin and Death, born in the first fall and actualized in the second, self-consciousness, the obsessive habit of anguished soliloquizing, and an inward, spiraling fall into ever-expanding depths of terror, loss and loneliness. Satan learns this terrible lesson in his earliest moments alone with himself, when he first has leisure to pause and take stock:

> Me miserable! Which way shall I fly
> Infinite wrath, and infinite despair?
> Which way I fly is Hell; myself am Hell;
> And in the lowest deep a lower deep
> Still threat'ning to devour me opens wide,
> To which the Hell I suffer seems a Heav'n.
>
> (4.73–78)

Although the inward self can become a paradise, it can also become a hell. The contrast is stark: "a paradise within thee," or "Myself am Hell." Such is the fallen Satan's realization as he turns his eyes inward for the first time and, with that mental act, arrives at a terrible precipice from which he falls ever deeper and deeper into subjectivity and solipsism. "The mind is its own place," he had boasted earlier to Beelzebub in a mood of pride, determination and stubborn defiance, "and in itself / Can make a Heav'n of Hell, a Hell of Heav'n" (1.254–55). At that time, however, he was making outward rhetoric, talking and persuading more than thinking, not allowing himself to pause in self-examination or to look within the mind he characterizes. His early confidence in the power of the self-reliant mind to exert control over objective reality proves sorely misplaced. The autonomous mind cannot, of its own power, even retreat safely within the fortress of its thoughts when fate is outwardly adverse, a Stoic practice that Milton rejects. As long as the would-be autonomous individual rejects divine love and grace, which the poem informs us are the necessary supports of free will and of the power to cultivate a paradise within, it turns out that the mind ceases to be its own place. It loses control not only over the outward world of matter and events but even over its own inward mental processes.

The failure of the will to achieve its intention is accompanied by a corresponding failure of the intellect to comprehend its situation. When he makes his defiant boast Satan is in effect denying not only the true nature and limitations of the mind but the objective reality of hell. Yet all the while he boasts, he stands within hell, sees it with his eyes, hears it with his ears and feels it through the soles of his feet. As long as he denies the objective reality of any part of the created universe — consequent on his hatred and denial of the Creator of the universe — he rejects the only available foundations upon which his reason might rest. Although he is supremely intelligent, Satan utterly lacks workable principles on which to base his logic. He lacks the Christian-Aristotelian virtue of prudence, which Milton sometimes refers to in his prose works as "Christian prudence," and the Christian-Platonic faculty of right reason. The Aristotelian-Thomistic tradition, which Milton inherited and upon which he drew, understood that logical reasoning relies on the cardinal virtue of prudence, that virtue which enables its possessor to comprehend truth, reality, that which exists.[5] The related Platonic tradition, on which Milton also draws, speaks of *recta ratio*, or right reason. God exchanges his golden scepter for an iron rod to punish Satan and his followers precisely because they "reason for their law refuse, / Right reason for thir Law" (6.41–42). Since the time of Machiavelli, the word "prudence" has in common usage become increasingly more instrumental and pragmatic, not to say cynical. It is seldom thought of as a virtue but rather as an aid to *virtù* or as an amoral means of achieving desired results. Since the rise of the New Science, reason has in common usage likewise been divorced from rightness, to become more instrumental, less ethical and moral.[6] A comparable rejection of rational foundations on which to build their arguments explains why the devilish philosophers, despite their presumably superior logical powers, are like Satan condemned to circle perpetually in their thoughts and find "no end, in wand'ring mazes lost" (2.561). Since Satan, like the other fallen angels, loses control of the foundations of reason and will, he falls inevitably into helpless spirals of inward despair, as Milton so vividly shows us in his soliloquy. For the damned, the mind is not a stoic refuge but an inescapable trap leading further and further downward into helpless despair.

Like Satan, Adam also falls into isolation and the habit of soliloquy after his fall. He first resolves to eat the forbidden fruit and commit the original sin because, drawn by his intense love of Eve, he firmly determines that they "never shall be parted, bliss or woe" (9.916). "Certain my resolution is to Die," he exclaims, "How can I live without thee?" (9.908–09). He would rather part from God and from life than from Eve. Nevertheless, the Fall soon evolves into precisely what he most feared and condemned himself to death to avoid: the loss of her company, separation, isolation. It turns out that there is no true community outside of the love of God. As yet the human community consists of only two people, who no longer speak to each other. In book 10 we find Adam, having quarreled bitterly with Eve at the end of book 9, where each blamed the other for his loss, alone, driven into himself in the manner of Satan. Adam is appropriately described as "hid in gloomiest shade, / To sorrow abandon'd, but worse felt within, / And in a troubl'd Sea of passion tost" (10.716–18). His lengthy soliloquy that follows, extending for 142 lines, although modeled on dramatic convention, is unprecedented for the subtlety, reach and comprehensiveness with which it depicts inward thoughts and feelings. It is precisely what Milton had promised to do, some 20 years earlier, as soon as he had leisure to write poetry again: "to paint out and describe . . . with a solid and treatable smoothness . . . the wily subtleties and refluxes of man's thoughts from within."[7] With the exception of Augustine's *Confessions*, and briefer passages in Shakespeare, nothing approaching the extraordinary depth of Milton's portrayal of the inward workings of the mind can be found in literature until after the ripening of the novel at the hands of Samuel Richardson and Jane Austen, or until Wordsworth's *Prelude* — a work pervasively conscious of and in rivalry with *Paradise Lost*.

As soon as Adam turns his thoughts inward, they lead him inevitably to the same awful brink discovered by Satan, and Adam likewise falls into the terrible depths of uncontrollable subjectivity. When Eve fell earlier, she echoed Satan's patterns of speech because she had heard him talk and his mode of language suited her new thoughts and aspirations.[8] Adam cannot have overheard Satan's soliloquy, yet his own soliloquy echoes Satan's words because he endures the same experience:

> Thus what thou desir'st
> And what thou fear'st, alike destroys all hope
> Of refuge, and concludes thee miserable
> Beyond all past example and futúre,
> To *Satan* only like both crime and doom.

O Conscience, into what Abyss of fears
And horrors hast thou driv'n me; out of which
I find no way, from deep to deeper plung'd!

(10.837–44)

For Milton, there is no way for the individual to escape from
the endless abyss of subjectivity, into which all the efforts of
his mind to escape only plunge and entangle him further: no
way, that is, except by means of an external rescue. The theological situation, similar to the familiar poststructuralist dilemma of absence and *différance*, is that there is no way for
mortal man to reach God past the barrier of transcendence or
difference, into a region that Augustine in the *Confessions*
argues is beyond time and the material universe. If man cannot reach God, then the only possible solution to his dilemma
is for God to reach man.

So says Augustine: "You were with me, but I was not with
you. . . . You called me; you cried aloud to me; you broke my
barrier of deafness. You shone upon me; your radiance envel-
oped me; you put my blindness to flight."[9] The philosophical
or metaphysical situation is similar to the theological situation. There is no way to transcend the I-centered world of the
self, of language, of the perceived phenomena, to encounter
the underlying substrate of reality, unless reality pierces the
barrier from the other side and intrudes itself upon the self.
That is clearly impossible unless we assign to "reality" qualities of agency and intentionality which, without romantic
mystification, belong properly only to a person — that is, unless we assume that reality is or resembles God. Descartes
claimed that he could ascertain with confidence the existence
of God within a philosophical system beginning with the
thinking self, but few if any philosophers who have succeeded
him have been able to elucidate this crucial yet highly dubious
aspect of his thought or to build further on it. For example,
from a related position Thomas Nagel has argued recently that
to escape the utter relativism of the post-Cartesian subject

one must posit the existence of objective rationality, without which philosophical argument is pointless. But, Nagel continues, universal rationality, in which human thinking accords significantly with the nature of things at a deep level, is hard to account for without bringing God into the picture, a philosophical move he raises but strongly prefers to avoid.[10] One may argue, as Milton implicitly does, that without the divine Logos rationality is meaningless, but to one who begins by positing certainty only in the existence of the thinking subject such an argument will almost certainly be found unpalatable. One might begin with the subject but be forced at the end of the argument to deny the subject's certainty or centrality. Or, to put it another way, if God exists at all, he — as the Alpha and Omega of Revelation, "from whom / All things proceed, and up to him return" (5.469–70) — is far too important to remain at the level of a contingent, secondary proof. That is not where Descartes says he wishes to put God, at the periphery, but on this point his argument is incoherent.

Related to the sheer inward fall into subjectivity, in both Satan's soliloquy and Adam's, are elements that are familiar from traditional Christian analyses of the inward discourses of guilt. The experience of guilt can spiral downward into an abyss of damnation or it can point upward from the abyss toward the possibility of renewal, by means of examination of conscience, conviction of sin, contrition, repentance and the painful mental processes that lead to conversion, regeneration and the paradise within. Mortal man can repent and resume his journey; Satan cannot. Unable to respond to love with love, he is incapable of repentance, compunction or softening of the heart. A commonplace of Christian psychology is that one of the chief functions of conscience is, when it is disregarded, to inflict inward pain on the guilty, to "heap coals of fire" on their heads. Echoing Proverbs 25.22, Saint Paul advises the Romans not to take vengeance on their enemies and persecutors but instead to rouse their consciences by returning good for evil, which will work on their enemies from within, moving them to reconsider their ways, either to continue suffering or to repent. "Therefore if thine enemy hunger, feed him; if he thirst, give him drink: for in so doing thou shalt heap coals of fire on his head" (Rom. 12:20). Satan can only suffer, while Adam can repent. But both begin by suffering the same inward experience: guilt wakens conscience, conscience wakens pain, terror and despair, and the soul falls into the inner abyss. Satan's plunge into the depths begins precisely when "conscience wakes despair / That slumber'd" (4.23–24). The same thing happens to Adam: "Conscience, into what Abyss of fears / And horrors thou hast driv' me" (10.842–43). To the painful "coals of fire" provided by the Bible, Milton adds his own characteristic trope: disorientation, nausea and vertigo, a fall into the void.

In *Paradise Regained*, when Satan tempts Jesus to expel the monstrous Emperor Tiberius from his throne by force as punishment for his sins, Jesus replies: "Let his tormenter Conscience find him out" (4.130). In its way, conscience is a worse punishment than vengeance, more inward, intimate and inescapable. Unlike vengeance, however, its torments may point the victim toward repentance. Milton often portrays the inward workings of guilt leading to conviction of sin and repentance as excruciatingly painful, sometimes as a throbbing disease of the soul, sometimes as a sharp, medicinal probing that wounds as it cures. In Spenser's *Faerie Queene*, when Penance and his associates work their cure on Red Crosse the curative process that Spenser describes is intensely — even morbidly — painful. As the spiritual physicians or torturers starve and excise Red Crosse's ulcers and his gangrenous flesh, "his torment often was so great, / That like a Lyon he would cry and rore, / And rend his flesh, and his owne synewes eat" (1.10.28).[11]

Milton often uses imagery similar to Spenser's to describe the painful lashings of conscience in a guilty soul. The *locus classicus* is *Samson Agonistes*:

My griefs not only pain me
As a ling'ring disease,
But finding no redress, ferment and rage,
Nor less than wounds immedicable
Rankle, and fester, and gangrene,
To black mortification.
Thoughts my Tormentors arm'd with deadly stings
Mangle my apprehensive tenderest parts,
Exasperate, exulcerate, and raise
Dire inflammation. . . .

(617–26)

At this stage in his life Samson feels that no "cooling herb" or "med'cinal liquor," "Nor breath of Vernal Air from snowy *Alp*" (626–28) can cure him or ease his pain. These are Paul's coals of fire. Only repentance, forgiveness, grace and regeneration can ease the pain. What Samson does not yet recognize is that his cure is already at work, that the medicinal probing has begun, which is why his pain is more intense at this stage than it was when the play began.

When Satan falls, he brings into existence new things with new names. Among the dreadful things and names that spring from his head, proceeding from his first inward act of defiance and rejection, are "sin," "death," "guilt," "shame" and "pain." When the sword of Michael shears deeply into his right side during the war in heaven, "then Satan first knew pain, / And writh'd him to and fro convolv'd" (6.327–28). He is carried from the battle "Gnashing for anguish and despite and shame" (6.340). So, after their fall, Adam and Eve first know shame, guilt, pain and mortality. Along with physical pain, mental and spiritual pain enter the world. They are both penalties and cures for sin. Just as God provides death both as the just punishment for transgression and as the bitter cure for sinful suffering ("so Death becomes / His final remedy" [11.61–62]), he provides physical and mental pain as necessary gifts to warn sufferers, so they will seek a cure for their wounds, their diseases, their sinful states, while there is yet time. Although contemporary man is more than usually reluctant to suffer pain, yet physicians recognize it to be an indispensable symptom revealing deeper problems, therefore a salutary warning.

After his fall Adam's condition so closely resembles Samson's that Milton calls our attention to the resemblance in his well-known simile of the "Harlot-lap" (9.1059–62). Yet, unlike Samson, Adam says little about pain, disease or torment in his soliloquy. He is filled with "dread," "fear," "misery," "shame," "woe" and "horror" — key words on which his thoughts ring changes. The closest he comes to suffering pain is in his anxious wish that he could die at once, so that "no fear of worse / To mee and to my offspring would torment me / With cruel expectation" (10.780–82). That is, his chief suffering is not present pain but anticipation of future pain, when the torturer will begin to do his work in earnest. But those who are physically diseased can experience two different and distinct kinds of suffering. One is pain. The other, which can be even worse, is vertigo, dizziness, and nausea. As we have already seen, Milton adds to the biblical trope of pain his own characteristic trope of vertigo. This is true from the first moment of the Fall when Satan first experiences both pain and vertigo not in his duel with Michael or his soliloquy on Mount Niphates, but at the initiating subjective moment of his revolt, as described to him by his daughter Sin:

> All on a sudden miserable pain
> Surpris'd thee, dim thine eyes, and dizzy swum
> In darkness, while thy head flames thick and wide
> Threw forth.
>
> (2.752–55)

I would argue that just as Milton uses spiritual pain as the natural signifier for the guilty pangs of conscience, so he uses vertigo, dizziness and the sense of falling as a signifier for spiritual loss and disorientation, for forfeiture of faith, certainty and mental foundations, for precisely what I would call the fall into subjectivity. Sartre speaks from the heart of a similar kind of alienation in *La Nausée*. In a conversation with Arthur

Kinney, I mentioned that I meant to reconsider in this essay the "fall into subjectivity." He laughed on hearing the phrase, because we have both heard it before. Yet the fall into subjectivity has a particular richness of meaning in connection with *Paradise Lost*. Some of the pain of falling into sin is suggestively evoked in Milton's first description of Satan's fall, when the "Almighty Power" hurls him "headlong flaming from th' Ethereal Sky / With hideous ruin and combustion down / To bottomless perdition" (1.44–47). It is painful, certainly, to imagine being set on fire and thrown down like a burning brand. More than pain, however, what the passage evokes is vertigo. The first thing we are told is that Satan is hurled from heaven upside down, head first; the next, that the abyss into which he is thrown is "bottomless."

Numerous readers have remarked how, in his second recollection of the angels' fall, Milton appeals to our sense of kinesthesia. He imaginatively evokes our sense of balance and of bodily orientation, a sense additional to the five traditional senses. When things go awry, physically or spiritually, the sense of orientation is transformed into a sense of disorientation. As Mulciber falls, he tumbles and rotates in a leisurely, strangely beautiful fashion, until we see as if from below how swift his fall really is. As he falls we participate with him in what it feels like to be thrown bodily from an immense height, to plunge through vast reaches of space, to hurtle downward faster and faster as subjective time slows to a crawl.

> And how he fell
> From Heav'n, they fabl'd, thrown by angry *Jove*
> Sheer o'er the Crystal Battlements: from Morn
> To Noon he fell, from Noon to dewy Eve,
> A Summer's day; and with the setting Sun
> Dropt from the Zenith like a falling Star,
> On Lemnos th' Aegean Isle.
>
> (1.740–46)

The tales of Marsyas and Philomel have taught generations of artists how to transform painful suffering into beautiful artifacts. But Milton does not allow us to rest even in that consolation:

> Thus they relate,
> Erring; for he with this rebellious rout
> Fell long before; nor aught avail'd him now
> To have built in Heav'n high Tow'rs; nor did he scape
> By all his Engines, but was headlong sent
> With his industrious crew to build in hell.
>
> (1.746–51)

Milton gives us another taste of helpless, vertiginous motion when Satan, after standing for a moment poised "on the brink of Hell" (2.918) to survey Chaos, hurls himself outward into the primal abyss:

> At last his Sail-broad Vans
> He spreads for flight, and in the surging smoke
> Uplifted spurns the ground, thence many a League
> As in a cloudy Chair ascending rides
> Audacious, but that seat soon failing, meets
> A vast vacuity: all unawares
> Flutt'ring his pennons vain plumb down he drops
> Ten thousand fadom deep, and to this hour
> Down had been falling, had not by ill chance
> The strong rebuff of some tumultuous cloud
> Instinct with Fire and Nitre hurried him
> As many miles aloft.
>
> (2.927–38)

It is hard to believe that anyone could have captured these dizzying sense experiences who lived long before it was possible to fly in bad weather and feel the sudden lurch of a downdraft, who never even felt the sensation of an elevator lurching to a stop.[12]

Milton tells us that Satan's dizzying and disorienting flight is governed by "chance." Perhaps Chaos is one of those regions, physical or spiritual, from which God tells us that he has voluntarily withdrawn his presence, thus relinquishing to chance and fortune all who dare to enter and put themselves outside his providential protection. If so, Satan's experience argues, as Boethius and others had long argued, that chance is not a reliable supporter of free agency, for it renders Satan passively helpless. Luckily for him, but unluckily for us, he escapes the threatened fate of falling forever into "vast vacuity," a hapless journey that would have begun in the first days of the world and lasted more than 5,500 years "to this hour" in which Milton wrote. But although Satan escapes falling forever into Chaos, this daunting moment serves as an outward sign of a similar, inward fall that he cannot escape: the loss of faith and certainty, the loss of intellectual footing and control, the loss of free will, as he plunges deeper and deeper into irremediable subjectivity. The inner life, potentially a way up to salvation, is also potentially a way down into bottomless perdition. The dizzy, nauseous, disorienting fall of Satan and Adam alike plunges them into the solipsistic void of the self.

The inward fall is potentiated by sin and guilt but in *Paradise Lost* not actualized until that moment when the eyes of the mind turn inward. Then the "Abyss of fears / And horrors" opens and reveals itself. Yet, as the blind poet tells us, inward vision is also necessary for the spiritual life:

> So much the rather thou Celestial Light
> Shine inward, and the mind through all her powers
> Irradiate, there plant eyes, all mist from thence
> Purge and disperse, that I may see and tell
> Of things invisible to mortal sight.
>
> (3.51–55)

Since the time of Plato philosophers have said that the unexamined life is not worth living. *Nosce teipsum*, "know thyself," has undergone many philosophical and religious revisions. In the middle ages, the Platonic ideal of self-knowledge, mediated and revised by Augustine, was chiefly realized in examination of conscience as a step leading to confession and conversion. By Milton's time introspection and examination of conscience were well established as salutary spiritual activities, necessary preludes to repentance and forgiveness. If anything, Protestantism rendered them more inward and private, concerns for the individual rather than the community. Yet as the present age has grown more and more inward-turning, self-consciousness and self-study have come to seem less satisfying and revitalizing. C. S. Lewis was something of an authority on this modern dilemma, as Stephen Logan points out in a recent essay. From Samuel Alexander's *Space, Time, and Deity* Lewis picked up the distinction, which he subsequently called an "indispensable tool of thought," between participating fully in an experience from within it and consciously examining an experience from outside of it.[13] An analogy would be the difference between looking at a natural scene through a pair of eyeglasses or refocusing your eyes on the glasses. Or we might consider the twin poles of reading and of literary criticism as represented by Victorian enthusiasts and postmodern deconstructionists, one type of reader giving himself with uncritical enjoyment to the experience, the other suspiciously holding back, fearful of ideological contamination, preferring to demystify and dissect. As Logan argues, "The essential point is that these two forms of attention are mutually exclusive. If you analyze the taste of strawberries you are no longer experiencing it. You are experiencing instead the act of analysis." If this is true of the habit of analysis directed outward, it is even more true when analysis is directed inward. "If you become over-interested in the emotions produced in you by attention to a loved one, you cease attending to the loved one and cease to experience the emotions" (72). To put the matter in broader terms, if you spend too much time analyzing your life, you cease to live. In this regard, living is primary, analysis is secondary.

Yet Milton, like most of his contemporaries, would argue that, in a fallen world, some degree of analysis and introspection, some thoughtful distinguishing between good and evil so as to choose the good, is necessary. In practice, such analytical activity may sometimes need to get very detailed, wearisome and tedious, as in the myth of Psyche, upon whom, as Milton reminds us in *Areopagitica*, Venus imposed the burden of "incessant labor to cull out and sort asunder" "those confused seeds." Acute analytical attention is often necessary to achieve the good life because "Good and evil we know in the field of this world grow up together almost inseparably; and the knowledge of good is . . . involved and interwoven with the knowledge of evil." The origin of this knotty problem, and therefore of the need for constant close analysis and introspection, was of course the Fall. "It was from out the rind of one apple tasted, that the knowledge of good and evil, as two twins cleaving together, leapt forth into the world."[14] It suits Milton's purpose in *Areopagitica* to leave the matter at that, so as to give no grounds for the advocates of prior censorship to make their case for suppressing certain kinds of knowledge. We must be free to study and sort out as wide a selection of texts as possible, so as to make informed decisions. We must analyze to live. But we may remember that in Apuleius's version of the myth Psyche would never have finished the tedious, soul-destroying work of sorting out the seeds if she had not been helped by friendly ants. Human powers blanch and fail at such an impossible analytical task. In *Areopagitica*, Milton is confident that careful reasoning can sort out the seeds, can know good by looking very closely at evil and carefully distinguishing between the two. "Let her and Falsehood grapple; who ever knew Truth put to the worse, in a free and open encounter?" (746). Yet the case is much different in *Paradise Lost*. After the failure to reform English government and religion, Milton is far less confident in the power of analytical reason to discriminate and choose correctly between truth and falsehood. As history unfolds in *Paradise Lost*, far from prevailing over falsehood, "Truth shall retire / Bestuck with sland'rous darts" (12.535–36). There is no likelihood that the seeds can be properly sorted.

In general, self-analysis and introspection work best when dealing with faults and failures. As Logan suggests, watching yourself love is unhealthy, but "If . . . you want to free yourself from a bad emotion, such as resentment, you can at least interrupt it by contemplating the emotion itself and know its cause" (72). Which is to say that ideally you should know yourself by focusing analytically on your faults, while refraining from too close or lingering an analysis of your strengths and virtues. But if Milton and the Christian-classical tradition are right, that would be impossible. How can we distinguish our faults from our virtues in the first place? Discrimination, that is analysis, is the first task. It is difficult for people to weigh their faults impartially, or even to see them. Such is the danger of the unexamined life. Moreover, Michael does not instruct Adam only to peruse his inward faults and consult his conscience as he combs through his mind for sins to be purged and avoided, but above all to seek for the positive spiritual experience of "a paradise within thee happier far." No longer is it possible for a newly created Adam simply to "feel that I am happier than I know" (8.282). Once having fallen, he cannot escape the two-sided trap and gift of self-consciousness.

Although Milton was certainly an individualist by instinct and conviction, his poetry also reveals that he feared isolation and loneliness. Fallen subjectivity entails isolation and loneliness. Before the Fall, Adam and Eve evidently wandered apart from time to time, as Eve does during Adam's conversation with Raphael, but without ever thinking or feeling that they were alone. After the Fall comes a new sense of separation, of exile, of "distance and distaste" (9.9), of banishment and alienation. We may think of "alienation" as a modern concept, perhaps as a Marxist term, but Milton's use of the word anticipates its modern sense of internal exile and estrangement from the community. Uriel, looking down from the sun, recognizes Satan's true nature not only from the passions that are revealed in his face, on which many Miltonists have remarked, but from his look or posture of alienation; he "soon discern'd his looks / Alien from Heav'n, with passions foul obscur'd" (4.570–71). Satan is out of place; he no longer belongs. Similarly Abdiel addresses Satan as "alienate from God" (5.877). Whole nations and churches can fall away from God and community in this manner, as is the case with "alienated *Judah*" and its "dark Idolatries" (1.456–57). At the opening of book 9, alienation is one aspect of the chasm that opens between heaven and earth, god and man: "foul distrust, and breach / Disloyal on the part of Man, revolt, and disobedience: On the part of Heav'n / Now alienated, distance and distaste" (9.6–8). As Satan tells Sin and Death, God has withdrawn his presence from the world, "Retiring, by his own doom alienated" (10.378), giving the hellish trio room to bridge the abyss from below and claim the abandoned world as their conquered empire.

With withdrawal and alienation come loss of community and a new sense of loneliness. Milton was well acquainted with loneliness. It is implicit in *Lycidas*, where the singer who once experienced youthful friendship, companionship and community, has been forced by his encounter with death and loss to exchange companionable needs and pleasures for isolation:

> Meanwhile the Rural ditties were not mute,
> Temper'd to th'Oaten Flute;
> Rough *Satyrs* danc'd, and *Fauns* with clov'n heel
> From the glad sound would not be absent long,
> And old *Damaetas* lov'd to hear our song.
>   But O the heavy change, now thou art gone,
> Now thou art gone, and never must return!
>
>   (32–38)

Not even the religious consolation of Christ's Resurrection, the vision of Edward King's salvation and reception into the company of the saints, or the implied prospect of his own eternal life after death "In the blest Kingdoms meek of joy and

love" (177) provides the singer of this "Monody" with relief
from isolation or — at least at the moment — with a renewal
of the communal companionship he once had and now has
lost. His thoughts are eager, his music Doric, his mood hopeful as he confronts the future and pursues his chosen vocation. Still he remains alone in an empty landscape.

It was, of course, the death of his close friend, Charles
Diodati, that most strongly brought home to Milton the essential loneliness of human beings in this world, painfully
alienated from one another, discordant in their feelings, and —
should they find companionship — faced with inevitable loss:

> Nos durum genus, et diris exercita fatis
> Gens, homines, aliena animis, et pectore discors,
> Vix sibi quisque parem de millibus invenit unum,
> Aut, si sors dederit tandem non aspera votis,
> Illum inopina dies, qua non speravis hora
> Surrupit, aeternum linquens in saecula damnum.
>
> (106–11)

> [But we men are a painful race, a stock tormented by fate, with
> minds mutually alienated and hearts discordant. A man can
> hardly find a comrade for himself in a thousand; or, if one is
> granted to us by a fate at last not unkind to our prayers, a day
> and hour when we apprehend nothing snatches him away,
> leaving an eternal loss to all the years.][15]

The problem, for Milton as for modernity in general, arises
from an absence of mediation and subsidiarity in the society
he envisages. The Middle Ages were rich in mediating institutions and overlapping communities: feudal bonds of loyalty
and obligation, the local parish with its rites and sacraments,
burial societies, and especially the various guilds and voluntary
associations.[16] The Middle Ages had a more communal sense
of prayer and reconciliation, especially of intercessory prayer
for others, including the dead. Since religion was then at the
heart of the culture — and was at least the remote foundation
of our present secular culture — this loss of intermediation is

most readily seen in the realm of prayer and intercession. Dante's *Commedia* shows us a universe of intermediation and intercession, represented most obviously by Beatrice but also by Mary and the angels and saints whom we encounter in the *Paradiso*. Prayer by one person for another is constant and efficacious. Only the damned in the *Inferno* are lost to the communion of saints, cut off, individualized, isolated within themselves, unable to love and be loved. The angels and saints are given active parts to play in the economy of salvation. With the help of Virgil and through the mediation of Beatrice, Dante is led along his journey upward. With Beatrice's aid and the intercession of Bernard and Mary, Dante is able at the end of his journey to gaze at last on the heavenly radiance of the Trinity. All is accomplished through divine grace, without which nothing would be possible; but Dante's God freely and generously delegates his grace to his servants and is ready to hear intercessory prayers.

By contrast, Milton's God uses angelic messengers to convey his word but never gives them any power to act in the economy of salvation. They do his will, carry out his orders unquestioningly, and communicate information but, as exemplified most clearly by the outcome of the first two days of the war in heaven and by Satan's encounter with the angelic guard in Eden, they have no apparent power or opportunity to further God's providential plans. Nor are they asked or permitted to intercede with God for grace. In England Anglicans and Puritans alike rejected the legitimacy of praying to the saints or of asking them to pray for them or their loved ones. Accordingly, in *Paradise Lost* only the Son has such delegated powers. He is the sole high priest, king, intercessor, and advocate (11.14–44).

Milton's mentality is, of course, Protestant, but he carries matters further toward a fundamental individualism than many of his fellow Protestants as a result of his strong belief in the total individuation of grace. Just as Milton's angels and saints are essentially excluded from the active economy of salvation, so in his view are churches and nations. The first duty of the Church is to get out of the way and to let God work. There are perhaps two significant exceptions to this principle of total focus on the individual. One — rarely found in this life — is friendship, as exemplified by the figure of Diodati. The other is marriage. Before the Fall, Adam and Eve are helpmeets, mutual supports and loving companions. After the Fall they resume their close companionship. Even the line that feminists find most troubling in the poem, "Hee for God only, shee for God in him" (4.299), seems determined to suggest, although with awkward asymmetry, what would otherwise be unthinkable to Milton, that grace can be mediated. Certainly it suggests that their communal relationship, in and under God, is close. Just so Eve's closing words to Adam: "thou to mee / Art all things under Heav'n, all places thou" (12.617–18). Milton further suggests that, after the Flood, there was a time when men lived "in joy unblam'd . . . / Long time in peace by Families and Tribes / Under paternal rule" (12.22–24). So the intimate community provided by marriage might conceivably extend to family and even to whole tribes. But Nimrod brings this period of primitive peace to an end with his invention of tyranny, glory and empire, and seemingly it is never repeated. The possibilities for community and companionship are limited. Instead of focusing on communities, Milton gives us a vision of salvation history that famously puts all its emphasis on singular election and accomplishment, on a succession of figures representing the "one just Man" (11.818, 890), anticipated and exemplified among the angels by Abdiel. This theme is, of course, biblical, but Milton noticeably elides any concomitant emphasis, which would be equally biblical, on Israel as the chosen community.

The sociologist David Riesman coined the telling phrase "the lonely crowd" to characterize what he describes as the typically modern condition of man: isolated individuals in a faceless, anonymous nation-state, with few mediating institutions.[17] Thomas Hobbes's frightfully inhuman image of Leviathan anticipates this typically modernist relationship between the individual and the state, with no vital communal institutions to intervene between them and moderate the psychological pressures. When he looks at humanity, Hobbes can see nothing but selfish individuals, who if given the chance would pit themselves against one another in a war of all against all. Therefore they must consent, from motives of self-protection, to be forcibly squeezed together willy-nilly into the gigantic body pictured in the frontispiece to the first edition: a strange, monstrous mutation of the more human "body politic" posited by classical and medieval political thinkers.

When we look for the phenomenon of the lonely crowd in *Paradise Lost* we find it everywhere depicted after the fall: threatening, anonymous crowds, huge numbers of faceless angels or men, and among them lonely, isolated individuals. It is the characteristic situation of hell, where Satan complains there is "neither joy nor love, but fierce desire" (4.509). Satan and Beelzebub consult with each other as fellow officers and politicians, but not as friends. Typical is the mass rally convened when Satan addresses his defeated troops, which strangely anticipates the mass political rallies staged by modern totalitarian states under the leadership of Hitler, Stalin or Mao:

> All in a moment through the gloom were seen
> Ten thousand Banners rise into the Air
> With Orient Colors waving: with them rose
> A Forest huge of Spears: and thronging Helms
> Appear'd, and serried Shields in thick array
> Of depth immeasurable; Anon they move
> In perfect *Phalanx* to the *Dorian* mood
> Of flutes and soft Recorders.
>
> (1.544–51)

As Milton shows us, the devils can work together, can move in unison in perfect military order. Similarly they can agree after debate on a plan of action at the Great Consult. But Milton is surely ironic in his words of praise: "O shame to men! Devil with Devil damn'd / Firm concord holds" (496–97). What he shows us is not something admirable: it is based on military and imperial convenience, not loving fellowship or community. The "concord" of the devils precisely resembles the situation of individuals in Hobbes's nation-state as leviathan.

Such a monolithic nation-state is the end product of Hobbes's argument for submission of the individual will to the general, since the contractual agreement or implied covenant to obey an absolute monarch is the surest means that a single person, thrust into a lawless and loveless world and concerned above all for his own survival, has to ensure self-protection and self-gratification. Hobbes does not advocate mediating or subsidiary institutions or voluntary associations of any kind. Suspicious of faction, he would consider them potentially divisive. They would undermine absolute power, which the state requires, in his view, to keep the peace against the disruptions of individual ambition, division of opinion and the threat of civil war. For Hobbes, liberty consists paradoxically in absolute, arbitrary, unquestioning obedience to the sovereign power of the state: "The Liberty of a Subject, Lyeth therefore only in those things, which in regulating their actions, the Soveraign hath prætermitted. . . . [N]othing the soveraign Representative can doe to a Subject, on what pretence soever, can properly be called Injustice, or Injury."[18] Milton, who certainly had no love of absolute rule, shows us in his hell an exaggerated picture of the perfect Hobbesian state, exhibiting the perfectly disciplined unity of perfectly self-centered individuals. Completely absent from his hell are personal freedom, love, concern for others and the possibility of personal relationships, such as any true community would allow and support.

That the angels had another kind of life, a more personal, intimate kind of companionship with one another before they fell, is suggested by several of Milton's scenes set in heaven among the loyal angels and by Raphael's hint to Adam concerning angelic lovemaking. "Let it suffice thee that thou know'st us happy," Raphael tells Adam, and then he extends the logic of that supposition: "without Love no happiness" (8.621–22). Evidently for Milton unhindered enjoyment of the beatific vision and basking in the love of God will not suffice for full happiness. There must also be close companionship among the inhabitants of heaven, a true society and a loving community. Whether we take Raphael's description of angelic lovemaking literally as a kind of sex or, with C. S. Lewis, more allegorically and spiritually,[19] it is evident that Milton wants the inhabitants of heaven to escape the burden of loneliness, isolation and frustration in love so often experienced in this world. There is a world of meaning in the earliest words that Satan speaks in *Paradise Lost*. He addresses them to Beelzebub the evening before the war in heaven: "sleep'st thou, Companion dear?" (5.673). His question must be read as the sugared beginning of a rhetorically skilled seduction to revolt and damnation, but if that is true then it must also be read as his expected and customary way of addressing his once dear and intimate friend, perhaps we should say his beloved friend, with whom he says he was used to share his inmost thoughts: "Thou to me thy thoughts / Wast wont, I mine to thee was wont to impart; / Both waking we were one; how then can now / Thy sleep dissent?" (5.676–79). Satan's rebellion, like Adam's, begins in, and is entangled with, a sense of estrangement from his closest companion and soul mate. It even begins with the avowal of hurt affection that characterizes a lovers' quarrel.

We cannot imagine Satan or any of the devils speaking to each other in such a loving and intimate fashion after their fall. Satan's first words to Beelzebub in hell are: "If thou beest hee; But O how fall'n! how chang'd / From him, who in the happy Realms of Light / Cloth'd with transcendent brightness didst outshine / Myriads though bright" (1.84–87). Among the many implications of the terrible (and mutual) transformation with which Satan's eyes are confronted is this: that Beelzebub, like his former "darling" Sin, is no longer good looking, no longer conceivable as an object of his love. In Satan's mind the past is instantly revised. He remembers or pretends to remember Beelzebub merely as a close military associate, a fellow rebel, a sharer in the desperate cause. After his fall, Satan can produce at best only a menacing, ironic parody of love, as he does in thoughts addressed silently to the unfallen Adam and Eve: "League with you I seek / And mutual amity so strait, so close, / That I with you must dwell, or you with me / Henceforth" (4.375–78). Never again will Satan or his fellows be able to love each other truly, or even to speak to anyone about love and intimacy, as once they did in heaven.

So also to a lesser extent with fallen men. Although human beings are still capable and needful of love, they will seldom find it. They will typically confuse love with lust and desire, "Marrying or prostituting, as befell, / Rape or adultery" (11.716–17). As incapable of true fellowship and community as of loving marriages, they will become the anonymous, slavish followers of tyrants or the willing dupes of churches. Even the most virtuous among them, as they walk hand-in-hand with a devoted and loving spouse must, like Adam and Eve, pursue the "paradise within" them "with wand'ring steps and slow," and along a "solitary way" (12.648–49). Thus they will be spiritually solitary even in the closest of company. The poet himself, who imagines and builds for us his marvelous vision of a paradise within, and who confidently declares that this new inward paradise can be happier far than the Paradise that was lost, is nonetheless moved to compare himself to a bird that "Sings darkling, and in shadiest Covert hid" (3.39–40). He tells us that he is "cut off" "from the cheerful ways of men" (3.46–47). He is alone in the dark not only because he is blind but also because he writes from within the darkness and corruption of the fallen world, of which his blindness is emblematic: "On evil days though fall'n, and evil tongues; / In darkness, and with dangers compast round, / And solitude" (7.26–28). He finds some relief from the encroachments of solitude, isolation and loneliness — he is "yet not alone" altogether — only because of the nightly visitations of his muse, a figure who (if not imaginary) represents both his divinely appointed vocation — the satisfaction of great things well made and well done — and the personal grace and enlightenment of the Holy Spirit. But to speak of his social nature, man is *durum genus*, a hard race, congenitally lonely. Seldom may true friendship and companionship be found in this life. In the modern, individualist world toward which *Paradise Lost* points, religion will diminish from something found in churches and parishes as well as within the soul, something with social and communal as well as private aspects, into something found only within the minds of the fit few. Indeed those were the only places, according to Milton's severely Protestant, revisionist view of history, where true religion was ever to be found.

So it was even from the beginning, when God drove Adam and Eve from the Garden, when he sent Abraham into exile from his home and family, and when the Son resolved to be a messiah who would let inward persuasion, individual by individual, do the work of outward fear. In the future, toward which Milton sets his face along with Adam and Eve, true community and companionship of any real depth will be absent or rare. As Milton acknowledges concerning his epic vocation in *Epitaphium Damonis*, "Quid enim? omnia non licet uni, / Non sperasse uni licet omnia" [What then? One man cannot do everything, nor (can one man) so much as hope to do everything].[20] He firmly resolves to try, but the task will be lonely. If a man falls from grace into sin, he will tumble into dizzying inward depths of alienation and estrangement and may never again escape the bottomless pit of subjectivity. If aided by grace he rises again, he can expect only inward consolation of his hurts and continuing loneliness. As he journeys toward the future, a whole world will unfold before him "where to choose." The possibilities are endless. The distant goal of his journey, Michael assures Adam — perhaps in due course even the present inward state of his mind — will be "happier far" than the Paradise he has lost. Every exile, however, must fall into himself or travel onward alone, aided sometimes by a companion, but still essentially alone.

Bugswords
Epilogue

Edward W. Tayler

My topic is bugswords. In my day, in my old-fashioned graduate school, the reigning orthodoxy was philological, centered
in textual and historical scholarship; the emerging, and liberating, orthodoxy was the New Criticism. In discussing Marvell's "Horatian Ode upon Cromwell's Return from Ireland,"
we understood that we were to take our stand with the Christian humanism of Douglas Bush of Harvard and to treat the
ironic ambiguities found in the ode by Cleanth Brooks of Yale
with the proper mix of alarm and contempt. This mock dichotomy, between something called scholarship and something
called criticism, seemed real enough to us at the time because it seemed that our jobs depended on it. The more recent
mock dichotomy, between something called totalizing essen-
tialism and something called theoretical discourse, seems
real enough to graduate students because it seems that jobs
depend on it.

During and after World War II, teachers of my generation
tended more and more to confine their academic attentions

to the work of art as heterocosm, a little world made cunningly on the model of a Rolex with a transcendental battery. Although we were receiving our instructions from the British (Richards, Empson) and from displaced Southern agrarians like Brooks and Tate, many of us felt that our jobs were on the line, and most of us remained mindful of what had happened to the departments of classics.

We had learned from our teachers, those textual scholars who are now known as historical positivists, to suspect the individual words of the text, and in a pinch we could hazard a guess as to whether Hamlet wanted his too solid or his too sullied flesh to melt. The New Criticism transformed our pedagogy and transported us into a brave new world of publication: instead of suspecting some of the words of the text we now held the *entire* text under an all-encompassing suspicion. *Lycidas* was no longer a pastoral elegy lamenting the death of Edward King; it was really about Milton the aspiring poet. "The Canonization" was no longer about religion, sex and a lover and his lass; it was about poetry and Donne the poet. Instead of coming into class to say, I have discovered the secret meaning of "too too solid" in *Hamlet*, I could now go in to class and say, I will reveal to you the secret meaning of the entire play, its oedipal urges and its formal enigmas. I would also feel morally obligated to qualify my pedagogical triumph by pointing out that we must respect the mysterious genesis of the work of art in the artist's dissociated or undissociated sensibility, which issues in functional ambiguities, in telling ironies, and in the artistic unity that derives, paradoxically, from the "language of paradox," and which instantly realigns the whole tradition in relation to the individual talent of the artist. The preeminent bugswords, which allowed us to think and to write with confidence, that shaped our responses and judgments, were "ambiguity," "paradox" and "irony."

This new and liberating theory rapidly calcified and introduced, as always, its own protocols, its own limits and constraints, its own attempts at censorship, its own bugs-words. In order to teach the great poems we had to commit fallacies, like the intentional, and subscribe to heresies, like that of paraphrase. Some of us still had authors, though it was not very sophisticated to mention them (that would be the biographical fallacy); and some allowed as how there might well be a world outside the poem, though only undergradu-ates assumed that it was real (that would be the fallacy of imitative form).

The Francophiliac connections began to be exploited during the sixties and seventies; first a brief phase of phenomenology (Georges Poulet); then the anthropological and structuralist theories of Lévi-Strauss, along with the anthropological, Marx-ist, narratological and linguistic admixtures of Roland Barthes; then Derrida's meditations on Heidegger and the logocentric tradition that eventuated in the kind of Nietzschean "decon-struction" popularized by Paul de Man and J. Hillis Miller at Yale; along with the feminist linguistic Freudianism of Lacan and the linguistic, discontinuous epistemes of Foucault, some-times combined uneasily with the neo-Marxism of Louis Althusser — all of them united only in their hyperbolical misreadings of Saussure. Most of these theories denied that anything had an answer to anything but nevertheless man-aged to provide, perhaps necessarily, an answer to everything: everything is reducible to the binary oppositions of cultural structures, everything is reducible to economic structures, everything is reducible to power, everything is reducible to language, everything is reducible, in short, and perhaps nec-essarily. . . . It might have gone many another way, the arc of the bugswords might well have described another course.

For example: between, say, 1973 and 1983 in the United States, and depending of course on whether the critic hailed from the provinces or from Yale, the word "deconstruction" seemed always-already prepared for canonization; but the rebarbative technicalities advocated by Derrida proved too rigorous for Americans, who in any case invariably turn the theoretical into the methodological; and so the word quickly lost its talismanic power, seemingly content to decline into dictionary meanings synonymous with "unmask" or "de-mystify." Or, to take another example, Hillis Miller, while still at Yale, tried to stake out some territory within the im-perium of Derrida and de Man: Miller boldly, and endearingly, proposed to divide the entire world of words, which is to say the world, into two rhetorical figures — catachresis and pro-sopopoeia. How is this possible, some of you may ask? Easy. Prosopopoeia, by which we may, for example, make the dead speak, signifies the presence of absence; and catachresis, by which we may, for example, lend a leg to a table, signifies the absence of presence. Two tricks make game. Easy.

But Miller's words, unlike the word "deconstruction," from, say, 1973 to 1983, never attained the exalted status of bugs-words. Everybody gets to be famous for 15 minutes but only a professor can coin a bugsword for a decade. Gerald Prince, aware of these matters but lacking the concept of bugsword, has pointed to the way, in France and in anticipation of its deployment here, the one word "narrative" became an impe-rial term and "commence à déloger d'autres termes," such as explication, argument, fiction, art, message, even theory and ideology; and how the term "narrative" then infiltrated phi-losophy, anthropology, sociology and other disciplines — un-til eventually we find ourselves explaining that the Kurds are in big trouble because they lack their own narrative. The word, no longer synonymous with story, becomes a means of estab-lishing legitimacy and constituting authority: the word has become a bugsword.

In a manuscript note to his elucidation of the faculties of reason, will and appetite in *The Lawes of Ecclesiasticall Pol-ity*, the judicious Hooker allows that "There are certaine wordes, as Nature, Reason, Will, and such like, which where-soever you find named, you suspect them presently as bugs wordes, because what they mean you do not indeed as you ought apprehend." Bugwords, more often bugswords, resemble the "working words" of Tamburlaine, born to exercise imperial sway: they are bogey, boogeyman words; like Milton's bullyboys, these words are "flown with insolence and wine," and they make the streets their own; their function is to threaten, swagger, intimidate — to coerce, even to menace, with the nightmare of a Big Meaning that "you do not indeed as you ought apprehend." The totemic word "narrative" breathes and moves, becomes predatory flesh, devours its sibling wordlings, and then spawns: narrative, narrativity, narrativizing, narratology. Finally, with its insemination into more and more specialized areas, the bugsword crystallizes into particulate meanings, into usages susceptible of exact definition; and then it loses what Wallace Stevens would call its "glamour" and its "flash."

The bugsword, shorn of its beams, needs to be replaced by a neologism or, preferably, with an old word that has been emptied — for the initiated — of its older meanings: it is a process of inverted kenosis, in which the word empties itself of its ordinary-language content in order to assume godhead. For instance, the word "discourse." With the publication of *Ècrits* in 1966, written in prose that embodied his dictum that the structure of the unconscious is the structure of language, Lacan helped to ensure, through the exercise of his own passionate opacity, that "discourse," as in the "discourse of the unconscious" or the "discourse of the hysteric," would be elevated to the rank of bugsword. In this unconscious effort he found an unwitting but powerful accomplice in Foucault. Since, according to Foucault, the "analysis of statements operates . . . without reference to a cogito," the word "discourse" must not be understood as the "majestically unfolding manifestation of a thinking, knowing, speaking subject, but, on the contrary, a totality, in which the dispersion of the subject and his discontinuity with himself may be determined." Discourse no longer emanates from speaker or author, no longer even from the unconscious: it has no determinate source, not even an ascertainable direction, for it surrounds us as a totality, the only totality there is; Lacan's identification of the world with the world of words has become "discourse," "discourse" that is surround sound that mouths and mumbles the "dispersion of the subject" into an infinitude of gaps, fissures, discontinuities and ruptures. The word "discourse" thus becomes a mighty noise, a bugsword. Again, as with Hillis Miller, it might have turned out differently. With his compelling notion of "interpellation" and his emphasis on the *imaginary* relations of ideology (Marxism for English professors), Althusser might have succeeded in emptying the word "ideology" of enough significance so that it could become a free-floating signifier, a bugsword. It didn't happen. Now we know that "discourse," having replaced "narrative," will be the imperial word that exercises hegemony over weaker words like "colonialism" or "feminism," demoting them to adjectival status, as in "subaltern discourse" and "feminist discourse," or relegating them to the genitive, as in "discourse of colonialism." The word "discourse" will then — the verbal equivalent of libido dominandi — censor or even displace still weaker words, such as "author," "individual," "self," and even "subject." The word "discourse," being now a kenotic, talismanic term, prosecutes its anonymous censorship while going about its assigned task, a task once assigned to that long-gone bugsword "deconstruction," of demystifying the sources of power: the subject becomes that which is subjected (in a variety of "subject positions"), and the power of discourse becomes the discourse of power. And so on: professors and graduate students excitedly engaged, without quite being aware of it, in automatic thinking and writing. Language, which is to say bugswords, speaks professors.

Theoretical positions devolve from, or at least intimately involve, feelings about what constitutes the human subject, which is to say, feelings about oneself. Ben Jonson, anticipating the "classical Classical Philologist" whom I shall quote in a moment, felt that *"Language* most shewes a man: speak that I may see thee." Heidegger, anticipating Foucault, felt that "language speaks man." Elizabethans talked a lot about order because they didn't have any; modern academics talk about power for roughly the same reason. Having read "theory" for at least a decade, I can testify that there's nothing much wrong with it unless one seeks to apply it.

Since "discourse" shows signs lately of going the way of "deconstruction" and "narrative," I feel free to introduce a new theoretical bugsword — not that I think it's likely to catch on. It still possesses a definable if disreputable meaning. I know. No more meanings, only indeterminacies endlessly deferred; no more books, only texts bandying signs with other texts, spasms of semiosis that engender what Meyer Abrams calls a "ceaseless echolalia, a vertical and lateral reverberation from sign to sign of ghostly nonpresences emanating from no voice, intended by no one, referring to nothing, bombinating in the void." Into this buzz and roil of Rabelais's *in vacuo bombinans* I want to introduce an always-already brand-new old-style bugsword: *intention,* as in the Intention of Another Human Being.

James Vincent Cunningham, with an insistency unparalleled in its passion among American and British scholars of his generation, wanted to know what the other person *meant,* what the other person *intended.* Cunningham, who liked to refer to himself as a "classical Classical Philologist," predictably argues that historical interpretation ought not to bruise the work of art into a configuration of theoretical abstractions, nor should it pander to the reader as Narcissus by appealing to universal values — or to any number of other specious principles — in order to render the past "relevant." Rather, the practice of historical interpretation ought "to enable us to see how we could think and feel *otherwise* than we do" [my emphasis].

And then Cunningham draws the atheoretical analogy that

alone lends human significance to our reading and teaching: "In fact," says Cunningham, "the problem that is here raised with respect to literature is really the problem of any human relationship: Shall we understand another on his terms or on ours? It is the problem of affection and truth, of appreciation and scholarship. . . ."

"Now, it is common experience," continues Cunningham, "that affection begins in misunderstanding."

> We see our own meanings in what we love and we misconstrue for our own purposes. But life will not leave us there, and not only because of external pressures. What concerns us is naturally an object of study. We sit across the room and trace the lineaments of experience on the face of concern, and we find it is not what we thought it was. We come to see that what [Shakespeare or Milton] is saying is not what we thought he was saying, and we come finally to appreciate it for what it is. Where before we had constructed the fact from our feeling, we now construct our feeling from the fact. The end of affection and concern is accuracy and truth, with an alteration but no diminution of feeling.

Cunningham not only assumes that we may find ways to reach toward an understanding of persons now gone from us but also implies that we may in some measure learn from the past how to know and how to love; and my personal experience allows me to suppose that Cunningham's "alteration but no diminution of feeling" might well read "with an alteration and augmentation of feeling." Many a man and woman, after all, "lives a burden to the earth," or so Milton felt; "but a good book," he goes on to say, "is the precious lifeblood of a master spirit, embalmed and treasured up on purpose to a life beyond life." So maybe we should live it up a little. . . . As Marvin Mudrick liked to say, books aren't life, but then what is?

Notes

Notes to Introduction/Berley

1. Ralph Waldo Emerson, "Self-Reliance," in *Emerson's Essays*, ed. Irwin Erdman (1926; reprint, New York: Harper and Row, 1951), 32.

2. Martial, Epigram 1.38, in *Epigrams*, ed. D. R. Shackleton Bailey (Cambridge: Harvard University Press, 1993), 66.

3. Ben Jonson, "To the Reader," in *Ben Jonson: The Complete Poems*, ed. George Parfitt (New Haven: Yale University Press, 1975), 35.

4. Later published as "The Patience of Shakespeare" in Frank Kermode, *Shakespeare, Spenser, Donne* (London: Routledge and Kegan Paul, 1971), 149–63.

5. C. A. Patrides, ed., *Milton's Epic Poetry* (Middlesex, England: Penguin, 1967), 9.

6. Edward W. Tayler, *Nature and Art in Renaissance Literature* (New York: Columbia University Press, 1964), 1.

7. Edward W. Tayler, *Milton's Poetry: Its Development in Time* (Pittsburgh: Duquesne University Press, 1979), 1–2.

8. Tayler, *Milton's Poetry*, 2.

9. Tayler, *Nature and Art*, 9.

10. Edward W. Tayler, *Donne's Idea of a Woman: Structure and Meaning in "The Anniversaries"* (New York: Columbia University Press, 1991), 8.

11. Denis Donoghue, *Reading America* (New York: Alfred A. Knopf, 1987), offers an apt account: "Reader-response theory seems to me a tautology: it proposes to give polemical force to the self-evident proposition that a reader reads a poem, say, pretty much as he wishes" (x).

12. Linda Hutcheon, in her introduction to the MLA's *Profession 2001* (New York: Modern Language Association, 2001), refers to "both the

capitalist notion of ownership and the Romantic concept of genius" as "now-questioned ideologies" the profession would do well to end (5).

13. Francis Bacon, *The Proficience and Advancement of Learning,* in *A Selection of His Works,* ed. Sidney Warhaft (1964; reprint, Indianapolis, Ind.: Bobbs-Merrill, 1984), 230; "Circles," in *Emerson's Essays,* 213.

14. John Milton, *Areopagitica,* in *Complete Poems and Major Prose,* ed. Merritt Y. Hughes (New York: Macmillan, 1957), 720.

15. *Re-membering Milton: Essays on the Texts and Traditions,* ed. Mary Nyquist and Margaret W. Ferguson (New York: Methuen, 1987).

16. D. W. Winnicott, *The Child, the Family, and the Outside World* (1964; reprint, New York, Addison-Wesley, 1987).

17. Montaigne, "On the Education of Children," in *Essays,* trans. J. M. Cohen (Middlesex, England: Penguin, 1958), 56.

18. "Circles," in *Emerson's Essays,* 226.

19. I quote the beginning of chapter 2, "Classical Backgrounds," in *Nature and Art in Renaissance Literature,* 38.

20. Francis Bacon, *The New Organon,* in *A Selection of His Works,* 340.

21. As Virginia Woolf tells us, "The Leaning Tower," in *The Moment and Other Essays* (1948; reprint, New York: Harcourt Brace Jovanovich, 1974), "we are in the dark about writers; anybody can make a theory; the germ of a theory is almost always the wish to prove what the theorist wishes to believe. Theories then are dangerous things" (129).

22. Anne Lake Prescott, "Through the Cultural Chunnel," in *Opening the Borders,* ed. Peter C. Herman (Newark, Del.: University of Delaware Press, 1999), 146.

23. Montaigne, *Essays,* 51.

24. Wallace Stevens, "Of Modern Poetry," in *The Collected Poems* (1954; reprint, New York: Vintage, 1983), 239.

Notes to Chapter 1/Kermode

1. John Milton, *Samson Agonistes,* in *Complete Poems and Major Prose,* ed. Merritt Y. Hughes (New York: Macmillan, 1957) 1.1692.

2. Edward W. Tayler, "Milton's Firedrake," *Milton Quarterly* 6:3 (1972): 7–10.

3. Edward W. Tayler, "*Measure for Measure*: Its Glassy Essence," *Cithara* 37:1 (1997): 3–21; all quotations of Shakespeare are from the Riverside Shakespeare, 2nd edition (Boston: Houghton Mifflin, 1997), hereafter cited in the text.

4. Here I must exempt Stephen Orgel and Jonathan Goldberg, who cite the Tayler note *ad loc.* in their Oxford Authors Milton, *John Milton: Selections* (Oxford: Oxford University Press, 1991), 957.

5. Edward W. Tayler, *Milton's Poetry: Its Development in Time* (Pittsburgh: Duquesne University Press, 1979), 275.

6. *The Tempest*, ed. Frank Kermode (London: Methuen, 1954).

7. *The Tempest*, ed. Stephen Orgel (Oxford: Oxford University Press, 1987), 190.

8. Walter Whiter, *Specimen of a Commentary on Shakespeare*, ed. Alan Over and Mary Bell (1794; London: Methuen, 1967); hereafter cited in text.

9. Walter Whiter, *Etymologicon Universale*, 3 vols. (Cambridge, England, 1822–25).

10. Caroline Spurgeon, *Shakespeare's Imagery, and What It Tells Us* (Cambridge: Cambridge University Press, 1935), 4.

11. Arthur M. Eastman, *A Short History of Shakespearean Criticism* (New York: Random House, 1968), 257.

12. R. B. Heilman, *Magic in the Web: Action and Language in Othello* (Lexington: University of Kentucky Press, 1956); *This Great Stage: Image and Structure in King Lear* (Baton Rouge: Louisiana State University Press, 1948).

13. L. C. Knights, *Some Shakespearean Themes*, (Stanford: Stanford University Press, 1960), 121.

14. Frank Kermode, *Shakespeare's Language* (New York: Farrar, Straus and Giroux, 2000), 64–69.

Notes to Chapter 2/Berley

1. The principal sources of Shakespeare's *King Lear* have long been known. From Raphael Holinshed's chronicles Shakespeare got the main story of King Leir, "a prince of right noble demeanor" with three daughters named "Gonorilla, Regan, and Cordeilla" who, "nothing content" with his youngest and favorite daughter's failure in a contest of flattery, puts his trust in the other two, only to incur their filial "unkindness" and "unnaturalness." From Sir Philip Sidney's *Arcadia* Shakespeare got the large subplot of Gloucester — blinded by his "unlawful and unnatural" bastard son, saved by his loyal son, who is "worthy of a more virtuous" father — and his tears "both of joy and sorrow." See Raphael Holinshed, *The Chronicles of England, Scotlande, and Irelande*, in *Shakespeare's Holinshed*, ed. W. G. Boswell-Stone, ed. (1896; reprint, New York: Benjamin Blom, 1966), 1–4, hereafter cited in the text, and Sir Philip Sidney, *Arcadia*, 2.10, passim, excerpted in *King Lear*, ed. Kenneth Muir (London: Methuen, 1972), 229–35.

2. Scene 3, lines 112–15, in *A Critical Edition of The True Chronicle History of King Leir and His Three Daughters, Gonorill, Ragan and Cordella*, ed. Donald M. Michie (New York: Garland, 1991), 79. Hereafter cited in the text by page number.

3. As Kenneth Muir notes in *Shakespeare's Sources: Comedies and Tragedies* (London: Methuen, 1961), Shakespeare "knew most of Sidney's work — *Astrophel and Stella, The Defence of Poesy,* and *Arcadia*" (13). Muir's only suggestion of Shakespeare's direct use of the *Defence* is his version of "Menenius's fable of the Belly and the Members of the Body" in *Coriolanus.* Both Shakespeare and Sidney, observes Muir, begin "with the words 'There was a time'; both use the word 'mutinous'" (223).

4. Sir Philip Sidney, *An Apology for Poetry,* ed. Forrest G. Robinson (New York: Macmillan, 1970), 15. Hereafter cited in the text.

5. Horace, *Ars Poetica,* in *Satire and Epistles,* ed. Edward P. Morris, (1939; reprint, Norman: University of Oklahoma Press, 1967). Compare Cicero, *De Oratore,* 2.27.115.

6. Horace, *Satires and Epistles,* 1.1.25.

7. Alfred Harbage, ed. *King Lear* (1958; New York: Penguin, 1986), 17. Hereafter cited in the text.

8. Samuel Johnson, *Johnson on Shakespeare,* ed. Bertrand H. Bronson and Jean M. O'Meara (New Haven: Yale University Press, 1986), 239. Hereafter cited in the text.

9. Frank Kermode, *Shakespeare's Language* (New York: Farrar, Straus and Giroux, 2000), 197. Hereafter cited in the text.

10. I do not attempt here to solve the problem of the two texts, Q and F. Shakespeare's interest in fore-conceit is evident in each, as it is in the text I am using.

11. Francis Bacon, "Of Great Place," *The Essayes or Counsels, Civill and Morall 1625,* in Francis Bacon, *A Selection of His Works,* ed. Sidney Warhaft (Indianapolis: Bobbs-Merrill, 1984), 70.

12. See Edward W. Tayler, "*King Lear* and Negation," *English Literary Renaissance* 20:1 (1990), 17–39.

13. Coppélia Kahn, "The Absent Mother in *King Lear,*" in *Rewriting the Renaissance,* ed. Margaret W. Ferguson et al. (Chicago: University of Chicago Press, 1986), observes that "we are shown only fathers and their godlike capacity to make or mar their children" such that "the children owe their existence to their fathers alone" (35). Her further point, however, that "the mother's role in procreation is eclipsed by the father's, which is used to affirm male prerogative and male power," ignores a central aspect of the play. The mother's absence makes Lear the parent responsible for the trait he most hates in the daughters he would disown: the rampant will to conceive.

14. Compare Sophocles, *Oedipus,* trans. David Greene (Chicago: University of Chicago Press, 1942), 74, where Oedipus sees the curse of his daughters' barrenness as a natural break in the cycle of evil.

15. Sigmund Freud, *Three Essays on the Theory of Sexuality* (New York: Basic Books, 1962), 15.

16. Lear questions the legitimacy of their conception, but Goneril and Regan are very much his daughters. They share with their father the excessive need to conceive the world.

17. Julia Kristeva, *Powers of Horror*, trans. Leon S. Roudiez (New York: Columbia University Press, 1982), 77.

18. See J. L. Austin, *How to Do Things with Words* (1962; reprint, Cambridge: Harvard University Press, 1975).

19. On Kent serving Lear, compare Richard Strier, "Faithful Servants: Shakespeare's Praise of Disobedience," *The Historical Renaissance*, ed. Heather Dubrow and Richard Strier (Chicago: University Chicago Press, 1988), 104–33.

20. Compare Stephen Booth, *King Lear, Macbeth, Indefinition, and Tragedy* (New Haven: Yale University Press, 1983): "Lear learns nothing in the course of the play" and "*King Lear* has nothing to teach us" (162).

21. Aristotle, *The Poetics*, in *On Poetry and Style*, trans. G. M. A. Grube (1958; reprint, Indianapolis, Ind.: Hackett, 1989), 22. Hereafter cited in the text.

22. Sigmund Freud, "Repression (1915)," in *General Psychological Theory*, ed. Philip Rieff (1963; reprint, New York: Simon & Schuster, 1991), 105.

23. Maynard Mack, "We Came Crying Hither," in *Everybody's Shakespeare* (Lincoln: University of Nebraska Press, 1993), 155.

24. Tayler, "*King Lear* and Negation," 37–39.

25. Those who identify with Goneril and Regan, seeing them perhaps as culturally produced slanders against all women, are beyond my scope here.

26. Sigmund Freud, "The Moses of Michelangelo (1914)," in *Character and Culture*, ed. Philip Rieff (New York: Macmillan, 1963), 81.

27. See Kermode's introduction to the Arden edition of *The Tempest*, ed. Frank Kermode (1954; reprint, London: Routledge, 1989), lxxxv, and Tayler's *Nature and Art in Renaissance Literature* (New York: Columbia University Press, 1964), 2.

28. John Keats, not coincidentally, defines his notion of "Negative Capability" in a letter about viewing *Lear*.

29. See Sidney: "There is no art delivered to mankind," writes Sidney, "that hath not the works of nature for his principal object, without which they could not consist, and on which they so depend, as they become actors and players, as it were, of what nature will have set forth" (13).

Notes to Chapter 3/Mack

1. See J. M. Nosworthy, "The Narrative Sources of the *Tempest*," *Review of English Studies* 24 (1948): 281–94; Jan Kott, "The *Aeneid* and the *Tempest*," *Arion* n.s., 3 (1976): 424–51; John Pitcher, "A Theatre of the Future: The *Aeneid* and the *Tempest*," *Essays in Criticism* 34 (1984): 193–215; and the most comprehensive and sophisticated treatment of the relation between the works, Robert Wiltenburg, "The *Aeneid* in the

Tempest," Shakespeare Survey 39 (1986): 159–68. See also Frank Kermode's introduction to his Arden edition of the *Tempest* (London: Methuen, 1954) and Stephen Orgel's introduction to his Oxford edition (Oxford: Oxford University Press, 1987). For book-length studies, see Barbara Bono, *Literary Transvaluation: From Vergilian Epic to Shakespearean Tragicomedy* (Berkeley and Los Angeles: University of California Press, 1984), and Donna Hamilton, *Virgil and the* Tempest*: The Politics of Imitation* (Columbus: Ohio State University Press, 1990).

2. For evidence of this iconographic tradition, see Kott, "The *Aeneid* and the *Tempest*," 428–29.

3. Although she focuses on *Antony and Cleopatra* rather than the *Tempest*, Bono, *Literary Transvaluation*, gives the fullest treatment of Shakespeare's response to the story of Dido and Aeneas.

4. *Tempest*, 1.2.424–25; *Aeneid*, 1.328. Quotations of Shakespeare are from the Riverside edition, ed. G. Blakemore Evans (Boston: Houghton Mifflin, 1974); hereafter cited in the text. English quotations of the *Aeneid* are from Robert Fitzgerald, trans. *The Aeneid* (New York: Random House, 1990). Latin quotations are from the Loeb edition, Virgil, *Aeneid*, ed. and trans. H. R. Fairclough (Cambridge: Harvard University Press, 1978); hereafter cited in the text by the line numbers of the Latin.

5. For Wiltenburg's identification and analysis of this parallel, see "The *Aeneid* in the *Tempest*," 166–68.

6. See Wiltenburg, "The *Aeneid* in the *Tempest*," who recognizes this pervasive atmosphere of loss but focuses his discussion on the trope of widowhood.

7. On the exclusion of Venus and Cupid from the masque, see Robert Egan, "This Rough Magic: Perspectives of Art and Morality in the *Tempest*," *Shakespeare Quarterly* 23 (spring 1972): 171–82; David Brailow, "Prospero's 'Old Brain': The Old Man as Metaphor in the *Tempest*," *Shakespeare Studies* 15 (1981): 285–303; and Lynne Magnusson, "Interruption in *The Tempest*," *Shakespeare Quarterly* 37 (1986): 52–65.

8. Hamilton, *Virgil and the Tempest*, offers a more involved reading of the masque, in which she compares the vision to the vision of the future of Rome presented to Aeneas in the underworld (78–85). Much closer to my reading is that of Pitcher, "A Theater of the Future," who sees the masque as a comic rewriting of the tragedy of Dido.

9. Alvin Kernan, "The Playwright as Magician," in *Shakespeare's Image of the Poet in the English Public Theater* (New Haven: Yale University Press, 1979), offers a similar interpretation of the scene: "A play, baseless fabric of a vision though it may be, is finally a true image of human life and the world. . . . It is a paradoxical triumph for art, in which the theater's illusory status, which had troubled Shakespeare for so long, becomes finally the source of the play's ability to mirror reality. Plays are not real, but then neither is the world itself" (144–45).

10. Wallace Stevens, "The Snow Man," *The Collected Poems of Wallace Stevens* (New York: Knopf, 1954), 9–10. See Edward W. Tayler, "*King Lear* and Negation," *English Literary Renaissance* 20 (1990): 17–39, for a fuller understanding of the connection between "knowing" and "nothing."

11. On the arrangement of the scenes in the *Tempest*, see Mark Rose, *Shakespearean Design* (Cambridge: Harvard University Press, 1972), 172–74.

12. For other opinions on the exchange between Ferdinand and Miranda, see Bryan Loughrey and Neil Taylor, "Ferdinand and Miranda at Chess," *Shakespeare Survey* 35 (1982): 113–18; R. F. Fleissner, "The Endgame in the *Tempest*," *Papers on Language and Literature* 21 (1985): 331–35; Gary Schmidgall, "The Discovery at Chess in the *Tempest*," *English Language Notes* 23 (1986): 11–16.

Notes to Chapter 4/Martz

Quotations from the *Anniversaries* have been taken from *The Epithalamions, Anniversaries, and Epicedes of John Donne*, ed. W. Milgate (Oxford: Clarendon Press, 1978). Portions of this essay have been adapted from a lecture delivered in November 1997, at Brigham Young University: "Metaphysical and Meditative: Donne's *Anniversaries* and Eliot's *Quartets*." The lecture was published in *Literature and Belief* 19 (1999): 25–42. I am grateful to the editors of this periodical for permission to incorporate certain portions of this lecture in the present essay.

1. Edward W. Tayler, *Donne's Idea of a Woman: Structure and Meaning in "The Anniversaries"* (New York: Columbia University Press, 1991); *The Variorum Edition of the Poetry of John Donne*, vol. 6 (Bloomington: Indiana University Press, 1995); Barbara Kiefer Lewalski, *Donne's Anniversaries and the Poetry of Praise: The Creation of a Symbolic Mode* (Princeton: Princeton University Press, 1973).

2. Jeffrey Johnson, *The Theology of John Donne* (Cambridge: D. S. Brewer, 1999); see esp. 13–16 for the differences between Donne and Calvin. For Donne's emphasis upon Memory, see the famous passage in *The Sermons of John Donne*, ed. George R. Potter and Evelyn M. Simpson, 10 vols. (Berkeley and Los Angeles: University of California Press, 1953–62; reissued, 1984), 2.72–74, where Donne opens his sermon by defining the interior trinity: "As the three Persons of the *Trinity* created us, so we have, in our one soul, a *threefold impression* of that image, and, as Saint *Bernard* calls it, *A trinity from the Trinity*, in those *three faculties* of the soul, the *Understanding*, the *Will*, and the *Memory*." For Donne's trinitarian theology see also *John Donne and the Theology of Language*, ed. P. G. Stanwood and Heather Ross Asals (Columbia: University of Missouri Press, 1986), 138–66; also Achsah Guibbory, "John Donne and

Memory as 'the Art of Salvation'," *Huntington Library Quarterly* 43 (1980): 261–74.

3. *Augustine: Later Works*, trans. John Burnaby (London: SCM Press, 1955), 102–03.

4. See, for example, *Sermons*, 3.110, where Donne challenges the Calvinists in his audience by saying, "you are here, and yet you think you could have heard some other doctrine of down-right *Predestination*, and *Reprobation* roundly delivered somewhere else with more edification to you"; 5.53–54, where Donne sharply attacks the doctrine of predestined reprobation; 1.313, where he attacks the doctrine of irresistible grace; or 6.161, 163, where Donne declares in the words of Revelation that the saved may be not a few, but rather "a multitude that no man can number."

5. See Johnson, *Theology of John Donne*, 125–27, for examples of Donne's use of the term "co-operate" in relation to grace: *Sermons*, 7.63; 4.224. "It is precisely," says Johnson, "this inclusion of human efforts in the action of grace that distinguishes Donne's understanding of the doctrine from that of Calvin."

6. The importance and extent of Donne's early experience of Catholicism in his family has now been demonstrated in the impressive study by Dennis Flynn, *John Donne and the Ancient Catholic Nobility* (Bloomington: Indiana University Press, 1995). Especially significant for the present discussion is Flynn's evidence for the long exposure of Donne to Jesuit influence, both in England and in the years from ages 12 to 15 that he seems to have spent on the Continent.

7. See especially the book by Nicholas Tyacke, *Anti-Calvinists: The Rise of English Arminianism, c. 1590–1640* (Oxford: Clarendon Press, 1987), along with the other studies of religious conflict in Donne's era cited by Achsah Guibbory in *Ceremony and Community from Herbert to Milton* (Cambridge: Cambridge University Press, 1998). See also the more detailed listing of these historical studies in the notes to Jeanne Shami, "John Donne and the Pulpit Crisis of 1622" *John Donne Journal*, 14 (1995): 1–58.

8. See my introduction to Manley's edition of the *Anniversaries* (Baltimore: Johns Hopkins University Press, 1963), 41–44, and my essay in *From Renaissance to Baroque* (Columbia: University of Missouri Press, 1991), 59–60.

9. Joseph Hall, chap. 16 in *Works* (London, 1628); I have taken quotations from this edition, which contains some revisions.

10. In his *Conversations with Drummond of Hawthornden*, Jonson says that Hall was "the Harbinger to Donne's Anniversary"; literally this refers only to the title of the prefatory poem to the *Second Anniversary*, but it has been assumed that the authorship applies also to the other prefatory poem, which is stylistically similar. See Ben Jonson,

Works, ed. C.H. Herford, Percy and Evelyn Simpson, 11 vols. (Oxford: Clarendon Press, 1925–52), 1:149. Leonard D. Tourney, "Joseph Hall and the *Anniversaries," Papers on Language and Literature* 13 (1977): 25–34.

11. See appendix 1 in my *The Poetry of Meditation* (New Haven: Yale University Press, 1954). In his dedication, Hall says, "In this Art of mine, I confesse to have received more light from one obscure nameless Monke, which wrote some 112. yeres agoe, then from the directions of all other Writers." Dating back from 1606 brings us to the year 1494, when the *Rosetum* of Mauburnus was published, anonymously. That this is the work referred to is made clear by Hall's marginal translation of the preparatory steps and the steps of the Understanding in the "Scala" (chap. 16); the latter steps Hall discards, preferring to give some logical exercises of his own for the Understanding. But when he comes to the "degrees of affection" and the "Conclusion" he follows very closely the steps of the "Scala," though without acknowledgment (chaps. 28–36). Frank Livingstone Huntley, in his modernized edition of Hall's treatise, *Bishop Joseph Hall and Protestant Meditation in Seventeenth-Century England* (Binghamton, N.Y.: Medieval and Renaissance Texts and Studies, 1981), 27–28, attempts to argue that this book published "112. yeres agoe" was not Mauburnus, but was *The Imitation of Christ,* for which he has found an anonymous edition of 1492 — "close enough," he says. But, aside from the fact that the *Imitation* contains nothing like the "Scala," Hall, as a learned man of 30, would have known that the *Imitation* was a work of the early or mid-fifteenth century, attributed to both Thomas à Kempis and Joannes Gerson.

12. Lewis and Short, *Latin Dictionary.*

13. For a detailed analysis of Hall's *Arte* see Richard A. McCabe, *Joseph Hall: A Study in Satire and Meditation* (Oxford: Clarendon Press, 1982), 172–84. McCabe describes Hall's treatise as "designed to introduce to English readers meditative techniques already well established on the Continent." He finds affinities with the Jesuit *Exercises* and accepts the influence of Mauburnus, along with the influence of Gerson's *La Montaigne de Contemplation.* McCabe's study may suggest that Hall's dual role as satirist and meditative writer would make him especially responsive to Donne's union of these two genres in the *Anniversaries,* especially the *Anatomy,* which is strongly satiric

14. See Tayler, *Donne's Idea of a Woman,* 38, 40. His citation from *Sermons,* 3.154 is especially significant in this context; Donne advises, "accustome thy selfe to meditations upon the Trinity, in all occasions, and finde impressions of the Trinity, in the three faculties of thine owne soule, Thy Reason, thy Will, and thy Memory."

15. O. B. Hardison, Jr., *The Enduring Monument* (Chapel Hill: University of North Carolina Press, 1962), 180–81.

Notes to Chapter 5/Labriola

1. All of the preceding information and quotations concerning fragrances were obtained from the brochures and other advertisements distributed by fragrance promoters or available on countertops.

2. For Aquinas's commentary on angels, see *Summa Theologica,* First Part, Question 50 ("Whether an angel is altogether incorporeal?"), article 1; first part, question 50 ("Whether an angel is composed of matter and form?"), article 2; first part, question 50 ("Whether the angels are incorruptible?"), article 5; first part, question 51 ("Whether the angels have bodies naturally united to them?"), article 1; first part, question 51 ("Whether angels assume bodies?"), article 2. Available at http://www.knight.org/advent/summa/105001.htm. See also 105002.htm, 105005.htm, 105101.htm. Retrieved April 15, 1998.

3. For a general overview of representative critical commentary on "Aire and Angels" (from Herbert J. C. Grierson's edition of Donne's poetry in 1912 to the present), see John R. Roberts's "'Just such disparitie': The Critical Debate about 'Aire and Angels'," in *John Donne Journal 9* (1990): 43–64. The endnotes comprise a virtual bibliography of significant and influential commentary on the poem. In fact, that issue of *John Donne Journal* is devoted exclusively to "Aire and Angels," with eleven other essays on the poem, in addition to the one by Roberts.

4. For background on the *Donna Angelicata,* see Leo Spitzer, "Understanding Milton," *The Hopkins Review* 4 (1951): 16–27.

5. *Marsilio Ficino: Three Books on Life,* ed. and trans. Carol V. Kaske and John R. Clark (Binghamton, N.Y.: Medieval & Renaissance Texts & Studies, 1989), esp. 249–91.

6. Paracelsus, Theophrast von Hohenheim, *The "Herbarius" of Paracelsus,* trans Bruce T. Moran, in *Pharmacy in History* (Madison, Wis.: American Institute of the History of Pharmacy, 1993), 35, 117.

7. Michael T. Murray, *The Healing Power of Herbs,* 2nd ed. (Rocklin, Calif.: Prima Publishing, 1995), 45.

8. Omer Englebert, *The Lives of the Saints,* trans. Christopher and Anne Fremantle (New York: David McKay Company, Inc., 1953), 45.

9. Jacobus de Voragine, *The Golden Legend: Readings on the Saints,* trans. William Granger Ryan (Princeton: Princeton University Press, 1993), 2:204.

10. "Angelica"; available at http://www.mothernature.com/Family/ Thirdway/ angel.htm. Retrieved April 15, 1998.

11. "Angelica"; available at http://home.it.net.au/~darke/windwolf/ Herbalism/ angelica.html. Retrieved April 15, 1998.

12. Ibid. In addition to the citations in endnotes 9–11, further documentation concerning *archangelica* and angels in Scripture, especially Michael, Raphael and Gabriel, includes the following: *Pictorial Lives of*

the Saints, ed. John Gilmary Shea (New York: Benziger Brothers, 1899); S. Baring-Gould, *The Lives of the Saints,* rev. ed. (Edinburgh: John Grant, 1914); Gordon Hall Gerould, *Saints' Legends* (Boston: Houghton Mifflin Company, 1916); *The Book of Saints,* comp. Benedictine Monks of St. Augustine's Abbey, Ramsgate (London: A. & C. Black, 1934); Alban Butler, *The Lives of the Fathers, Martyrs, and Other Principal Saints,* vol. 3 (Chicago: The Catholic Press, Inc., 1954); Donald Attwater, *The Penguin Dictionary of Saints* (Baltimore: Penguin Books, 1965); Christina Hole, *Saints in Folklore* (New York: M. Barrows and Company, 1965); John J. Delaney, *Dictionary of Saints* (Garden City, N.Y.: Doubleday, 1980); *Saints and Their Cults,* ed. Stephen Wilson (Cambridge: Cambridge University Press, 1983); George Every, *Christian Legends,* rev. ed. (New York: Peter Bedrick Books, 1987).

13. In addition to the citations in endnotes 7, 11 and 12, further documentation concerning *angelica* — its use and effects from the Middle Ages and Renaissance to the present era — includes the following items from folklore, history and pharmaceutical science: Willyam Bulleyn, *Bulleins Bulwarke of Defence againste all sicknes sornes and woundes* (1562; reprint, Amsterdam: Da Capo Press, Theatrum Orbis Terrarum, 1971), h.iii; John Gerard, *The Herball or General History of Plants* (1597; reprint, Amersterdam: Theatrum Orbis Terrarum, 1974), 847; John Gerard, *Gerard's Herball,* The Essence thereof distilled by Marcus Woodward from the edition of TH Johnson, (1636; reprint, London: Spring Books, 1964), 157–58; Benjamin H. Barton and Thomas Castle, *The British Flora Medica,* rev. ed. by John R. Jackson (London: Chatto and Windus, 1877), 13–17; David Ellis, *Medicinal Herbs and Poisonous Plants* (London: Blackie and Son, 1918), 89–90; Warren R. Dawson, *A Leechbook or Collection of Medical Recipes of the Fifteenth Century* (London: Macmillan and Co., 1934), 251; Siri von Reis Altschul, *Drugs and Foods from Little-Known Plants* (Cambridge: Harvard University Press, 1973), 213–14; Nelson Coon, *The Dictionary of Useful Plants* (Emmaus, Pa.: Rodale Press, 1974), 258; Walter H. Lewis and Memory P. F. Elvin Lewis, *Medical Botany* (New York: John Wiley & Sons, 1977), 81, 323, 338, 389, 394; Nelson Coon, *Using Plants for Healing* (Emmaus, PA: Rodale Press, 1979); James A. Duke, *CRC Handbook of Medicinal Herbs* (Boca Raton, Fla.: CRC Press, 1985), 43–44, 391; James A. Duke and Edward S. Ayensu, *Medicinal Plants of China,* vol. 1 (Algonac, Mich.: Reference Publications, 1985), 77, 660–63; Gervase Markham, *The English House-wife,* ed. Michael R. Best (Kingston: McGill-Queen's University Press, 1986). Hundreds of scientific essays have been written on *angelica.* See Cambridge Scientific Abstracts under the database "Plant Science" and the query "angelica"; available at http://www.csa2.com/htbin/txtdisp.cgi?filename=/tmp/ftp/pub.csaAAAaavFka.bin. Retrieved May 30, 1998.

14. Herrick's poetry is cited from *The Complete Poetry of Robert Herrick*, ed. J. Max Patrick (Garden City, N.Y.: Doubleday, 1968). Line numbers are cited parenthetically.

15. For extensive commentary on the apparitional appearances of angels in Scripture (light, fire, luminous clouds), see Pascal P. Parente, *The Angels* (St. Meinrad, Ind.: Grail Publications, 1958); Theodora Ward, *Men and Angels* (New York: The Viking Press, 1969).

16. *The Third Dayes Creation. By that most excellent, learned, and divine Poet, William, Lord Bartas*, trans. Thomas Winter (London: Thomas Clerke, 1604), 19.

17. *Bartas: His Devine Weekes and Works*, trans. Joshua Sylvester (1605; reprint, Gainesville, Fla.: Scholars' Facsimiles & Reprints, 1965), 98.

18. William Denny, "The Shepherd's Holiday," in *Unedited Poetical Miscellanies 1584–1700*, comp. W. C. Hazlitt (London: Chiswick Press, 1870), 25.

19. "Aire and Angels" is cited from *The Complete Poetry of John Donne*, ed. John T. Shawcross (Garden City, N.Y.: Doubleday, 1967). Line numbers are cited parenthetically.

20. *Paradise Lost* is cited from John Milton, *Paradise Lost: An Authoritative Text, Backgrounds and Sources and Criticism*, 2nd ed., Scott Elledge (New York: W. W. Norton, 1993). Book and line numbers are cited parenthetically.

Notes to Chapter 6/Prescott

1. See George Klawitter, "Verse Letters to T. W. from John Donne: 'By You My Love Is Sent,'" in *Homosexuality in Renaissance and Enlightenment England: Literary Representations in Historical Context*, ed. Claude Summers (New York: Haworth Press, 1992), 85–102. On Donne's probable knowledge of Sappho, see Stella Revard, "The Sapphic Voice in Donne's 'Sapho to Philænis,'" in *Renaissance Discourses of Desire*, ed Claude J. Summers and Ted-Larry Pebworth (Columbia: University of Missouri Press, 1993). On the performance of cross-dressing in verse and its consequent blurring of gender lines, see the sympathetic and thoughtful introduction to *The Routledge Anthology of Cross-Gendered Verse*, ed. Alan Michael Parker and Mark Willhardt (London: Routledge, 1996), which includes Donne's "Sapho." I quote Donne from his *Complete English Poems*, ed. C. A. Patrides (New York: Knopf, 1991).

This essay derives from a talk first given at Victoria College, Toronto, in January 2000. I thank Konrad Eisenbichler for inviting me and for showing me his paper on the love between Laudomia Forteguerri and Margaret of Austria.

2. See, for example, Stephen Greenblatt, "Fiction and Friction," in

Reconstructing Individualism: Autonomy, Individuality, and the Self in Western Thought, ed. Thomas C. Heller et al. (Stanford: Stanford University Press, 1986). On a criminal case noted in Henri Estienne's *Apologie pour Hérodote* (1566) that involved a woman with an unsuspecting bride, see C. Annette Grisé, "Depicting Lesbian Desire: Contexts for John Donne's 'Sapho to Philænis,'" *Mosaic* 29, no. 4 (1996): 41–57. Critics of theatrical cross-dressing feared the effeminization of men, argues Laura Levine in *Men in Women's Clothing: Anti-Theatricality and Feminism* (Cambridge: Cambridge University Press, 1994).

3. This is not the only poem by Donne with an interest in lesbian or, to use the once preferred term, "tribade" relations: a poem to "T. W." suggests that the poets' muses have engaged in a "chaste and mistique tribadree" and that T. W.'s muse then "gott this Song on mee"; see Grisé, "Depicting," 49.

4. Philaenis appears in the Greek anthology, the epigrams of Martial, and dialogues by Lucian and pseudo-Lucian as the author of a sexual manual or as a lady confused with her. On how Donne might have come to link Philaenis to Sappho, see Elizabeth Harvey, "Ventriloquizing Sappho, or the Lesbian Muse," in *Reading Sappho: Reception and Transmission*, ed. Ellen Greene (Berkeley and Los Angeles: University of California Press, 1996), 79–104. Lucian's possible role in Donne's view of tribadism and Philænis has been obscured by faulty citations and a misplaced trust in available translations. Usually cited is the pseudo-Lucianic "Affairs of the Heart" (*Amores*) in Lucian's works, trans. M. D. Macleod (Cambridge: Harvard University Press, 1967) vol. 8, which has a passage on tribadism that mentions Philaenis. Lillian Faderman's useful and oft-cited *Surpassing the Love of Men: Romantic Friendship and Love Between Women from the Renaissance to the Present* (New York: William Morrow, 1981) solemnly ascribes the latter's refusal to say what goes on between lesbians to male ignorance; but it could be knowing humor. A girl in the less often noted "Dialogues of the Courtesans" by Lucian himself will buy red beads like those of Philaenis with her first earnings (7:387). But especially relevant to Donne, one would think, is "The Mistaken Critic" ("Pseudologista"), which asks those who use fancy terms where they get such words as "bromologous" or "anthocracy." From a composer of dirges? "Or from the Tablets of Philaenis, which you keep in hand?" The mention of "hand" — "cheiros" — may hint at what the tablets are good for. If so, Lucian links Philaenis, failed language and autoeroticism. See vol. 5, ed. A. M. Harmon, 1936, p. 401.

5. Arthur Weigall, quoted in *The Love Songs of Sappho* ed. Paul Roche (New York: New American Library, 1966). Roche denies that Sappho was a "pervert."

6. George Klawitter, *The Enigmatic Narrator: The Voicing of Same-Sex Love in the Poetry of John Donne* (New York: Peter Lang, 1994), 47–61.

7. Maria Prendergast, *Renaissance Fantasies: The Gendering of Aesthetics in Early Modern Fiction* (Kent, Ohio: Kent State University Press, 1999), 126; Prendergast's book is not without error (for example, mistaking François I for Henri II), but it can be clever.

8. On Donne's implied links among lesbian egalitarian erotics, flatness of style and failures of signification, as well as on the "tolerant patriarchalism" that reduces lesbianism to a preliminary erotic stage and, by means of the name "Sapho," to the classical past, see James Holstun, "'Will You Rent Our Ancient Love Asunder?': Lesbian Elegy in Donne, Marvell, and Milton," *English Literary History* 54 (1987): 835–67. Harvey, "Ventriloquizing," also focuses on Donne's effort to imitate a female voice, an effort she reads rather frostily as an effort to overgo and cannibalize his rival Ovid as well as a homosocial commodification, erasure, and colonization of a threatening female writer. William West, "Thinking with the Body: Sapho's 'Sappho to Philænis,' Donne's 'Sapho to Philænis,'" *Renaissance Papers 1994* (1995): 67–83, associates the poem's lack of metaphor (and hence its minimizing of difference) with this voice; but West reads Donne's move positively, finding it fruitfully ambiguous because it is itself metaphoric. Writing in a female voice was, of course, an old story; for many examples and a learned survey, see John Kerrigan, *Motives of Woe: Shakespeare and "Female Complaint": A Critical Anthology* (Oxford: Clarendon Press, 1991). For Barbara Correll, "Symbolic Economies and Zero-Sum Erotics: Donne's 'Sapho to Philænis,'" *English Literary History* 62 (1995), who seems to find the poem irksome, Donne produces a backfiring and "programmatically failed poem" about "a crisis of signification," one that "voids signification and paints the ventriloquizing poet into a corner" and responds to what Correll calls an "economically embedded cultural masculine crisis." A heavy load for one paradoxical elegy to carry. More sympathetic is Paula Blank, "Comparing Sappho to Philænis: John Donne's Homopoetics," *PMLA* 110 (1995), 358–68, who argues that Donne calls into question not "lesbian desire" itself but "the homoeroticization of desire, the effort to re-create the other as the self and the self as other" (364). Blank's essay is refreshing for its judicious and crisply expressed empathy, although I am not fully convinced that Donne means to question Sappho's affection rather than imagine it. Cecilia Infante, "Donne's Incarnate Muse and His Claim to Poetic Control in 'Sapho to Philænis,'" in *Representing Women in Renaissance England*, ed. Claude J. Summers and Ted-Larry Pebworth (Columbia: University of Missouri Press, 1997), stresses Sappho's onanism. Yet moralists and satirists have long accused male lovers of narcissism. When it comes to misreading passion for oneself as passion for another, Cupid is an equal-opportunity archer.

9. Blank, "Comparing Sappho," 365. H. L. Meakin, *John Donne's Articulations of the Feminine* (Oxford: Clarendon Press, 1998), whose

commentary on "Sapho" is subtle and sympathetic, calls it "astonishingly anomalous within classical and Renaissance literature generally" (88). Moderately anomalous, yes. Meakin also thinks the pseudo-Lucian's "Affairs of the Heart" is innovative in using "Lesbian" and "Sapphic" to describe tribadism (195). But these are the translator's words. The fourth-century author has "tribade" and "androgynous." On the terminology for same-sex female eros in ancient and medieval times, see Bernadette J. Brooten, *Love between Women: Early Christian Responses to Female Homoeroticism* (Chicago: Chicago University Press, 1996), 4–9; on Sappho and her premodern reputation, see 9–41.

10. *The Latin Poems of Jean Dorat*, trans. David R. Slavitt (Alexandria, Va.: Orchises Press, 2000), 12.

11. Janel Mueller, "Lesbian Erotics: The Utopian Trope of Donne's 'Sapho to Philænis,'" in *Homosexuality in Renaissance and Enlightenment England: Literary Representations in Historical Context*, ed. Claude Summers (New York: Haworth Press, 1992), 103–34. I agree with Mueller that Donne is conducting a quasi-utopian "thought-experiment" and that his poem has connections with the Renaissance paradox. Faderman, *Surpassing the Love of Men*, mentions Tyard and quotes several lines.

12. Kenneth Borris is editing an anthology that includes translations of these three French poems. Joan DeJean, *Fictions of Sappho 1546–1937* (Chicago: University of Chicago Press, 1989), traces the ways Sappho was imagined and reconstructed. She does not deal with these French poems, I assume because they do not mention Sappho. She argues that Renaissance poets usually took Sappho to be a heterosexual love poet. Yet thanks to Medieval annotations on Ovid, the heterosexual Sappho did not entirely erase memories of the lesbian one; for quotations from commentators and relevant Renaissance translations of Ovid, see Harriette Andreadis, "Sappho in Early Modern England," in Greene, *Re-Reading Sappho*, 105–21.

13. See the chapter on Ronsard in my *French Poets and the English Renaissance: Studies in Fame and Transformation* (New Haven: Yale University Press, 1978), and, with caution, various studies by Hugh Richmond.

14. Pierre de Ronsard, *Oeuvres complètes*, ed. Jean Céard, Daniel Ménager, and Michel Simonin, 2 vols. (Paris: Gallimard, 1993–94), 2:421–26; for poems to English dignitaries, see 2:51–64, 100–04. From 1567 to 1573 a sonnet (Céard, 1:514) followed the elegy, likewise in celebration of the love between Anne and Diane. On a parallel sonnet by Etienne Jodelle from the same period and perhaps alluding to the same "lesbian" affair, see Richard Griffiths, "'Les Trois Sortes d'Aimer': Impersonation and Sexual Fantasy in French Renaissance Love Poetry," *Journal of the Institute of Romance Studies* 3 (1994–95), 111–27.

15. On dildos and tribadism at court, see Pierre de Bourdeille, sieur

de Brantôme, *Recueil des dames, poésies et tombeaux*, ed. Etienne Vaucheret (Paris: Gallimard, 1991); this includes the memoirs sometimes called the "Vies des dames gallantes." *Recueil* I2.1, "Sur les dames qui font l'amour et leurs maris cocus" has much on tribadism. As is often remarked by those who note his delicious and chatty gossip, Brantôme, who cites Lucian on the matter, assumes that tribadism — love "donna con donna" (is there a multilingual pun here on "con"?) — is imitative, that one woman plays the man's valorous part, that the practice came from Italy, that rubbing is harmless but dildos can cause damage, and that lesbianism is a preliminary to heterosexual relations because women will prefer running water to the stagnant and because any doctor can tell you that a wound needs probing, not rubbing.

16. See *Aeneid*, 2.341.

17. When I read a version of this essay at Yale University, Edwin Duval suggested that there may be a pun on "vit" — "lives" but also "penis" — in this line. Such a pun would seem unsuitable for the poem's time, but it would not be unlike a Pléiade poet to make it, especially in so problematic a context. Professor Duval also noted the move from the heterosexual Corœbus and Cassandra to the male Pylades and Orestes.

18. Brantôme, *Recueil des dames*, 363.

19. On some (ambiguous) evidence for lesbian marriages in the ancient world, though, see Brooten, *Love between Women*.

20. Daniel Ménager, "L'Amour au féminin," in *Sur des vers de Ronsard (1585–1985): Actes du colloque international, Duke University 11–13 Avril 1985* (Paris: Aux Amateurs de Livres, 1990), 105–16. Ménager mentions the 1565 elegy but not this one.

21. Eva Kushner tells me that she and other scholars who work with Tyard are struck by how anomalous the poem seems in its volume.

22. One of Ronsard's love poems foresees a closely similar postmortem fame and temple (see my *French Poets*, 115). Tyard's poem may be found in *Poètes du XVIᵉ siècle*, ed. Albert-Marie Schmidt (Paris: Gallimard, 1953), 403–05, and in Pontus de Tyard, *Oeuvres poétiques complètes*, ed. John C. Lapp (Paris: Didier, 1966), 246–50. The translation is mine.

23. The passage is quoted by Faderman, *Surpassing the Love of Men*, 35, who notes Fiordispina's assumption that such a love cannot be satisfied.

24. See the quotations from Fallopius and others in Andreadis, "Sappho in Early Modern England."

25. Priestess of Apollo, but "Peitho," the name of the goddess of persuasion and, sometimes, a surname for Aphrodite, makes better sense. The ear-chaining recalls the Gallic Hercules.

26. On the friendship of Hopleus and Dymas, see *Thebaid* 10:347–448.

27. Brooten, *Love between Women*, 29–50, describes many classical comments on this point.

28. Meakin, *Articulations*, 107–08, thinks Donne perhaps read Brantôme on tribades: admiring Rabelais and Aretino, he may have, in the 1590s, "sought out what soft-pornographic writing was available in Europe and England." Neither Meakin nor, I think, anyone else writing on Donne, notes that Brantôme mentions Philaenis ("Filenes," 363).

29. From *Le cabinet secret du Parnasse . . . Théophile de Viau et les libertins*, ed. Louis Perceau (Paris: Cabinet du Livre, 1935), 139. The headnote to Saint-Pavin notes that his nickname was the "King of Sodom." I thank Kenneth Borris for sending me these and several similar libertine poems on "tribades."

30. "Amour, je ne me plains de l'orgueil endurcy," withdrawn in 1584 from *Les Amours diverses*; in *Oeuvres*, ed. Céard, 1:466. The poem complains of the mistress' "godmicy," her dildo, and the "faux plaisir" it gives her all night. She should, says the speaker, be altogether a Laïs rather than employ such means to feign being Portia. For Ronsard, as for Saint-Pavin, the pleasure from a dildo is imitative, unreal. Thomas Nashe, in his notorious "Choise of Valentines" raises, at greater length and with more self-mockery, the same issue. On Ronsard's poem and its possible relevance to Hélène de Surgères, subject of Ronsard's *Amours de Helene*, see Gregory de Rocher, "Ronsard's Dildo Sonnet: The Scandal of Poissy and Rasse de Nœux," in *Writing the Renaissance: Essays on Sixteenth-Century French Literature in Honor of Floyd Gray*, ed. Raymond C. La Charité (French Forum Monographs 77, 1992), 149–64.

Notes to Chapter 7/Stewart

1. Elizabeth D. Harvey and Katharine Eisaman Maus, introduction to *Soliciting Interpretation: Literary Theory and Seventeenth-Century English Poetry* (Chicago: University of Chicago Press, 1990), ix; hereafter cited in the text.

2. David Norbrook, "The Monarchy of Wit and the Republic of Letters: Donne's Politics," Harvey, *Soliciting Interpretation*, 15.

3. The quotation that figures so prominently in current "theoretical" commentary is from the apochryphal *The Will to Power*, which William Kaufmann edited from Nietzsche's Nachlass. For a discussion of the spurious place of this work in the Nietzsche canon, see Bernd Magnus, "The Use and Abuse of *The Will to Power*," in *Reading Nietzsche*, ed. Robert C. Solomon and Kathleen M. Higgins (New York: Oxford University Press, 1988), 218–35; see also Bernd Magnus, Stanley Stewart and Jean-Pierre Mileur, *Nietzsche's Case: Philosophy as/and Literature* (New York: Routledge, 1993), chap. 1.

4. Edward W. Tayler, *Donne's Idea of a Woman: Structure and Meaning in "The Anniversaries"* (New York: Columbia University Press, 1991), 71; hereafter cited in the text.

5. Ronald Corthell, *Ideology and Desire in Renaissance Poetry: The Subject of Donne* (Detroit: Wayne State University Press, 1997), 110; hereafter cited in the text.

6. Louis Montrose, "The Elizabethan Subject and the Spenserian Text," in *Literary Theory / Renaissance Texts*, ed. Patricia Parker and David Quint (Baltimore: Johns Hopkins University Press, 1986), 307.

7. For a more extensive discussion of this point, see Stanley Stewart, *"Renaissance" Talk: Ordinary Language and the Mystique of Critical Problems* (Pittsburgh: Duquesne University Press, 1997), chap. 1; hereafter cited in the text.

8. George Klawitter, "Verse Letters to T. W. from John Donne: 'By You My Love Is Sent,'" in *Homosexuality in Renaissance and Enlightenment England: Literary Representations in Historical Context*, ed. Claude J. Summers (New York: Haworth Press, 1992), 85–102.

9. Thomas Overbury, *The "Conceited Newes" of Sir Thomas Overbury and His Friends*, ed. James. E. Savage (Gainesville, Fla.: Scholars' Facsimiles & Reprints, 1968), 166.

10. For a discussion of the possible irony in Donne's misogyny, see Theresa Kenney, "John Donne's Conversion from Misogyny," *English Renaissance Prose* 6 (1997–98): 1–17, esp. 5; see also her introduction to *"Women Are Not Human": An Anonymous Treatise and Responses*, ed. and trans. Theresa M. Kenney (New York: Crossroad, 1998).

11. Thomas Docherty, *John Donne, Undone* (London: Methuen, 1986), 174; hereafter cited in the text.

12. See Jonathan Crewe, *Trials of Authorship: Anterior Forms and Poetic Reconstruction from Wyatt to Shakespeare* (Berkeley and Los Angeles: University of California Press, 1990), 95–98; for a response to Crewe's argument, see Stewart, *"Renaissance" Talk*, chap. 6.

13. John Donne, *The Poems of John Donne*, ed. Herbert J. C. Grierson (1912; reprint, London, Oxford University Press, 1951), 1, 15; hereafter cited in the text.

14. See, for instance, Paul Cantor, "Stephen Greenblatt's New Historicist Vision," *Academic Questions* 6, no. 4 (1993): 21–36.

15. Ricardo J. Quinones, *The Ben Jonson Journal: Literary Contexts in the Age of Elizabeth, James, and Charles* 5 (1999): 187–88.

16. Joseph Glanvill, "An Essay Concerning Preaching" (1677), in *Literary Criticism of Seventeenth-Century England*, ed. Edward W. Tayler (New York: Alfred A. Knopf, 1967), 353, hereafter cited in the text.

Notes to Chapter 8/Gilman

1. *Ben Jonson*, ed., C. H. Herford and Percy and Evelyn Simpson, 11 vols. (Oxford: Clarendon Press, 1947). Hereafter cited in the text by the abbreviation HS, the volume, page number and, where applicable, line number.

2. Thomas Dekker, *The Plague Pamphlets of Thomas Dekker*, ed., F. P. Wilson (Oxford: Clarendon Press, 1925), 76. All quotations from Dekker's plague pamphlets (he published six in all between 1603 and 1630) are from this edition, cited hereafter in the text by page. As the series of pamphlets represents a continuing project, and are now gathered in a single edition, for convenience individual titles are not noted.

3. Charles F. Mullett, *The Bubonic Plague and England* (Lexington: University of Kentucky Press, 1956), 86; Paul Slack, *The Impact of Plague in Tudor and Stuart England* (Oxford: Clarendon Press, 1985), 146. Hereafter cited in the text.

4. David Riggs, *Ben Jonson: A Life*. (Cambridge: Harvard University Press, 1989) 170. Hereafter in the text.

5. See Leeds Barroll, *Politics, Plague, and Shakespeare's Theater: The Stuart Years* (Ithaca: Cornell University Press, 1991, (esp. chap. 3, "Pestilence and the Players," Cheryl Ross; "The Plague of *The Alchemist*," *Renaissance Quarterly* 41 (1988): 434–58; and Michael Neill, *Issues of Death: Mortality and Identity in English Renaissance Tragedy* (Oxford: Clarendon Press, 1997): The action of *The Alchemist* "implicitly equates the pestilence raging outside Lovewit's usurped house with the moral disease rampant within it. The Alchemist's den is not merely a microcosm of the city, of course; it is also presented as a type of fraudulent theatre — to the point where Face's epilogue actually identifies his ill-gotten pelf with the takings of the playhouse itself" (24).

6. John Davies (of Hereford). *Humours Heau'n on Earth; With The Ciuile Warres of Death and Fortune. As also the Triumph of Death; or, The Picture of the Plague, according to the Life; as it was in Anno Domini. 1603* (London, 1605), 245. Hereafter cited in the text. Compare Dekker on the kingdom as a vast plague playhouse: "These are the Tragedies, whose sight / With teares blot all the lynes we write, / The Stage wheron the Scenes are plaide / Is a whole Kingdome" (96).

7. I. H. *This Worlds Folly; or, A Warning-Peece discharged upon the Wickedness thereof* (London, 1615), sig. B3, quoted in Neill, *Issues of Death*, 25, who comments: "In its blurring of moral distinctions, its counterfeitings, its violations of vestimentary order, its breaking of the accepted boundaries of hierarchy and gender—and perhaps even in its promiscuous creation of a mass audience, heaped together in a pit — playing constituted, in fact, a kind of metaphoric plague for which the actual disease was the proper and inevitable retributive substitute" (26).

8. Cited in Alan D. Dyer, "The Influence of Bubonic Plague in England 1500–1667." *Medical History* 22 (1978): 323, from J. W. Blench, *Preaching in England in the Fifteenth and Sixteenth Centuries* (Oxford: Oxford University Press, 1964), 307.

9. Thomas Lodge, *A Treatise of the Plague* (London, 1603).

10. "S. H." *A New Treatise of the Pestilence, containing the Causes, Signes, Preseruativies and Cure thereof* (London, 1603), A2v.

11. Henoch Clapham, *An epistle discovrsing vpon the present Pestilence: Teaching what it is, and how the people of God should carrie themselves towards God and their Neighbor therein* (London, 1603), considers these matters scrupulously, providing an array of ingenious reasons why "some Beleeuers die of the pestilence, and some vnbeleeuvers scape it" (B2r–B2v). Hereafter in the text.

12. Scriptural passages repeatedly cited include Lev. 26, Num. 14.11–12, Deut. 28.21–22, 1 Sam. 5–9, 2 Sam. 24.12–13, and Ps. 106.29–30, showing that all bodily sickness proceeds from God, as punishment for transgression of his commandments; 2 Sam., chronicling the plague visited on David for numbering the people (as London did, by posting bills of mortality); Jer. 16.4, showing that those dead of pestilence "shall be as dung vpon the earth" (Davies, 237); and in the New Testament, John 9.23 and Luke 13.12, instructing us, somewhat troublingly, that "those which are afflicted, are not alwayes greater sinners than others" (Dekker, 5).

13. Alfred W. Crosby, *The Columbian Exchange: Biological Consequences of 1492* (Westport, CT: Greenwood Publishing Company, 1972); William H. McNeill, *Plagues and Peoples* (New York: Doubleday, 1977); Sheldon Watts, *Epidemics and History: Disease, Power and Imperialism* (New Haven: Yale University Press, 1997).

14. The title of Laurie Garrett's *The Coming Plague: Newly Emerging Diseases in a World Out of Balance* (New York: Penguin, 1994), reflects the shift from an older, pre-AIDS narrative that assumed that all infectious disease would soon fall before the weapons of medical research, to one which at its most nightmarish sees the inevitable breakout of Ebola, Lassa Fever, and an untold number of future biohorrors (including smallpox, once thought eradicated) as an imminent threat to the existence of humankind. Her reportage is greeted by Larry Kramer as a "magnificent attempt to make people realize that the future health of the world is in great danger" (ii). One reviewer finds in it a moral lesson very much in the spirit of seventeenth century plague Jeremiads: sexual carelessness, the "widespread misuse of antibiotics" and the "destruction of the rainforest" have planted "the seeds of the next plague in humanity's hubris" (iii).

15. Katherine E. Maus, *Ben Jonson and the Roman Frame of Mind* (Princeton: Princeton University Press, 1984), 119.

16. Martial, *Epigrams*, trans. Walter C. A. Ker, 2 vols. (Cambridge: Harvard University Press, 1943). Hereafter cited in the text.

17. Wesley Trimpi, "'BEN. JONSON his best piece of poetrie,'" *Classical Antiquity* 2 (1983): 147, 149.

18. Dennis Flynn, "John Donne: Survivor," *The Eagle and the Dove: Reassessing John Donne*, eds. Claude J. Summers and Ted-Larry Pebworth (Columbia: University of Missouri Press, 1986), seeing Donne as "a 'survivor' of the Elizabethan persecution" of Catholics (17), cites Bruno Bettelheim's insight that the threat of being killed, and the knowledge that one's "closest friends and relatives are being killed," raises the "unsolvable riddle of 'Why was I spared,' and also with completely irrational guilt about having been spared" (24). Quoted from Bettelheim, "Trauma and Reintegration," in *Surviving and Other Essays* (New York: Knopf, 1979), 26.

19. Margaret Healy, "*Discourses of the Plague in Early Modern London*," *Epidemic Disease in London*, ed. J. A. I. Champion, Center for Metropolitan History, Working Paper Series no. 1 (London, 1993), 30.

20. For this reading of the final line I am indebted to Ted Tayler, to whom I owe all that I am in arts.

21. One may speculate on the appearance of a plague play by Jonson in 1610 — when, had he lived, young Ben would have celebrated his second seven years of life.

22. Compare Dekker's preface to *The Wonderfull Yeare*: "If you read, you may happlie laugh; tis my desire you should, because mirth is both Phisicall, and wholesome against the Plague, with which sicknes, (to tell the truth) this booke is, (though not sorely) yet somewhat infected" (3).

23. Pliny, *Letters and Panegyricus*, trans. Betty Radice, 2 vols. (Cambridge: Harvard University Press, 1969): "*Observatur oculis ille vir quo neminem aetas nostra graviorem sanctiorem subtiliorem tulit*". All English translations are those of the Loeb edition.

24. In the ode to Cary and Morison, Jonson's "Brave Infant of *Saguntum*" represents the opposite of these long-suffering Romans: foreseeing "lifes miseries" from the womb, this "Wise child" took his own life by refusing to born (8:242–43, 1, 19, 7).

25. Indeed, in *Emma*, the very absence of any awareness of the uneasy post-Revolutionary English political climate on the part of the residents of Austen's provincial and self-satisfied Highbury helps us to appreciate both her affection for, and her ironic attitude toward, the little world she has created.

26. Edward Said, *Culture and Imperialism* (New York: Knopf, 1993).

Notes to Chapter 9/Elsky

This essay is dedicated to Edward W. Tayler, who first introduced me to Erich Auerbach in a seminar on seventeenth century lyric in 1971.

1. Erich Auerbach to Walter Benjamin, September 23, 1935. Auerbach's letters to Benjamin appear in Karlheinz Barcke, ed., "5 Briefe Erich Auerbachs an Walter Benjamin in Paris," *Zeitschrift für Germanistik* 6 (1988): 688–94. The citation here appears on 689–90. The letters are discussed in Hans Ulrich Gumbrecht, " 'Pathos of the Earthly Progress': Erich Auerbach's Everydays," in *Literary History and the Challenge of Philology: The Legacy of Erich Auerbach*, ed. Seth Lerer (Stanford: Stanford University Press, 1996), 13–35. The contextual information he supplies is invaluable for understanding them. Among other degradations, the constant threat of dismissal and its psychological impact is recorded in Victor Klemperer, *I Will Bear Witness: A Diary of the Nazi Years, 1933–1941*, trans. Martin Chalmers (New York: Random House, 1998). A student of Vossler, Klemperer was a Jewish Romanist who converted to Protestantism, and was Auerbach's rival for the position in Istanbul. When Vossler supported Auerbach for the position, Klemperer broke with Vossler. See entry for December 28, 1937 (243).

2. *Mimesis: Dargestellte Wirklichkeit in der Abendländischen Literatur* (Bern: Francke Verlag, 1946). It is known in English translation as *Mimesis: The Representation of Reality in Western Literature* (Princeton: Princeton University Press, 1953). All citations are from this edition.

3. The essays I will discuss appear in Erich Auerbach, *Gesammelte Aufsätze zur Romanischen Philologie* (Bern: Francke Verlag, 1967).

4. "Racine und die Leidenschaften," in Auerbach, *Gesammelte Aufsätze*, 196–203. Originally published in *Germanisch-romanisch Monatsschrift* 14 (1927): 371–80.

5. *Mimesis*, 370–94. To be sure, the seeds of his critique of Racine in *Mimesis* are here too, in the contrast between the concretely represented passions of ordinary people (see 200) and the abstract passion of Racine's character types who are removed from any daily activities (203).

6. For the intense cultural polemics waged between by Germans and French between the wars, see David Carroll, *French Literary Fascism: Nationalism, Anti-Semitism, and the Ideology of Culture* (Princeton: Princeton University Press, 1995).

7. Martin Chalmers, introduction to Klemperer, *I Will Bear Witness*, xii–xiii. See also xxii n. 10 for further references concerning Klemperer and French culture. For a detailed treatment of the subject, see Frank-Rutger Hausmann, "Die Nationalsozialistische Hochshulpolitik und ihre Auswirkungen auf die Deutsche Romanistik von 1933 bis 1945," in *Deutsche und Österreichische Romanisten als Vervolgte des Nationalsozialismus*, ed. Hans Helmut Christmann, Frank-Rutger Hausmann, and Manfred Briegel (Tübingen: Stauffenburg Verlag, 1989), 9–54. See

25–26 for the German reaction against Romance philology after World War I. For Romanist Herbert Dieckmann's anti-Germanocentrism, see Jochen Schlobach, "Aufklärer in Finstere Zeit: Werner Krauss und Herbert Dieckmann," in Christmann, *Deutsche und Österreichische Romanisten*, 136.

8. "Der Schriftsteller Montaigne," in Auerbach, *Gesammelte Aufsätze*, 184–95. Originally published in *Germanisch-romanische Monatsschrift* 20 (1932): 39–53.

9. "Passio als Leidenschaft," in Auerbach, *Gesammelte Aufsätze*, 161–75. Originally published in *PMLA* 56 (1941): 1179–96.

10. Eugen Lerch, "'Passion' und 'Gefühl,'" *Archivum Romanicum* 17(1938): 320–41. Auerbach's "Figura" appears in the same issue. The journal was published in Florence by Olschki. For an overview of Lerch's intellectual interests and achievements, see Edmund Schramm, "Gedächtnisrede," in *Studia Romanica: Gedenkschrift für Eugen Lerch*, ed. Charles Bruneau and Peter M. Schon (Stuttgart: Port Verlag, 1955), 7–21.

11. In *Mimesis*, where Auerbach's emphasis shifts from the structure of feeling to realistic representation, Balzac replaces Racine as the quintessential modern figure. Here too the connection to the gospel is important: Balzac's style is the ultimate development of the gospels' *sermo humilis.*

12. Erich Auerbach, "Epilogomena zu Mimesis," *Romanische Forschungen* 65 (1954): 1–18. Auerbach relates that he could write "Figura" and "Passio als Leidenschaft" only because he was allowed into the Dominican monastery to use a copy of Migne's *Patrologia* (10 n. 12).

13. There is perhaps an unspoken interaction going on here between Auerbach and Lerch. By the time of his article "'Passion' und 'Gefühl,'" Lerch had also suffered at the hands of the Nazis. He was forced to retire from the University of Mainz in 1935 for having an affair with a Jewish woman. His dismissal is mentioned by Klemperer, *I Will Bear Witness* (123, 125, 129). I am indebted to Max Grosse for pointing this out.

14. After leaving Germany, Auerbach published only two works in European journals before the war: "Remarques sur le mot 'passion,'" *Neuphilologische Mitteilungen* 38 (1937): 218–24; and "Sprachliche Beiträge zur Erklärung der Scienza Nuova von G. B. Vico," *Archivum Romanicum* 21 (1937): 173–84. During the war, of the five works he published one appeared in neutral Switzerland (*Neue Dantestudien* [Zürich: Europa-Verlag, 1944]), and one in the United States ("Passio als Leidenschaft," *PMLA* 56 [1941]: 1179–96. The three others were "Figura," *Archivum Romanicum* 22 (1939): 436–89; "Sacrae Scripturae Sermo Humilis," *Neuphilologische Mitteilungen* 42 (1941): 57–67; and "St. Francis of Assisi in Dante's *Commedia*." *Italica* 22 (1945): 166–79.

Between the time he left Germany and the end of the war, he published only one review, which appeared in 1938 in *Literaturblatt für Germanische und Romanische Philologie.* See "Schriftverzeichnis Erich Auerbachs," in *Gesammelte Aufsätze,* 365–69.

15. The Romanist Liselotte Dieckmann, who was in Istanbul with her Romanist husband Herbert Dieckmann, describes the "atmosphere of all around distrust" [die Atmosphäre allseitugen Misstrauens]. See Schlobach, "Aufklärer in Finstere Zeit," in Christmann, *Deutsche und Österreichische Romanisten,* 130–31.

16. "5 Briefe Erich Auerbachs an Walter Benjamin in Paris," March 1, 1937, 692.

17. "5 Briefe Erich Auerbachs an Walter Benjamin in Paris," March 1, 1937, 692.

18. Erich Auerbach to Walter Benjamin, "5 Briefe Erich Auerbachs an Walter Benjamin in Paris," October 6, 1935, 690. Auerbach is writing from Florence. For Marburg in the Nazi period, see Werner Krauss, "Marburg unter dem Naziregime," *Sinn und Form* 35, no. 5 (1983): 943; Rudy Koshar, *Social Life, Local Politics, and Nazism: Marburg 1880–1935* (Chapel Hill, N.C.: University of North Carolina Press, 1986); Schlobach, "Aufklärer in Finstere Zeit," in Christmann, *Deutsche und Österreichische Romanisten,* 124.

19. I have developed this idea at greater length in "Church History and the Cultural Geography of Erich Auerbach: Europe and Its Eastern Other," in *Opening the Borders: Inclusivity in Early Modern Studies, Essays in Honor of James V. Mirollo,* ed. Peter C. Herman (Newark, Del.: University of Delaware Press, 1999), 324–49.

20. "Entdeckung Dantes in der Romantik," in Auerbach, *Gesammelte Aufsätze,* 176–83. Originally published in *Deutsche Vierteljahrsschrift für Literaturwissenschaft und Geistesgeschichte* 7 (1929): 682–92.

21. He specifically refers to the early nineteenth century poet, Wilhelm Friedrich Waiblinger.

22. Auerbach himself would repeat precisely this idea, except that he would connect it to typological biblical hermeneutics. See "St. Francis of Assisi in Dante's *Commedia," Italica* 22 (1945): 166–79, later reprinted in *Scenes from Drama of European Literature* (New York: Meridian, 1959); and "Farinata and Cavalcante," a chapter from *Mimesis* that first appeared in English in *Kenyon Review* 14 (1952): 207–42.

23. "Dante und Vergil," in Auerbach, *Gesammelte Aufsätze,* 115–22. Originally published in *Das Humanistiche Gymnasium* 42 (1931): 136–44.

24. For the impact of the Nazis on Auerbach's view of Roman conquest in his *Introduction to Romance Languages and Literature,* see Arnulf Stefenelli, "Ein Werk aus dem Exil: Erich Auerbachs *Introduction aux Études de Philologie Romane,*" in Christmann, *Deutsche und Österreichische Romanisten,* 105.

25. Paul Mendes-Flohr, *German Jews: A Dual Identity* (New Haven: Yale University Press, 1999). Hereafter cited in the text.

26. Flohr-Mendes is here quoting Aleida Assmann, *Arbeit in Nationalen Gedächtnis: Eine kurze Geschichte der Deutschen Bildungsidee* (Frankfurt: Campus Verlag, 1993), 91.

27. Hermann Cohen taught at Marburg from 1873 to 1912.

28. "5 Briefe Erich Auerbachs an Walter Benjamin in Paris," October 6, 1935, 690.

29. Klemperer, *I Will Bear Witness*, October 5, 1935, 134. For his insistence that he writes on the history of ideas from a thoroughly German perspective, see July 9, 1933 (24); for his fear that he has deluded himself about his German identity, see July 8, 1936 (174).

Notes to Chapter 10/Low

1. Louis L. Martz, *The Paradise Within: Studies in Vaughan, Traherne, and Milton* (New Haven: Yale University Press, 1964), 106, 166. Further along these lines, see also Martz's *The Poem of the Mind: Essays on Poetry English and American* (London: Oxford University Press, 1966).

2. John Milton, *Complete Poems and Major Prose*, ed. Merritt Y. Hughes (New York: Odyssey Press, 1957). All quotations of Milton's poetry and prose, except where noted, refer to this edition. Hereafter cited in the text.

3. For more on Milton's rejection of any and all Churches in historical time see my *The Reinvention of Love: Poetry, Politics and Culture from Sidney to Milton* (Cambridge: Cambridge University Press 1993), 158–77, 180–84.

4. See my "'Umpire Conscience': Freedom, Obedience, and the Cartesian Flight from Calvin in *Paradise Lost*," *Studies in Philology* 96 (1999): 348–65.

5. Milton speaks often and favorably of prudence. See s.v. "prudence" and "prudent" in *A Concordance to the English Prose of John Milton*, ed. Laurence Sterne and Harold H. Kollmeier (Binghamton, N.Y.: Medieval & Renaissance Texts & Studies, 1985). Milton speaks of "Christian prudence" and "sacred prudence," and several times associates prudence with liberty, for example, "prudence guides us in the liberty which God hath left to us"; *Tetrachordon*, 2:688, in *Complete Prose works of John Milton*, ed. Don M. Wolfe et al., 18 vols. (New Haven: Yale University Press, 1953–1982). He is familiar with the Thomistic rearrangement of the Aristotelian virtues, "Piety, Justice, Prudence, Temperance" (*Eikonoklastes*, 3:542, in *Complete Prose*, ed. Wolfe et al.), where piety corresponds with Spenser's Holiness in book 1 of *The Faerie Queene*, as well as the classical version, "valor, justice, constancy,

prudence" (*Eikonoklastes*, 3:348). Rarely does Milton use the word in its cynical, modern, Machiavellian sense, as when Satan abruptly adjourns the Great Consult, "Prudent," lest another take credit for his bold venture (*PL* 2.468). Since Satan parodies the virtues, this usage is not surprising.

6. On prudence, see Josef Pieper's excellent historical and philosophical analysis in *The Four Cardinal Virtues* (Notre Dame, Ind.: University of Notre Dame Press, 1966), 3–40; on *recta ratio* see Robert Hoopes, *Right Reason in the English Renaissance* (Cambridge: Harvard University Press, 1962).

7. *The Reason of Church-Government Urg'd Against Prelaty* (1642), in *Complete Poems and Major Prose*, ed. Hughes, 670.

8. See Peter Berek, "'Plain' and 'Ornate' Styles and the Structure of *Paradise Lost*," PMLA 85 (1970): 237–46.

9. Augustine, *Confessions*, trans. R. S. Pine-Coffin (London: Penguin Books, 1961), 10.27, 231–32.

10. Thomas Nagel, *The Last Word* (Oxford: Oxford University Press, 1999).

11. Edmund Spenser, *The Fairie Queene*, in *The Works of Edmund Spenser: A Variorum Edition*, ed. Edwin Greenlaw, Charles Grosvenor Osgood and Frederick Morgan Padelford, vol. 1 (1932–57; reprint, Baltimore: Johns Hopkins University Press, 1966). On the significance of this episode, see my "Sin, Penance, and Privatization in the Renaissance: Redcrosse and the True Church," the *Ben Jonson Journal* 5 (1998): 1–35.

12. Similarly, it has often been said that Milton's technique of "stationing" anticipates the movies. John Collier contributes to the efforts of many writers to naturalize the epic for their times in *Milton's Paradise Lost: Screenplay for Cinema of the Mind* (New York: Alfred A. Knopf, 1973).

13. Samuel Alexander, *Space, Time, and Deity, the Gifford Lectures at Glasgow, 1916–1918* (London: Macmillan, 1920); C. S. Lewis, *Surprised by Joy* (London: Geoffrey Bles, 1955), 206; cited by Stephen Logan, "Old Western Man for Our Times," *Renascence* 51 (1998): 72. Logan is hereafter cited in the text.

14. Hughes, *Areopagitica*, 728. Hereafter cited in the text.

15. Translated by Hughes, 135.

16. On the shift from communal to private religion, see my "Privacy, Community, and Society: Confession as a Cultural Indicator in *Sir Gawain and the Green Knight*," *Religion and Literature* 30 (1998): 1–20; and "*Hamlet* and the Ghost of Purgatory: Intimations of Killing the Father," in *English Literary Renaissance* 29 (1999): 443–67.

17. David Riesman, in collaboration with Reuel Denney and Nathan Glazer, *The Lonely Crowd: A Study of the Changing American Character* (New Haven: Yale University Press, 1950).

18. Thomas Hobbes, *Leviathan*, ed. C. B. MacPherson (London: Penguin Books, 1968), 2.21, 264–65.

19. C. S. Lewis, *A Preface to Paradise Lost* (London: Oxford University Press, 1942), 112–15.

20. *Epitaphium Damonis*, 171–72; in *Complete Poems and Major Prose*, ed. Hughes, 137.

About the Contributors

MARC BERLEY, adjunct associate professor of English at Barnard College, Columbia University, is president of the Foundation for Academic Standards & Tradition. He is the author of *After the Heavenly Tune: English Poetry and the Aspiration to Song* (Duquesne University Press, 2000) and articles on Milton and Shakespeare.

MARTIN ELSKY, professor of English at Brooklyn College, directs the Renaissance Studies certificate program at the Graduate Center of the City University of New York. He is the author of *Authorizing Words: Speech, Writing, and Print in the English Renaissance* (Cornell University Press, 1989) and articles on Bacon, Donne, Herbert and Shakespeare.

ERNEST B. GILMAN, professor of English at New York University, is the author of *The Curious Perspective: Literary and Pictorial Wit in the Seventeenth Century* (Yale University Press, 1978), *Iconoclasm and Poetry in the English Reformation* (University of Chicago Press, 1986), *Recollecting the Arundel Circle* (Peter Lang, 2003) and articles on Spenser, Shakespeare, Donne, Milton and the Arundel circle.

FRANK KERMODE, has written and edited numerous books, including *Romantic Image* (Routledge & Kegan Paul, 1957), *The*

Sense of an Ending (Oxford University Press, 1967), *Shake-speare, Spenser, Donne* (Routledge & Kegan Paul, 1971), *The Art of Telling* (Harvard University Press, 1983), *The Classic* (Harvard University Press, 1983), *Forms of Attention* (University of Chicago Press, 1985), *An Appetite for Poetry* (Harvard University Press, 1989), *Not Entitled: A Memoir* (Farrar, Straus and Giroux, 1995) and, most recently, *Shakespeare's Language* (Farrar, Straus and Giroux, 2000). He has taught at Cambridge University and University College, London and been a visiting professor at Columbia, Harvard, and Yale.

Albert C. Labriola is professor of English and Distinguished University Professor at Duquesne University. The editor of *Milton Studies*, he has written articles on Donne, Herbert, Milton, and Shakespeare, as well as edited variorum editions of Donne and Milton. He is coauthor of *Milton's Legacy in the Arts* (Penn State University Press, 1988) and coeditor of *The Bible of the Poor* (Duquesne University Press, 1990) and *The Mirror of Salvation* (Duquesne University Press, 2002).

Anthony Low, professor of English at New York University, is the author of *The Blaze of Noon: A Reading of Samson Agonistes* (Columbia University Press, 1974), *Love's Architecture: Devotional Modes in Seventeenth-Century English Poetry* (New York University Press, 1978), *The Georgic Revolution* (Princeton University Press, 1985) and *The Reinvention of Love: Poetry, Politics, and Culture from Sidney to Milton* (Cambridge University Press, 1993). He has published numerous articles on Renaissance literature.

Michael Mack, assistant professor of English at the Catholic University of America, received his Ph.D. from Columbia University. He is completing a book on Sir Philip Sidney.

Louis L. Martz was Sterling Professor of English at Yale University. During his distinguished career, he wrote numerous books and articles on Renaissance literature, including *The*

Poetry of Meditation (Yale University Press, 1954), *The Paradise Within: Studies in Vaughn, Traherne, and Milton* (Yale University Press, 1964), *The Poem of the Mind* (Oxford University Press, 1966), *Poet of Exile* (Yale University Press, 1980), and *Thomas More: The Search for the Inner Man* (Yale University Press, 1990). He also edited anthologies of poetry and criticism, including the *Anchor Anthology of Seventeenth-Century Verse* (Doubleday, 1969) and *George Herbert and Henry Vaughn* (Oxford University Press, 1986).

ANNE LAKE PRESCOTT is Helen Goodhart Altschul Professor of English at Barnard College, Columbia University. She is the author of *French Poets and the English Renaissance* (Yale University Press, 1978) and *Imagining Rabelais in Renaissance England* (Yale University Press, 1998) and coeditor of *Edmund Spenser's Poetry* (W. W. Norton, 1993), *Female and Male Voices in Early Modern England* (Columbia University Press, 2000) and *Spenser Studies*.

STANLEY STEWART, professor of English at the University of California, Riverside, is the author of *The Enclosed Garden* (University of Wisconsin Press, 1966), *The Expanded Voice: The Art of Thomas Traherne* (Huntington Library, 1970), *George Herbert* (Twayne, 1986) and *Renaissance Talk* (Duquesne University Press, 1997). Coeditor of *Jonson's Spenser: Evidence and Historical Criticism* (Duquesne University Press, 1995), *The Cambridge Companion to Ben Jonson* (Cambridge University Press, 2000) and the *Ben Jonson Journal*, he serves as president of the Association of Literary Scholars and Critics.

EDWARD W. TAYLER is Lionel Trilling Professor in the Humanities Emeritus at Columbia University, where from 1960 to 2001 he taught Shakespeare, Milton, Renaissance literature, and Humanities. He is the author of *Nature and Art in Renaissance Literature* (Columbia University Press, 1964), *Milton's Poetry: Its Development in Time* (Duquesne University Press,

1979), and *Donne's Idea of a Woman: Structure and Meaning in "The Anniversaries"* (Columbia University Press, 1991) and essays on Shakespeare and Milton. He is the editor of *Literary Criticism of Seventeenth-Century England* (Alfred A. Knopf, 1967).

Index

Aeneas, 57-77, 122

Aeneid (Virgil): parallel to *The Tempest*, 57–77; themes in, 59–72, 245–46n1

aestheticism, 131–32

"Aire and Angels" (Donne): Herrick on, 95; interpretations of, 93–94, 100; Labriola on, 103–08

The Alchemist (Jonson), 153–55, 164

Andrewes, Lancelot, 150

angelica, archangelica, 94–103, 251n13

angels: definition of, 93–94; in poetry, 94, 108

Anniversaries (Donne). *See also First Anniversary, Second Anniversary:* Corthell on, 4, 78, 136–37; Hardison on, 89; structure of, 84–89; Tayler on, 4, 78; and theology, 78–79

Annunciation, 99

Antony and Cleopatra (Shakespeare), 18–21, 25, 41–42

An Apology for Poetry (Sidney), 11, 28

Aquinas, Thomas, 93

archangelica, 98, 100, 106

archangels, 98–99

Areopagitica (Milton), 221

Aristo, Titius, 171

Aristophanes, 18

Aristotle, 28, 50–52, 135, 186

Armin, Robert, 46

Armstrong, E. A., 18

Ars Poetica (Horace), 29

Arte of Divine Meditation (Hall), 81–83

Auerbach, Erich: on Dante, 193–94; dismissal of, 176; on France, 179; on hermeneutics, 185; insight of, 13; and Klemperer, 182, 202–03; on Racine, 178–84; Said on, 177;

and Vossler, 178–79; *Mimesis*, 177-79, 187, 202

Augustine, Saint, 79–80, 83, 89, 187, 191

Augustus, 59, 62

Austen, Jane, 173

Bacon, Francis, 6-8, 37–38

Benjamin, Walter, 176, 182

Bernard of Clairvaux, 178, 187

Blake, William, 172–73

botanical, 95–96, 98, 103

Brantôme, Pierre de, 118

Bush, Douglas, 233

Calvin, John. *See also* Calvinism, 79–80, 163, 247n2

Calvinism, 79–81, 207, 248n4

Camden, William, 168–72

"Canonization, The" (Donne), 120, 135–36, 142–44

Catholic. *See also* Roman Catholic Church, 79, 126, 136, 161, 183–85, 248n6

Chalmers, Martin, 182

Christianity, 54–55, 177–78, 180, 185–88

Church of England, 81

Cicero, 114

Clapham, Henoch, 161, 164

Clemen, Wolfgang, 18

College of Physicians, 140

Comte, Auguste, 146

conception, 244n13, 244n16

contradictions, 141

Conversations (Drummond), 160–61

Corthell, Ronald, 136–42, 145, 189

Cotton, Sir Robert, 154, 163, 168

Crewe, Jonathan, 143

274